MEDIA AND THE RESTYLING OF POLITICS

MEDIA AND THE RESTYLING OF POLITICS

Consumerism, Celebrity and Cynicism

edited by
John Corner and Dick Pels

SAGE Publications
London • Thousand Oaks • New Delhi

First published 2003
Reprinted 2006

SAGE Publications Ltd.
1 Oliver's Yard, 55 City Road
London EC1Y 1SP

SAGE Publications Inc
2455 Teller Road
Thousand Oaks, California 91320

SAGE Publications India Pvt Ltd.
B-42 Panchsheel Enclave
Post Box 4109
New Delhi 110 017

British Library Cataloguing in Publication data

A catalogue record for this book is available from the British Library

ISBN-10 0-7619-4920-8
ISBN-10 0-7619-4921-6 (pbk)
ISBN-13 978-0-7619-4920-6
ISBN-13 978-0-7619-4921-3 (pbk)

Library of Congress Control Number Available

Typeset by C & M Digitals (P) Ltd., Chennai, India
Printed and bound in Great Britain by
Athenaeum Press Ltd., Gateshead, Tyne & Wear.

Contents

Notes on Contributors

Frank Ankersmit is Professor in Intellectual History at the University of Groningen, The Netherlands. He is the author of many books on the philosophy of history and political philosophy, including *History and Tropology: The Rise and Fall of Metaphor* (University of California Press, 1994), *Aesthetic Politics: Political Philosophy Beyond Fact and Value* (Stanford, 1997), *Historical Representation* (Stanford, 2001) and *Political Representation* (Stanford, 2002).

W. Lance Bennett is Professor of Political Science and Ruddick C. Lawrence Professor of Communication at the University of Washington, where he also directs the Center for Communication and Civic Engagement (www.engagedcitizen.org). Areas of current interest include the transformation of mass media news, Web-based political information networks, and the organisation of global activist networks and community information systems. Recent publications include *Mediated Politics: Communication in the Future of Democracy* (Cambridge, co-edited with Robert Entman) and *News: The Politics of Illusion*, fifth ed. (Longman).

John Corner is Professor in the School of Politics and Communication Studies at the University of Liverpool. His recent books include *Studying Media: Problems of Theory and Method* (Edinburgh, 1998) and *Critical Ideas in Television Studies* (Oxford, 1999). He has published articles and chapters on media analysis in a range of international journals and collections and is an editor of the journal *Media, Culture and Society*. Currently, he is working on the history of current-affairs television.

Peter Dahlgren is Professor of Media and Communication Studies at Lund University, Sweden. His current research interests focus on the themes of democracy, cultural theory and identity in late modern society. He has written for a range of international journals and collections and his book *Media and Civic Engagement* will be forthcoming from Cambridge University Press in 2003.

Dick Pels is Senior Research Affiliate at the Amsterdam School for Social Science Research and a Freelance writer. Until recently he was Professor of Sociology in the Department of Human Sciences at Brunel University. He has published widely in social and political theory, and is the author of *Property and Power: A Study in Intellectual Rivalry* (Routledge, 1998), *The Intellectual as Stranger: Studies in Spokespersonship* (Routledge, 2000) and *Unhastening Science: Autonomy and Reflexivity in the Social Theory of Knowledge* (Liverpool University Press, 2003).

Margaret Scammell is Senior Lecturer at media@lse, at the London School of Economics. She has published widely on politics, communication and political marketing and is the author of *Designer Politics* (Macmillan, 1995), *On Message: Communicating the Campaign* (Sage, 1999) with Pippa Norris, John Curtice, David Sanders and Holli Semetko, and *Media Journalism and Democracy* (Ashgate, 2000) with Holli Semetko.

Jon Simons is Senior Lecturer in Critical Theory. Previously, he has lived in Israel and the US. He is the author of *Foucault and the Political* (Routledge, 1995), as well as articles that have appeared in journals such as *Philosophy and Social Criticism*, *Society and Space*, and *Political Studies*. He has also contributed chapters to *Feminist Interpretations of Michel Foucault* (Penn State University Press, 1996) and *Reconstituting Social Criticism* (Macmillan, 1998). His current research concerns the nature of critical political theory.

John Street is Reader in Politics at the University of East Anglia. He has written several books, the most recent of which is *Mass Media,Politics and Democracy* (Palgrave, 2001); he is also co-editor of the *Cambridge Companion to Pop and Rock* (Cambridge University Press, 2001). His articles on political analysis and popular culture have appeared in a number of journals, across political, media and cultural studies.

Bronislaw Szerszynski is Lecturer in Environment and Culture at the Institute for Environment, Philosophy and Public Policy, Lancaster University. He is the author of *The Sacralisation of Nature: Nature and the Sacred in the Global Age* (Blackwell, 2004 forthcoming) and co-editor of *Risk, Environment and Modernity: Towards a New Ecology* (Sage/TCS, 1996), *The Reordering of Nature: Theology, Society and the New Genetics* (T&T Clark, 2002), and *Nature Performed: Environment, Culture and Performance* (Blackwell/Sociological Review, 2003).

Liesbet van Zoonen is Professor of Media Studies at the University of Amsterdam and director of the Centre for Popular Culture. She has published widely on gender and/in media and is currently working on the articulation of politics and popular culture. Among her books are *Feminist Media Studies* (Sage, 1994), *The Media in Question* (co-edited, Sage, 1998) and *Gender, Politics and Communication* (co-edited, Hampton Press, 2000).

1

Introduction

The Re-styling of Politics

JOHN CORNER AND DICK PELS

The 'Voting Paradox'

In recent times, political moralists have developed a steady habit of complaining about electoral withdrawal, apathy and cynicism, accumulating worries about a civic culture in decline. In the run-up to the 2001 general election, Tony Blair, for example, feared that political apathy would be the main obstacle to Labour regaining power. In the end, he need not have worried (but of course he worried a lot after the fact), because the second Labour victory was secured on the poorest voter turnout since the beginning of universal suffrage (53 per cent, while the 1997 landslide had still brought out 71 per cent of the electorate). After the polls, BBC director-general Greg Dyke ordered a wide-ranging review of political news coverage in the hope of regaining the interest especially of younger voters. But he might have pondered the following paradox: whereas politicians encounter the greatest difficulty in 'getting out the vote' in ordinary elections, the enthusiasm to vote for wannabe celebrities on reality shows such as *Big Brother*, *Popstars* and *Pop Idol* regularly reaches levels that border on collective frenzy. In our society, the level of direct engagement that characterised Athenian democracy may have become unattainable ... except in the playful interactivity which is afforded by modern mass entertainment.

In the February 2002 finals of the 23-week *Pop Idol* 'election campaign', the two remaining candidates together polled more votes than the Liberal Democrats in the general election. In the biggest-ever phone-in, which led to a near-meltdown of the BT network, 8.7m votes were cast, of which 4.6m favoured the winner, politics graduate Will Young. Starting in October 2001 with 5.6m viewers, the show's finale was watched by an audience of more than 15m (compare the average of 4.5m who watched the 10 o'clock news during the 'real' election campaign, or the 2.5m who watched the Paxman–Blair interview on *Newsnight*). The preceding weeks had seen the apotheosis of an absorbing competition in which, as the celebrity magazine *Heat* put it, 'Gareth and Will's different styles, appearances and personalities divided the nation' (as Tony and the other William [Hague] had conspicuously failed to do in the previous year). During the final week, the two front runners were sent on a a mock-political campaign, visiting newspaper offices and broadcasting studios, and diving into crowds from shiny battlebuses that carried slogans such as VOTE WILL or VOTE GARETH. Established celebrities came out in favour of one or the other, gaining a little extra publicity for themselves on the side. With some justice, Steve Anderson, ITV's news controller, suggested that Westminster still had a lot to learn from *Pop Idol*'s techniques of mass marketing and personality display.

But we should also notice that 'official' politics has been catching up, blurring the boundaries and levelling the hierarchy between 'high' political representation and 'low' popular entertainment. If manufactured pop has adopted some of the paraphernalia and conventions of political electioneering, politics has become more of a 'culture industry', increasingly resembling a talent show or popularity contest, where polling is as relentlessly continuous as in the music and film charts, and star-gazing and infotainment have become equally central as they are to the tabloids and the celebrity magazines. It is hardly accidental that political interest and electoral enthusiasm have generally picked up wherever politics has attained a high level of drama, offering spectacular storylines and flamboyant personalities rather than ideological standoffs or partisan bickering, as was evident during highly entertaining episodes such as the 2000 mayoral elections in London, the leadership contest in the Conservative Party subsequent to its 2001 election defeat, or the recent Dutch elections, which were entirely dominated by the dandyesque figure of Pim Fortuyn.

'Reality TV is not the end of civilisation as we know it; it *is* civilisation as we know it', as Germaine Greer has wittily put it. She was speaking about *Big Brother*, where ejecting somebody from the House has (now for the third time) become one of the most popular forms of 'single-issue voting'. This 'voting paradox' may appropriately focus some of the issues about the changing nature of political representation that we wish to make central to this book. The mass visibility that is afforded by modern mediated politics has foregrounded issues of 'style, appearance, and personality', breaking down some of the fences that separate politics from entertainment and political leadership from media celebrity. In turn, citizens have become political consumers who no longer 'buy' inclusive ideological packages or tried-and-trusted party brands, but are still mobilisable around strings of single issues and around 'singular' political personalities who represent these issues in a distinctive manner. What is too readily complained about as political cynicism or civic withdrawal, might more often be a rejection of traditional political divisions and of the arrogance of distanced, self-absorbed political professionals.

Political Communication and Political Culture

The primary aim of this book is to explore the nature and consequences of change in what can be seen, broadly, as two separate but related dimensions of political structure and process. First of all, there are the shifts in 'political communication' and in the whole nature of media-political relations. The growth of new forms of political marketing, the concern about news management and 'spin' and the emergence of new media options for political publicity have produced a revised agenda for inquiry here (many of the chapters that follow cite the rapidly growing literature). Questions on this agenda have become the subject of intensified scrutiny and debate, not only in political studies but in international media research too. This has brought a welcome dialogue between these previously rather disparate areas of scholarship; a dialogue that it is one of the aims of this book to further. Second, there are changes of various kinds at work in political culture, some of which we have already pointed to above. The term 'culture' has been put to a wide range of applications in recent academic writing and there is some cogency in the view that it has often been used rather evasively, conflating factors that might better be differentiated and becoming an enemy of sociological precision. Yet the word continues usefully to signal a range of things still too often left out of account in many conventional research perspectives, even though the situation is improving. In using the term here, we mean to indicate the realms of political experience, imagination, values and dispositions that provide the settings within which a political system operates, shaping the character of political processes and political behaviour. It is the elements of political culture that, among other things, interconnect the 'official' world of professional politics with the world of everyday experience and with the modes of 'the popular' variously to be found within work and leisure. One of the aims of this collection is not only to make a stronger link between questions of political communication and of political culture but to remedy the general neglect of the 'cultural' dimension and to show the importance for political analysis of attending to it more in the future.

It might now be useful to indicate in a little more detail what we see to be the agenda for further inquiry in each of the two areas identified above, before moving on to introduce some of the ideas that we had in mind when commissioning the essays that follow.

The relationship between media and politics has, of course, long been the subject of debate. It is possible to see one approach to this question as taking an 'enabling' perspective. Here, the assumption is that the media are necessary agents of the practice of modern, popular democracy. Subject to certain conditions (the question-begging economic and regulatory circumstances of a 'free press' being the most important, on this see the fine commentary of Baker, 2002), their circulation of knowledge, presentation of diverse views and critical scrutiny of those in power will act as a guarantor of political health and active citizenship. In its earliest versions, this is behind the Enlightenment or Liberal view of media-political relations. This is one in which, insofar as the question of 'influence' is raised at all, it is raised in a way that emphasises the potential for good. Kant's notion of the positive relationship between 'publicity' and the exercise of 'public reason' is one founding principle of the enabling view (on this in relation to press theory, see Splichal, 2002).

We can contrast such a position with what we might call the 'disabling' perspective. In this far more familiar view, the media are seen as variously undermining the practice of democracy or, at least, of having a strong propensity to do so. They perform their subversive function through such routes as the substitution of entertainment for knowledge, the closing off of true diversity, the pursuit of an agenda determined primarily by market factors and their susceptibility to control by government and corporate agencies. These can be alternative or combinatory factors within any given account. Although attempts to assert the case for the 'enabling' view are still to be found (if nearly always with considerable modification to the economic and regulatory arrangements thought necessary), it is the 'disabling' view that has provided the focus for the majority of studies in political communication. Indeed, unease about the political consequences of a developing media sector provides one clear reason for the growth of media research as a subfield of social science, particularly in the USA during the 1940s and 1950s. The key question has been: in what ways and to what extent do the media impact negatively upon political practice? The tones in which this question has been asked have ranged from the urgent and anxious to the more measured. However, even in those enquiries framed finally by a sense of positive reassurance it is important to note how address to the negative rather than to the positive has provided the primary point of reference.

Concern with the perceived negative character of media-political relations can be seen most often to work within the terms of one or other of two versions of 'imbalance', variously qualified. The first version might be called the notion of a *politicised media*. In this, the media's independence is seen to be almost entirely circumscribed by the controls of the political system. The realm of politics has effectively superimposed itself upon the realm of media. As independent agencies, the media have been 'shut down'. Many arguments about the effect of 'spin' and of political marketing work with a sense of this kind of imbalance as their basic scenario. The second version reverses the relationship and might be called the notion of a thoroughly *mediatised politics*. Here, it is the realm of politics that has become colonised by media logics and imperatives, losing its specificity and integrity. Politics has become an adjunct to show business. Debate about 'infotainment' and 'dumbing down' often uses this version as its base model, but it is of course entirely possible to regard 'spin' and 'political marketing' as indicators not of the political control exerted over the media but of the displacement of political values by those of the media system.

The two models are not the only option. Refusing any suggestion of separate realms involved in some kind of play-off of convergence or super-imposition makes good sense. It can be argued that the relationship between the media system and the political system is, in many countries, far too densely interpenetrating in character to admit of such a separate, spatial conceptualisation. Nevertheless, a commitment to seeing the complex mutuality of contemporary political and media systems still leaves questions of relationship, causality and value to be asked, even if these are now seen to be more 'internal', partial and contingent in character. This is a challenge for a new generation of researchers both in politics and in media studies. In facing it, the term 'political communication' will need to be rejected as the defining label for what is under scrutiny. It is both too limiting in its suggested scope (centred, sometimes exclusively, upon political publicity and political journalism and with a bias towards electoral campaigns) and too functionalist in its implications of a defined role self-consciously performed. Working terms that catch more at the breadth and complexity of mediated politics, and at the indirectness of much of what is significant, will be needed.

The second broad area in which this collection attempts to open up new lines of enquiry, political culture, clearly has a substantial overlap with the agenda, both established and emerging, around mediation. Questions of communication and of culture have always been hard to separate but never more so than now. Perhaps the most central question here concerns the changing terms upon which everyday life is lived and 'the public' and 'the private' defined in relation to each other. How do politics and politicians fit within these broader contours of experience, framed by new routines of work and leisure and producing their own forms of self- and social consciousness, of aspiration and anxiety, hope and disillusionment?

Consumerism, Celebrity and Cynicism

Three C's, consumerism, celebrity and cynicism, are key factors in need of attention here. In many countries, the emphasis on the consumer within relations of market provision has extended well beyond the core areas of trade and shopping. It has shaped revised forms of public service, including education and health, and it has inevitably placed politicians in the role, at least partly, of being 'service providers'. To some commentators, consumer-consciousness has brought an end to deference and a clearer sense of quality and choice. It has worked against producer controls and has thus exerted what can finally be seen as an empowering, democratising effect upon those social areas in which it has become prominent. Rather than undermining citizenship, it has reinforced it by supplying new kinds of awareness and expectations. To other writers, the prominence of the consumer and the language of consumerism indicate the continuing contradiction between market values and democratic development.

Forms of celebrity, involving sustained performance within conditions of expanded media visibility and, quite often, vigorous media scrutiny, are a major feature of contemporary culture. Alongside the more established 'public figures', a whole new range of people from television, sport, popular music and other areas of entertainment have become, if only temporarily, members of a celebrity system that extends to the international level. This is a system reinforced, indeed sustained, by the busy circuits of publicity and promotion within audio-visual and print culture. As we noted at the start of this introduction, among its latest recruits are the participants in television's new 'reality programmes'. These constitute a bottom level of regularly replenished celebrity, anchored in the ordinary by the very nature of their recruitment.

Political prominence, both as fame and as notoriety, has been substantially re-worked in terms of the broader pattern. A new aesthetics of the political self has been fashioned and it is to the further exploration of this, among other things, that we wish to point in our discussion below of the idea of *political style*. The examination of political performances, their settings and the kinds of response they receive are a common theme in a number of the pieces that follow.

Inter-linked both with questions of consumerism and of celebrity is the issue of political cynicism. For some commentators, as our opening remarks suggested, the increase in cynical disposition, perhaps most noticeable in low election turn-outs but by no means limited to electoral periods, is the single most worrying element of contemporary politics. Often, media treatment of politics is blamed for reinforcing if not causing the tendency, although some media managers have pointed to the difficulties they face in making politics interesting to their audiences and readerships, particularly to the young. Another often cited cause is the adoption of more aggressively commercial forms of political marketing in many countries and the negative and more distanced attitudes towards political activity that this is said to have encouraged. It is interesting to note just how much this mooted 'effect' contrasts with the idea of a happily compliant, misinformed citizenry projected in other accounts.

Behind the question of cynicism, and often entirely unaddressed, are assumptions about what kinds of investment people *should* make in politics and what kind of expectation they *should* have of politicians. Here, we connect with contemporary versions of a venerable issue – the rational grounds for political affiliation and action and the interplay of these with a more affective dynamics, with the realm of feelings and even of fantasy. Enquiry here begins to interrogate the very notion of political 'representation' and the forms of relationship and responsibility it supposes. A number of writers have recently revisited this topic, examining the kinds of criteria which particular versions of representation bring to the assessment of media performance and also to the performance of 'proper' citizenship. Again, this is a matter that a number of chapters pursue in different ways.

Political Style

Consumerism, celebrity, and cynicism (or political indifference), thus together restructure the field for political representation and good citizenship, downplaying traditional forms of ideological and party-based allegiance, and foregrounding matters of aesthetics and style. Political style increasingly operates as a focus for post-ideological lifestyle choices, which are indifferent to the entrenched oppositions between traditional 'isms' and their institutionalisation in the form of political parties (for example, left *vs.* right or progressive *vs.* conservative), and which favour more eclectic, fluid, issue-specific and personality-bound forms of political recognition and engagement. While all parties tend to become centre parties and reproduce the divisions of the political spectrum within themselves, voters increasingly float away from these empty cubicles in order to identify with public individuals or celebrities who condense particular themes and emotions in a spectacular display of character and style.

Increasingly, people want to vote for persons and their ideas rather than for political parties and their programmes. Their so-called 'apathy' or lack of interest (which is often a legitimate lack of interest in the interests of political professionals) is at least to some extent counterbalanced by a more distracted interest in political infotainment and celebrity, framed within the permanent campaigning, marketing and polling rhythms that characterise a fully grown media democracy. This interest is facilitated by new forms of visual and emotional literacy, which allow audiences to 'read' political characters and 'taste' their style, enabling them to judge their claims of authenticity and competence in a more effective manner. The continuous media exposure of political personae lends them a strange familiarity which, despite the sharp asymmetry that separates the visible few from the invisible many, still to some extent bridges the gap between them. In generating such new structures of proximity and distance, television democracy offers new risks but also new opportunities for democratic representation and accountability.

This new visibility of persons and the affective identification they attract represents a broader cultural shift that fits the individualisation of political trust into more general sociological patterns of de-institutionalisation and personalisation. The proliferation of differences *within* institutions (such as political parties) and social categories (such as class) spills over and tends to blur the boundaries *between* them, while individuals themselves travel more freely across these institutional and classificatory boundaries. Increasingly, institutions are represented and identified by the individual faces who 'front' them (Virgin = Branson; Labour = Blair), while (some) individuals turn into institutions as a result of their mediated ubiquity and universal fame. The central significance of celebrity culture for this new constellation is that public figures embody stylised forms of individuality, which offer a temporary focus for identification and organisation by fluid collectives (or 'audiences') in the 'classless', individualised, broader culture (Marshall, 1997). Such 'audience subjects', as Marshall calls them, appropriately express both a unique individuality and the social power of a particular group. Within this context, individuals attempt to make sense of social experience through celebrating and selectively identifying with the lifestyles of public personalities.

This system of celebrity power is progressively being translated from the popular entertainment industries towards more 'serious' fields such as business, politics, art and science. In this respect, the new forms of publicity that are generated by celebrity culture (and media culture more generally) also tend to blur the 'liberal' demarcations between the social spheres of culture, the polity, and the economy, pressing for a mutual interpenetration of formerly distinct 'field logics' or 'system codes'. Such a de-differentiation is, for example, promoted by the discourse about 'enterprise culture' which, as we have noted above, intrudes upon political reality in the form of performative metaphors about political marketing, branding, and citizen-consumership. Such a push for the 'economisation' of politics (and culture) is immediately flanked by a drive for the culturalisation of politics (and the economy), which defines some of the structural shifts which have been identified above. Both the new 'cultural economy' and the new 'cultural politics' evidence an intermeshing of formerly distinct values and codes, which brings out the new prominence of discursivity, symbol-making, and aesthetic design for economic and political practice. Media culture acts as a central energiser of this process of de-differentiation, forcing a 'style revolution' in other social domains that is simultaneously a process of aestheticisation, emotionalisation and celebrification. In this culture of universal promotion (Wernick, 1991), institutions such as parties and ideologies primarily survive as brands, while the only future for political personality is that of celebrity. Art and the artistic life turn into models for political (and economic) behaviour; and bohemian individuality and authenticity emerge as the core values of a thoroughly aestheticised capitalism.

Aesthetic Politics

That politics is not a science but an art, and that political representation follows an aesthetic rather than rationalistic logic, has been thematised more clearly by the Romantic than by the Enlightenment tradition in Western political thought. The idea of politics as theatre, focusing on spectacle, style, emotion, and the cult of personality, has been put into practice with particular force and flamboyance by radical right-wing movements and regimes. In the Wagnerian conception of political art, the state and the people were viewed as a *Gesamtkunstwerk*, which the charismatic political artist would shape out of the rough and disorganised matter of the popular mass. For a Marxist author such as Benjamin (1992) the aestheticisation of politics was therefore a logical corollary of the Fascist ploy to give the masses a grandiose expressive aim (radical nationalism and total war), which would conveniently deflect their energies from attacking the structure of capitalist exploitation. Horkheimer and Adorno's pessimistic analysis of the culture industries (Horkheimer and Adorno, 1979; Adorno, 1991) generalised this critique to encompass the modern cult of celebrity and pseudo-individuality in post-Fascist Western liberal democracies.

However, it can be argued that this negative or 'disabling' view of aesthetic politics fails to capture its true significance for our own media-saturated political culture. As Horkheimer and Adorno realised, the aestheticisation drive did not remain confined to right-wing political movements and regimes, but carried a much broader historical resonance that tied it in with long-term processes of massification and mediatisation. Indeed, Le Bon's analysis of the new emotive relationship between leader and mass (1960), Barrès's view of politics as emotional energy (cf. Hillach, 1979: 105–6), Durkheim's notion of 'collective effervescence' (1995), and Weber's account of charismatic 'leadership democracy' (1988, 1994) offered early pointers towards forms of theatrical, spectacular and performative politics that have meanwhile emerged across the whole breadth of the political spectrum. Pioneered by artistic movements such as Futurism and Surrealism, such new political styles and techniques were first consolidated and professionalised by the Fascist and National Socialist regimes, which turned mass propaganda and mass ritual into an art form and made unprecedented use of newly available technologies of communication and mobility. But already, during the 1920s and 1930s, the iconography and histrionics of right-wing political activism were successfully copied by centre-left movements such as Christian democracy and revisionist socialism, as was for example evidenced in the agitation for the Plan of Labour that swept Belgium and other European countries during the 1930s.

The subsequent evolution of political democracy has demonstrated that aesthetic stylisation is an inherent and inevitable feature of mass politics, particularly in its (post)modern mediated form. We cannot therefore leave the aestheticisation of politics to the historical (and contemporary) right, but must instead contemplate its role in enabling new forms of representation and a further democratisation of democracy. Instead of aggravating the dangers of spectacular politics, emotional identification and charismatic leadership, the unprecedented spread of new technologies of communication has in a sense neutralised their authoritarian risk, by 'lowering the political hero to our level' (Meyrowitz, 1985) and creating the peculiar intimacy-a -a-distance that characterises the relationship between modern media celebrities and their fan-like audiences. In conditions of democratic pluralism and mediated political competition, the single God-like political leader who embodies a sacralised national unity is replaced by a whole firmament of little gods who rise and fall in a never-ending game of public reputation-making-and-breaking, and who can mobilise only partial and fleeting forms of consensus, which lack an integrative nucleus of values or beliefs. Under such new conditions of mediated visibility and 'thin' solidarity, a politics of personal style may generate democratic effects, by expanding the platforms for engagement and citizenship, and by offering forms of popular appeal and emotional identification that cut through technocratic smoke-screens and institutional inertia. A performative politics foregrounds the politician as an actor, whose performance on the public stage is continuously judged in terms of authenticity, honesty and 'character'.

The Presentation of Political Self

Inevitably, therefore, questions concerning the nature of the political 'self', including questions about the nature of self-consciousness and of political performance, need to be raised at a number of different points in any study of political culture. Here, the work of Erving Goffman (classically, Goffman, 1959) provides an indispensable source of ideas and perceptions. For professional politicians, 'the presentation of self in everyday life' involves the management of a number of different roles, many of them performed in a cultural context where the relationship and interplay between 'public' and 'private' realms is indeterminate and changing. The 'styling of the self' in politics, the projection of political persona, is partly a matter of choice (a conscious 'branding' exercise designed to sharpen profile) and partly a required reaction to the terms of media visibility that now frame and interpret political action in many countries.

There are sociological issues here, certainly. We cannot understand contemporary political processes and settings unless we at least engage with the kinds of identity that politicians project and the relation of these to popular perceptions and judgements. Issues of 'strength' and 'weakness', of the 'trustworthy' and the 'sly', of the perceived limits of 'ambition' are central to the organisation of popular political feelings. The way in which politicians are assessed, both as members of a professional grouping and also as somehow representatives of the people, articulating differing versions of 'common sense', is crucial too. This assessment connects outwards to the broader identities they enjoy as celebrities, the subjects of political gossip and of speculation as to the deeper, more private, personalities that lie behind the personae adopted for the duties of office.

There is also a psychological dimension. As Andrew Samuels has observed (Samuels, 2001), politics has a 'secret life', a narrative of inner management and tension, of aspiration and fear. Although it is most often in the genre of autobiography and biography that this aspect is reflected upon in any sustained way, there are shifts in the personalisation of politics that may contrive to make the link between the 'inner' and the 'outer' more prominent in the future. Renewed interest in questions of 'trust', of 'sincerity', and of a politics that somehow escapes the distortions of 'system', is one feature of current changes in the terms of political culture.

The language that politicians use has, rightly, been seen as one key test of their integrity and quality and, perhaps less positively, of their strategic acumen. Finding the 'right' kind of language to address particular audiences on specific topics is among the primary challenges to those seeking and holding political office. The forms of language in use will necessarily reflect in part the broader shifts in public and cultural coinage. Terms and phrases can lose, or gain, credibility and cogency within the space of a year or so, while if we compared the political language of, say, Britain in the 1960s with Britain today, a whole shift in register, vocabulary and rhetorical organisation would become apparent (see for instance Fairclough, 2000). One key move has been towards more informal kinds of address, ones better suited to mediation through television than those deriving from older forms of public oratory. Informality suggests 'closer' relationships, and the move towards a more colloquial political language has often gone along with an attempt to reconfigure political relations in a way that goes beyond the hierarchy and the terms of deference and condescension characterising older models. The 'personal' has a long history in political appeal, strategically augmenting the 'public' when thought necessary, but many of our chapters show to what degree personal factors have become prominent in political life. This has shown itself in an increased use of personalised comment (in tone and in content) not only in the projection of political identity but also in the defence of policies.

Political Deceit

Perhaps the oldest questions to be asked about the political self are those to do with motive and with honesty. Politicians have come to be seen, internationally, as inveterate liars, creating an expectation against which 'honesty' is a novelty. This perception derives partly from an ancient scepticism about the guile of rulers (wonderfully articulated by Machiavelli, in an account that escaped its sixteenth century context to become defining). However, modern forms of democracy and the growth of new patterns of political communication have added to, and revised, the terms of suspicion. They have also reconfigured the conditions for being honest and for being truthful. In part, they have positioned politicians so deeply within the terms of *publicity*, within cross-currents of assertion, persuasion, denial and counter-assertion, that in many instances complete honesty might be judged as dangerously naive. One might say that the pragmatic contexts for political speech trade on a routine, professional insincerity in a manner not entirely unlike the conventions of the advertising industry (see Mayhew, 1997 for a striking re-examination of this comparison). It is the expanded circumstances of visibility and notional accountability within which modern politicians work that have, a little paradoxically, helped to create a more elaborate repertoire of deceit and evasion in political speech. The public speech of politicians is addressed to three broad categories of significant addressee – to other politicians, to journalists and to sections of the general public. In openly reported speaking, different priorities of combination will occur according to the situation. Of course, there are many subcategories here too, creating a complex dynamics of communicative design and anticipation.

In a suggestive essay, Arendt (1973) considers 'lying' as something partly to do with the very nature of the political imagination and its tendency towards the projection of aspirations and goals not qualified by compromise. Certainly, an openly ideological politics may display this utopian vein, but the more 'managerialist' politics with which many of us are now familiar seems to resort to deceit as much in its reactive moments as in its considered publicity. This is often in an attempt to pre-empt the bad news, to reassure on a point of growing anxiety, to hold a compromise position between shifting and mutually suspicious interest groups or points of view. The changing conditions of political trust and their relationship both to media practice and to codes of political honesty are an important aspect of political culture, which have so far received less attention than they deserve.

The Organisation of this Book

As indicated before, the 'aesthetics' of political representation and the salience of political style are central issues in the new approaches to political culture that are advanced this book. The next chapter by **Frank Ankersmit** develops an intriguing analogy between the notion of political style and Schumann's notion of the 'inner voice': a melody that is not actually played but strongly suggested by what is played. Political reality similarly arises in the gap between what is objectively there and what is merely suggested. While the 'classical' view defines political reality as basically transparent, unambiguous and consensual, leaving no room for the 'inner voice' of politics, 'romantic' political theory acknowledges its essential ambivalences and perspectival conflicts, from which political truth emerges as an 'inner voice' and in the form of a new political style. In the complex symphony of democratic politics, style is at work between political form and political content and between representers and represented, locating the source of political creativity in the interplay between the left hand and the right hand of the democratic process.

The following chapter by **Dick Pels** critically elaborates Ankersmit's aesthetic approach in a more sociological direction, by asking how the conditions of political identity and difference are changing under the impact of televisual technologies and the new prominence of style. The brief political life and dramatic death of Pim Fortuyn, the mediagenic political dandy who effected a major 'style break' in Dutch political culture, is used as a focus for discussing the new forms of personality politics, political celebrity and 'parasocial' quasi-intimacy that are presently restructuring the field of political recognition and (dis)trust. Parasocial identification stages a novel proximity between representers and represented that is counterbalanced by the dramatic distance that inevitably remains between celebrities and 'civilians'. While political personalities adopt more aesthetic forms of self-display, citizens increasingly judge them on the basis of 'emotional intelligence' and considerations of political taste. In this sense, the stylisation of politics bridges the representative gap and may inspire a further democratisation of democracy – even though the risk of false intimacy and obsessive identification remains.

As is clear from the above, issues around the new forms of the personal in politics are close to the centre of many chapters in this volume. **John Corner** makes this his primary focus. Taking up the idea of 'persona', he reviews the changing character of professional political identity, political performance and the interconnections with new forms of media portrayal. The approach is schematic, outlining features of structure and process that now interconnect 'private' and 'public' dimensions of political life both in political journalism and in the broader sphere of political gossip and celebrity culture. Corner assesses how popular political sentiment relates to ideas of political personality, a focus for cynicism yet a continuing point of attraction, and looks at new terms for considering the perennial debate about political honesty and political deceit. How far can personalisation be seen as a denial of proper democratic engagement and to what extent might it actually return politics to a more productive recognition of motives, values and beliefs?

John Street continues the focus on political personality by developing further the idea of 'political celebrity' and the relationship with popular culture. Street begins his chapter by reviewing a number of theories of democracy in relation to how the 'people' figure as arbiters of political value and as the addressees of political publicity. He then looks at contemporary features of political performance, linking them to other forms of cultural stardom both in their production and consumption. The idea of a 'cool politics' is explored critically, making reference to the attempt by the Blair government in Britain to link itself more closely with style and success in the popular arts. What kind of criteria might be used in assessing a politics that is more openly cultural and performative in its appeal? How would they differ from more established forms of political judgement?

This new articulation between political performance and entertainment culture is further explored by **Liesbet van Zoonen** in her chapter on the 'soaping' of politics. The ubiquitous presence of the soap opera as a frame of reference first of all operates as a critical metaphor, which positions the viewer at a distance from the superficiality, incompetence and obsession with scandal and spin that allegedly disfigure political life. This critique carries a gendered subtext since, over and against the traditional dominance of modernist and 'macho' metaphors of rationality, struggle and public presence, the generic features of soap are usually associated with feminine values, the private sphere and the emotional life. But the soap metaphor simultaneously expresses a sense of crisis, providing symbols that explore people's capacity to become emotionally involved and connected to interesting characters and storylines. In this more subtle understanding of politics, which suggests a more positive reconciliation between democracy and popular culture, virtues which were traditionally considered to be part of femininity become a central ingredient of political merit.

The relationship between citizenship and consumerism, one dimension of that broader tension between publics and markets, provides the focus for **Margaret Scammell**'s chapter. The central part of her account is given over to a critical examination of the case against 'marketing'. What precisely is the damage done to democracy by the use of this approach in politics? What do the terms of critique indicate about the presumed limits and liabilities of democratic practice? Older models of marketing presupposed the essentially passive role of the 'customer-consumer', but Scammell looks at recent shifts suggesting the idea of a much more active 'consumer republic'. She moves on to raise complementary questions about shifts beyond state-oriented politics towards forms of 'corporate citizenship' and suggests much that cannot usefully be viewed within the totalising terms of despair that have sometimes been adopted.

The re-positioning of citizenship, both as an identity and as a practice, is the main concern of **Lance Bennett**. As in Scammell, the convergence with consumer roles is seen as significant. His chapter maps some of the principal factors, including a decline in the role and status of civic institutions and an electoral politics drawing closer to marketing models, that underpin current changes. For him, as for other contributors, a 'new politics' is emerging that is more fragmented, more personalised and symbolic and far less predictable than the kinds of established practices it is replacing. Drawing primarily on his reading of the current situation in America, Bennett registers the problems of democratic value that this introduces, threatening to displace effective routes of civic involvement. At the same time he finds some hope in the newer critical energies, forms of activism and possibilities for re-building that do more than simply by-pass the present institutional connections between political involvement and the practices of government.

It is impossible to discuss current changes in political culture without making some connection with debates about 'new media' and about the uses and potential of the Internet. **Peter Dahlgren** gives this sustained treatment in a chapter that has a double focus. First of all, he offers a detailed, analytic commentary on the idea of 'civic culture', identifying the different dimensions that make up a 'circuit' of values and processes in which the media have inevitably become deeply implicated. He then moves on to look at how 'new media' are reconfiguring the dynamics of this circuit, in ways whose final direction and consequence can still only be the subject of speculation. How are online political actions related to offline citizenship? What is being opened up in the civic circuit and what is at risk of being closed down? Dahlgren concludes by surveying a number of websites, a selective trawl that allows a provisional reading of the various orientations and possibilities of the new political terrain, putting some hope in the 'new informal politics' that is becoming visible there.

Jon Simons pursues the link between the popularisation of culture and the democratisation of politics on a more general level, developing a case against elitist critics who despair about universal commodification and the pernicious influence of the media. This intellectual pessimism about popular democracy and the aestheticisation of culture should largely be understood as a lament about the loss of relevant cultural capital, which has traditionally been invested in typographic rather than televisual forms of communication. However, political elites necessarily operate in a risky arena, since electoral competition must be conducted with the help of aesthetic technologies and media formats that are largely oriented to visuality, emotionality, commercialism and entertainment. The dominant rationalistic orientation of these elites tends to obscure the critical and democratic potential that is offered by visual and emotional literacy and the contradictions of media culture, which inevitably conjure up the risks of sensationalism, parody, and scepticism.

In the final chapter, **Bronislaw Szerszynski** re-engages the central dilemmas of aesthetic representation and political style not so much from the 'elevated' perspective of political elites but 'from below', focusing upon the peculiar dramaturgy of ecological protest politics. Their political semiotics include a specific visualisation and aesthetic typing of protest actors, which facilitate the emotional identification with strangers who are clearly marked out as different from the norm, but who simultaneously claim to embody a higher moral legitimacy. Since this gap between particularity and universality is bridged by a political aesthetic, style display also makes these political actors vulnerable to being seen as acting out a particular identity or a private sentiment (for example, that of frustrated middle-class children, troublemakers, or youthful idealists), denying them the right to speak more representatively. Extending Sennett's historical parallel between theatre and public life, Szerszynski argues that contemporary protest actions exemplify artistic and expressive forms of public performance and citizenship, in which the expression of authenticity and the projection of universal values are made to coexist in a tensionful and risky balance.

Critical Tensions: Pessimism and Optimism

In different ways, all our contributors, therefore, work with a critical tension between modernist or rationalist conceptions of 'high' politics, 'high' journalism and 'high' science, and a variety of 'romantic', 'aesthetic' or 'performative' views which elaborate matters of representational style in order to level the traditional hierarchy with 'low' popular culture and more 'ordinary' practices and skills of world-making. Arguing against objectivism and foundational certainties in politics, political journalism and political science, they variously rehabilitate perspectivism, aesthetic styling, emotional intelligence, informality and visual culture as possible conduits for political representation and democratic citizenship. Such a performative restyling of politics may incorporate an interesting convergence between issues of linguistic performativity (such as elaborated by speech act theory or critical discourse analysis – see for example Fairclough, 2000) and sociological and anthropological theories of action which generalise the metaphor of artistic performance (Goffman, 1959; Turner, 1982) and fruitfully link up with 'performance theory' in theatre and music studies (see Carlson, 1996 for a critical survey). The latter influences consecrate a shift from a predominantly discursive or textual view of performativity and performance towards a more 'tacit', material, or 'practical' view which focuses upon aesthetic display, bodily encounters and 'libidinal' attachments to objects and spaces (Schieffelin, 1998; Thrift, 2000; Pels, Hetherington and Vandenberghe, 2002). In straddling the 'higher' dimension of political rationality and political speech and the 'baser' one that admits affect, body language, 'looks', dress code, and other stage props of political performance, this perspective immediately maps on to the inclusive concept of political style that we have made central to the book.

Such a notion of performativity also engages a different conception of political truth (and hence of the political significance of lying and deceit, see above), in recognising the ineradicability of perspectivism and the constructivist logic of descriptions that co-produce what they describe. The modernist discourse of politics (and of journalism and of science) still has regular difficulties in experiencing style because of its aspirations towards transparency. A performative and reflexive view, on the other hand, acknowledges this political naturalism as a singular example of a representational style that fails to recognise itself as such. This leads on to another important epistemological dimension of the notion of performativity: its capacity to harbour crossovers between judgements of value and judgements of fact. Indeed, while all our contributors venture beyond the realm of strict factual description, most of them also recognise the impossibility of 'scientifically' neutralising normative issues and political concerns. If facts and values find themselves in 'natural proximity' (Pels, 2002: ch. 4), there can be no time out from judgements about the 'enabling' or 'disabling' effects of current changes in the landscape of mediated politics. In a style-conscious epistemology, pessimism or optimism about the future of democracy and the state of civic culture cannot be relegated to an underworld of arbitrary sentiment and taste, but are intrinsically interwoven with those ostensibly more grounded analytical views that make up the conventional wisdom of 'high' science.

All of the contributions that follow therefore interconnect, if sometimes only indirectly and after fulfilling their descriptive and analytic tasks, around a question that in its most vulgar and direct form could be posed as 'is politics getting better or worse?' The reader will notice that most of our contributors explore an 'enabling' or optimistic perspective on the aestheticisation and 'popularisation' of politics, even though all of them take care to weigh the democratic opportunities afforded by the new intensity of media-political relations against its evident risks. It should be clear that the purpose of this book is to open up an area of enquiry and debate, one that has often got lost in the gaps between political and media studies, rather than to foreclose around any particular reading or assessment. The sheer complexity of the current phase of 're-styling', across its various dimensions, is such as to confound any attempt at the neat analysis or the elegance of the unqualified judgement. We have identified shifts in representation across its two meanings, both as mode of portrayal and as practice of delegation, and then in the relation between the two, as pivotal here.

That many countries are experiencing a new dynamics of change in their political life is hardly in question. Nor is the shift in the directness of the connections with popular culture and with commerce. Political structures, performances and experience are all in transformation and the bold form of our question resists an equally bold answer simply because of the mix of trajectories and values. Different kinds of what Raymond Williams called 'residual, dominant and emergent' elements are in process together. This is certainly true for many established democracies. Elsewhere, of course, history and more fundamental kinds of transition sometimes allow for a more decisive answer, at least for the time being. But the 'troubled' tone of many of the chapters, their sense of engaging with values in tension and sometimes in contradiction, we take to be the direct product of their perceptiveness of approach rather than a failure of evaluative resolve. For whatever else it does, the present re-styling of politics presents us (both as citizens and as scholars) with quite specific kinds of *difficulty*. Our hope is that this book provides some help in thinking that difficulty through.

References

Adorno, T. (1991) *The Culture Industry*. London & New York: Routledge.

Arendt, H. (1973) 'Lying in Politics', pp. 9–42 in idem, *Crises of the Republic*. Harmondsworth: Penguin.

Baker, C.E. (2002) *Media, Markets and Democracy*. Cambridge: Cambridge University Press.

Benjamin, W. (1992) *Illuminations*. H. Arendt (ed.). London: Fontana.

Carlson, M. (1996) *Performance: A Critical Introduction*. London & New York: Routledge.

Durkheim, E. (1995 [1912]) *The Elementary Forms of Religious Life*. New York: The Free Press.

Fairclough, N. (2000) *New Labour: New Language?* London: Routledge.

Goffman, E. (1959) *The Presentation of Self in Everyday Life*. New York: Anchor Books.

Hillach, A. (1979) 'The Aesthetics of Politics: Walter Benjamin's "Theories of German Fascism"', *New German Critique* 17: 99–119.

Horkheimer, M. and Adorno, T. (1979 [1947]) *Dialectic of Enlightenment*. London: Verso.

Le Bon, G. (1960 [1901]) *The Crowd: A Study of the Popular Mind*. New York: Viking.

Marshall, P.D. (1997) *Celebrity and Power. Fame in Contemporary Culture*. Minneapolis & London: University of Minnesota Press.

Mayhew, L. (1997) *The New Public: Professional Communication and the Means of Social Influence*. Cambridge: Cambridge University Press.

Meyrowitz, J. (1985) *No Sense of Place. The Impact of Electronic Media on Social Behaviour*. New York and Oxford: Oxford University Press.

Pels, D. (2003) *Unhastening Science. Autonomy and Reflexivity in the Social Theory of Knowledge*. Liverpool: Liverpool University Press.

Pels, D., Hetherington, K. and Vandenberghe, F. (2002) 'The Status of the Object: Performances, Mediations, and Techniques' in idem (eds) *Sociality/Materiality. The Status of the Object in Social Science*, special double issue of *Theory, Culture and Society* 19(5–6).

Samuels, A. (2001) *Politics on the Couch*. London: Profile Books.

Schieffelin, E.L. (1998) 'Problematizing Performance', pp. 194–207 in F. Hughes-Freeland (ed.) *Ritual, Performance, Media*. London: Routledge.

Splichal, S. (2002) 'The Principle of Publicity, Public Use of Reason and Social Control', *Media, Culture and Society* 24(1), 5–26.

Thrift, N. (2000) 'Afterwords', *Society and Space* 18: 213–55.

Turner, V. (1982) *From Ritual to Theater. The Human Seriousness of Play*. New York: Performing Arts Journal Publications.

Weber, M. (1988) *On Charisma and Institution Building: Selected Papers*. S.N. Eisenstadt (ed.). Chicago: University of Chicago Press.

Weber, M. (1994) *Political Writings*. P. Lassman and R. Speirs (eds). Cambridge: Cambridge University Press.

Wernick, A. (1991) *Promotional Culture*. London: Sage.

2

Democracy's Inner Voice

Political Style as Unintended Consequence of Political Action[1]

FRANK ANKERSMIT

> In any given case political style might be unimportant or dangerous, but obviously it can't be both. Robert Hariman, *Political Style* (1995)

The *innere Stimme* in Music and Politics

In Robert Schumann's *Humoreske* (1838) we encounter one of the most remarkable passages in the history of music. The historian of music Charles Rosen, in his brilliant *The Romantic Generation* (1996), wrote the following about this passage: 'there are three staves: the uppermost for the right hand: the lowest for the left, the middle, which contains the melody, is not to be played'. Hence, the pianist plays with right and left hands the accompaniment of a melody that is clearly and unambiguously suggested by the score and which the listener will also hear, while at the same time, the score explicitly forbids the pianist to play this melody. The melody is here, as Schumann indicates himself in the score, an *innere Stimme*, an inner voice, which the listener, without being aware of it, will furnish himself. Put differently, the melody, also for Schumann the heart of the composition, will be *listened to* by the listener, without actually being *heard* by him. Hence, what one listens to, according to Rosen, 'is the echo of an unperformed melody, the accompaniment of a song. The middle part is marked *innere Stimme*, and it is both interior and inward, a double sense calculated by the composer: a voice between soprano and bass, it is also an inner voice that is never exteriorised. It has its being within the mind and its existence only through its echo' (Rosen, 1996: 7).

Certainly, precedents can be found in polyphony for this paradox of inaudible music; indeed, for the more subtle composers in polyphony this was a musical trope as obvious as it was popular. We can think of the really 'shattering rest', louder than the loudest kettledrum beat, in the midst of the *Sind Blitze, sind Donner in Wolken verschwunden?* of Bach's *St. Mathew's Passion*. The classical tradition, on the other hand, with its emphasis on transparency and the unambiguous, forbade this paradox and therefore its theory of music left no room for it. It was only Romanticism that operationalised and eagerly exploited all the possibilities of making silence audible and of transforming into music what was not yet music.

Now, we may ask ourselves, is this *innere Stimme* a reality or a mere illusion, if we, as we have seen, did *listen* to it, but could not possibly actually have *heard* it? Probably the answer to this question will depend on what one's musical affinities happen to be. Whoever is used to classical music will undoubtedly prefer to see Schumann's invention as an illusion, as mere musical rhetoric: we were deliberately and artfully deceived, for we believed to have heard what we could not possibly have heard. Schumann achieved this invention by means of a reality effect, an *effet de réel* in the terminology of Roland Barthes, offending a healthy and recommendable sense of what reality is. And this certainly is how one could look at the matter.

But the romanticist will not be at a loss when confronted with this argument, pointing out that this melody that was listened to but could not be heard can be identified with just as much precision as what we actually did hear. There is an amount of quasi-mathematical precision in music ensuring that the *innere Stimme* is completely and unambiguously fixed by what we *could* or *did* hear. And, the romanticist continues, if we customarily associate reality with what can objectively be established, whereas fiction indeed permits us to leave this objective reality, then we should situate Schumann's *innere Stimme* in the domain of reality rather than in that of fiction and illusion. And that would also justify the amazing inference that what is *not* there, can nevertheless be part of reality.

But what has all this to do with politics? The main point of my argument will be that if we want to give content to the notion of 'political reality', and to define what we should see as such, the paradox of Schumann's melody that can be listened to without being heard will prove to be a most valuable and fruitful analogy. For, in a way much reminiscent of Schumann's *innere Stimme*, two answers can be given to the question about the nature of political reality. On the one hand we have, to use the musical terminology adopted above, those 'classical' political theorists and political scientists according to whom there is a measurable political reality that should be the basis and starting point of all reflection on politics. To press the analogy with music a little further, within the classical conception of politics, nothing can be *listened to* in politics that had not been actually *heard* before. Political 'input' on the one hand and political 'output' on the other, what 'really' happened in the domain of politics on the one hand and our perception of it on the other – at all times these two are most directly and intimately interconnected. There can and should be no 'gap' or 'discrepancy' between this input of objective political reality and the output of how we subjectively experience this reality. For if such a gap or discrepancy were to present itself, we would seem to perceive something in the political world that is not 'really' there; we would then have become the will-less plaything of illusions and of political myths. The fact that we naturally and immediately resort to this kind of pejorative qualification in this context clearly suggests already how objectionable we would tend to think such discrepancies to be. We are therefore naturally inclined to agree with the 'classical' political theorist's view that such a discrepancy would lack a *fundamentum in re* and must therefore be considered an expression of irrationality, of primitive instincts, if not worse.

On the other hand, there are the political 'romantics' who reject the input/output model of their 'classicist' opponents. They will not deny that in many cases, perhaps even most cases, the model will be adequate and helpful – just as in music we will ordinarily have listened to what we have actually heard – but they also want to leave room for cases in which in political reality something new is produced that transcends the input/output model. When such a new political reality comes into being, we seem to be listening to a political *innere Stimme* for which the classical input/output model is unable to account. And, as will become clear in this chapter, this disagreement between the 'classical' and the 'romantic' political theorist is not of mere academic significance; the sound functioning of our Western democracies requires that we are able and prepared to listen to that political *innere Stimme* in the complex symphony of democratic politics.

Perhaps we might observe here another argument in favour of the elective affinities between democracy and the market that have already been emphasised by so many writers. The value of a company or of a national currency will not be found by figuring out the values of the company's buildings, machines, assets, bank accounts, and so forth, nor by determining a country's natural riches, its trade balance, and national savings. All these things may seem to be very 'real' and determinate and therefore the obvious and solid basis for establishing value; nevertheless it will be the unpredictable and often unexplainable vagaries of the stock exchange that give us the best definition of the economic realities of a company or a nation. Hence, both in democracy and in economics it is in the *innere Stimme* of political and economic interaction that 'reality' reveals itself. And there is no surer way to disaster than the decision not to listen to this *innere Stimme* – as will invariably be the case when we decide to ignore what reality is like.

What is Political 'Reality'?

If we wish to determine our own position in this debate between 'classical' and 'romantic' political theorists, it will above all be necessary to propose a concretisation of the notions of political input and political output. A most suggestive example of such a concretisation is presented by Murray Edelman, when he writes that the citizens in a democracy are always urged 'to look upon government as a mechanism that is responsive to their wants and upon these in turn as rational reflections of their interest and moral upbringing and therefore as stable and continuing' (Edelman, 1971: 3). Put differently, on the one hand there is the input of the political interests and desires of the citizen, and, on the other, the output of political decision making. And the classical model of the nature of (democratic) political reality requires us to conceive of the output of political decision making in terms of the input of those interests and desires of the citizen. This does not in the least preclude, however, that in actual democratic practice this relationship between input and output may be very complex and untransparent.

This plausibility of the classical conception of the machinery of democracy is still further reinforced by what Combs and Nimmo recently referred to as 'the Myth of the Good Citizen'. That is to say, by the widespread presupposition that democracy is supported by 'peaceful citizens who by taste or by interest sincerely desire the well-being of their country' (Combs and Nimmo, 1996: 28). This myth of the Good Citizen seems to endow the classical political model with a solid and reliable foundation in the reasonable interests and desires of the citizen and presents democratic politics as a more or less complicated calculating machine that figures out the correct resultant of all these individual interests and desires – without adding anything of itself, if things go as they should. In short, there is a popular ideology of democratic politics – this myth of the Good Citizen – that seems to grant an immense plausibility to the 'classical' conception of democratic politics.

When the romantic political theorists wish to attack the input/output model two arguments are at their disposal. Or, rather, as will become clear in a moment, it is only the second argument that is really decisive. But since the first argument offers a few interesting perspectives, it deserves our attention within the present context as well.

Within the first argument the input/output model is rejected since it is said to be impossible in politics to identify clearly and unambiguously what functions as input for the output of public political action. Input and output are simply inseparable and the classical model therefore is an illusion. Even more so, it is an illusion that is at odds with the very nature and spirit of democracy; for is not this inseparability of input and output one of the greatest virtues of democracy? Is democracy not the political system attempting to link these two together more closely and intimately than any other political system? Does this classical principle of the separability of political input and political output not inevitably create a distance between the two which, in its turn, inevitably invites the danger that input and output no longer correspond? And if all this does not sound implausible, would that not justify the conclusion that the classical model is a denial of the very idea of all democracy?

Next, romantic political theorists will tend to be political realists and will therefore be little inclined to confuse some ideology – of democracy in this case – with what democracy is in actual historical reality. They will therefore not be content with the observation that the classical model contradicts some ideal of democratic politics. They will also want to demonstrate that democratic *practice* is at odds with the classical model. Murray Edelman has made clear in what respect democratic practice deviates from the classical notion of the separability of political input and political output. One may think here primarily of his thesis according to which 'political actions chiefly arouse or satisfy people not by granting or withholding their stable substantive demands, but rather by changing the demands and the expectations' (Edelman, 1971: 7). Put differently, the output (of political action) codetermines the nature of the input and cannot be separated from it; or, in Edelman's own formulation, 'the significant "outputs" of political activities are not particular public policies labeled as political goals, but rather the creation of political following and supports: i.e., the evocation of arousal or quiescence in mass publics' (1971: 4). And, in the second place, the reverse is true as well. For just as political action codetermines the desires of the citizens, the citizens' demands will codetermine the politician's action – a truth that Edelman puts into words by means of the provocative paradox that 'political leaders must follow their followers' (Edelman, 1988: 37). In summary, if we look at both the ideal and the practice of democracy, then the classical input/output model must be rejected as a technocratic illusion.

But it is unlikely that classical political theorists will be deeply impressed by this kind of argument. They will protest that romantic political theorists have demonstrated precisely the opposite of what they wanted to prove. For this argumentation, as they will go on to reason, succeeds not so much in demonstrating the *shortcomings* of the input/output model as its *omnipresence* in political reality. For what the romantic political theorist unintentionally showed has been that we will have to apply the model also in cases where we originally had been little inclined to make use of it. Apparently there is a continuous *interaction* or *interchange* between all the actors and factors that are operative in the political domain, and for a correct understanding of this interaction we will have to apply the input/output model even more intensively than hitherto.

An example may clarify the classical political theorist's rejoinder. Think of the situation in which two political parties that differ profoundly from an ideological point of view nevertheless see themselves forced to cooperate in order to prevent worse. One may think here of certain phases in the conflict between labour and capital in Western Continental democracies. Such a situation will often give rise to the paradoxical situation that precisely the extremist political die-hards of both parties discover themselves to be each other's 'objective' allies, to put it in the Marxist jargon of some thirty years ago. For those extremists will be most strongly opposed to compromise and cooperation and they will find the strongest argument for their intransigence in the extremism of their ideological antipodes. So, on the one hand, this presents us with the paradox that precisely the greatest political disagreement is conducive to the realisation of a shared political goal. On the other hand, as the classical political theorists will emphasise, in this realisation of an unexpectedly shared common political goal, we certainly cannot discern a political *innere Stimme*, as the romantic is apt to do. For the classical input/output model is perfectly well equipped to deal with this paradox. The input of political polarisation has caused the output of this rejection of compromise and cooperation desired by the extremists of both parties. In other words, the shared goal of political non-cooperation was already latently present in the extremist wings of both parties – and something really new, something that would, so to speak, transcend what is written in the political scores of the extremists of both parties and that would *not* be reducible to it, did not and could not make itself heard. In short, in spite of this surprising paradox of fruitfully cooperating political extremists, we still safely find ourselves here in the clear and transparent world of classical political rationality.

But precisely this example will also enable the romantic political theorist to demonstrate the deficiency in his classical opponent's position. He will begin by pointing out that his political conceptions have their natural biotope in the realm of political conflict – and that, if only for that reason, the example proposed by the classical political theorist suits him excellently. Just as Schumann's *innere Stimme* was only something that could be listened to at all thanks to the oppositions and the complex mutual interferences of what is played by the right and the left hands, so the political *innere Stimme* can only come into being thanks to political opposition and conflict. There is no room for this political *innere Stimme* in a society that is reigned by a universal consensus – whether this consensus actually exists or has been imposed by brute, totalitarian political force. Romantic political reality can only be observed, therefore, in a society of political struggle and conflict. If democracy is the political system aiming at the *juste-milieu* between conflicting political positions (see more extensively Ankersmit, 1997; 2002), this political *innere Stimme* can be listened to more often in democracy than in any other political system.

But let us return to the classical political theorist's example and focus now not on the ideological extremists, but on those within both parties who are prepared to compromise and cooperate. It is there that we will, for the first time, recognise those democratic mechanisms that can properly be accounted for only by the romantic conception of political reality – which also justifies, by the way, the inference that political renewal can never be achieved by extremists but only by those who are ready to cooperate with the political opponent. In the first place we should realise that this readiness to cooperate will make both parties look for compromise – and the notion of *compromise* should be clearly distinguished here from that of *consensus*.

For the latter notion is suggestive of actual ideological agreement; that is to say, from the perspective of different ideological positions discussion may reveal a set of political views that both parties will consider to be acceptable or even most rational. In the simplest case consensus will take the form of an identification of the common denominator of the ideological position of the parties involved. And in more complicated cases consensus will be a development of this common denominator into ideological directions that both parties had not foreseen when defining their own ideological positions and that had, therefore, been left unexplored. But in all cases the ideological conflict is not so much camouflaged, accepted or momentarily forgotten for the sake of cooperation; conflict really disappears here: where there was previously conflict, consensus now reigns. Obviously consensus will primarily be achieved where ideological differences turn out, on closer inspection, to be much smaller than was initially believed. In sum, in consensus the compatibility of different ideologies is exploited to the full. But precisely for this reason consensus cannot produce anything that was not already present in the existing ideologies; all the ingredients for consensus were already part of those ideologies. So even here we are still in the realm of classical political theory.

This process is different from that of compromise, which ocurs when two parties agree upon a political option that is explicitly at odds with the desiderata of the different ideologies involved, but both parties are nevertheless willing to take the political responsibility for this option. They recognise that the existence of other parties with other ideologies requires them to accept compromise as an unpleasant but inevitable fact about meaningful political decision making, if the even worse alternative of a total breakdown of the political machine is to be prevented. The paradox of political compromise is that, on the one hand, as in the case of consensus, one stands by one's ideological conviction, but, on the other hand, one is prepared to follow a line of political action more or less inimical to that conviction. Hence, it will be obvious that political compromise may produce something really *new*, something that was not yet present in the existing catalogue of political ideologies. This does not alter the fact that political compromise will always bear the marks or traces of the ideologies contained by that catalogue. And the important conclusion is that, as opposed to consensus, compromise invites the introduction of this political *innere Stimme* in the symphony of democratic politics.

Political compromise enables us, so to speak, to listen to the political *innere Stimme* that was not yet 'audible' in ideological conflict but that can indeed be discerned in it *from a later point of view* – the point of view embodied by the political compromise. Only compromise can make us aware of the point of view implicit in previously given political conflict and opposition. Like Schumann's *innere Stimme*, this is a reality that can also *become* a reality. This, then, is the kind of peculiarly ambivalent reality that is indispensable to the proper functioning of democracy – to this political system that cannot live without conflict.

Even more so, the very stability of democracy as such is not threatened by conflict but by consensus and agreement which, as we saw above, leave no room for the political *innere Stimme*. For, as Edelman puts it, 'when statements need not be defended against counterstatements, they are readily changed or inverted' (1988: 19). A state and society dominated by consensus is an unstable state and society, since little will be needed to make everybody change their opinion – with all the unpredictable and unpleasant consequences that this may have. By contrast, in a state and society where disagreement is dominant, the pros and cons of the conflicting opinions will be widely discussed and commented on. Under such circumstances public opinion will develop slowly but responsibly, and political disasters that may hurt everybody will be more easy to avoid. A society governed by consensus is a stupid society, given to erratic and counterproductive behaviour, whereas the society dominated by struggle and conflict will ordinarily succeed in avoiding the worst follies. As Montesquieu already put it: 'In an age of ignorance one has no doubts even if one commits the most serious mistakes; in an enlightened age one trembles even if producing the greatest benefits' (Montesquieu, 1973: 6).

But even more surprising is the typically romanticist political thesis that the conflict between political opinions shores up not only democracy but also those conflicting political opinions themselves. In a manner worthy of Tocqueville, Edelman formulates the insight as follows: 'as soon as ... bits of language circulate in a culture and present themselves for acceptance or rejection, it becomes evident that texts become bulwarks of each other while isolated texts, *unsupported by opposition*, are readily vulnerable to new language' (Edelman, 1988: 19; my italics). The force of political positions partly lies, paradoxically, in the opposition they will encounter because of the presence of other and rival political positions. It follows that in a democracy the political *innere Stimme* will be easier to discern and that it will play a more beneficial role, to the extent that political positions are more clearly delineated and easier to recognise for all concerned.

Indeed, nobody had a clearer eye for the kind of insight into the nature of democracy and of public debate expounded above than Alexis de Tocqueville. Though no oeuvre resists summary and recapitulation more than Tocqueville's, I may be allowed to indicate one constant in his observations on democracy that is relevant here. Tocqueville always likes to confront his readers with the paradoxes of democracy: he likes to impress on us that democracy often functions for reasons precisely opposite to what we tend to associate with that political system. He says, for example, that democracy is not inclined to revolutionary change but to conservatism, that public debate in a democracy is not a debate in the proper sense of the word but rather a *dialogue des sourds*, that political decision making is not decision making but rather the creative avoidance of it and that the democratic state does not execute what the people wish or decide, but that the people decide what the state achieves or tries to achieve (cf. Ankersmit, 1997: 294). And always the message is that we should not see these paradoxes as signs of a degeneration of democracy, but as the conditions of its successful functioning – though it is certainly true that Tocqueville also fears from democracy several threats to the cause of liberty.

I shall not dwell any longer here on Tocqueville's paradoxes, nor on whether we should always agree with him. Instead I want to point out the congeniality between this kind of paradox and our notion of the political *innere Stimme*. For as is generally the case with paradoxes, Tocqueville's paradoxes also make us aware of an unsuspected political reality that is, in some way or other, hidden or present in our naive discourse about democracy, but that we may only become aware of thanks to the conflicts and paradoxes in that discourse. Paradox is the figure of speech confronting us with these conflicts in our speaking and thinking and that requires us to look at reality itself in order to find our way out of the impasse into which paradox has led us. And *if* we follow this injunction of paradox and actually turn to reality itself, we shall see that what discourse made us believe to be incompatible can peacefully coexist in reality itself. For example, on the basis of what we associate with these words, egoism *seems* to be incompatible with the common interest, but if we may believe Bernard de Mandeville and Adam Smith, in *reality* these two things are in line with each other. In a similar way, Tocqueville often succeeds in demonstrating that what we initially believed to be at odds with the principles of democratic government is, in fact, a condition for its proper functioning.

If we wish to account for these paradoxes of democracy, Machiavelli's perspectivism will prove to be our best point of departure. This viewpoint has its origins in Machiavelli's attack on ethics that many people down to the present day have found so profoundly shocking. The point of Machiavelli's argument I have in mind here (see further Ankersmit, 1997: 115) is that in social-political reality there is no perspective or point of view that is uniquely privileged above all others in discovering and defining moral truth. Even more so, not only is there no such Archimedean point of moral truth that would enable us to justify our own moral and political action, it is often exactly *the other* who is in a better position to assess the merits of our action than we are ourselves. 'Real' moral truth chooses its home rather with the other than with ourselves (and the unsettling fact is that this is true for each determination of what should count as 'ourselves'). Hence, paradoxically, it is precisely our respect of the other that requires us to surrender our own moral certainties – and thus any certainty that we might have with regard to how we should properly demonstrate our respect for the other. 'Real' moral truth – in short, political truth – is not so much a matter of perky inner moral conviction as a matter of how 'the other' perceives 'the outside' of our action (regardless of our inner moral convictions that may or may not have inspired it); and we should therefore always consider with the greatest distrust our 'Cartesian' inclination to make ethics into a matter of conscience. Moral Cartesianism leads us away from 'real', essentially *political* moral truth to moral solipsism and the moral complacency of an ethical egocentrism, however sublime the ideals of Cartesian ethics may often seem to us at first sight.

But what Machiavelli affirms here about ourselves is obviously just as true for *the other* as it is for ourselves. And this justifies the conclusion that the source of moral (or, rather, political) rectitude cannot be located in ourselves, nor even in others, but instead *in the space between ourselves and the others*, so to speak. Much like Schumann's *innere Stimme*, moral and political rectitude can only come into being in the interaction, the interference and in the conflict between political and ideological convictions with regard to moral and political truth. Next, it is self-evident that democracy, more than any other political system, will have a natural affinity with Machiavelli's perspectivism as described. For is democracy not inspired by the belief that political truth can only be the result of the interaction of individuals and groups in a democratic society? The essentially *monological* discourse of ethics is therefore basically at odds with the *dialogue* of democracy and, hence, the notion of an ethical or moral *foundation* of democracy should be considered a *contradictio in terminis*. Thus, nothing has contributed more importantly to the construction of the political mentality of democracy than this ill-famed rejection of the pretensions of ethics that we find in Machiavelli's *The Prince*.

Political Style

Several conclusions about the notion of political style follow from the foregoing. In order to clarify these conclusions, I shall appeal to another less obvious source within the present context, namely Schiller's essay *Über naive und sentimentalische Dichtung* of 1796. Schiller distinguishes here between what he refers to as 'naive' and 'sentimental' poetry. He defines this distinction as follows: naive poetry is, above all, an expression of nature and should also be experienced as such. Put differently, in naive poetry we will find not only an expression of 'being that is free, that is, being which takes its existence out of itself', but also of the *awareness*, or of the very *idea* of this natural existence that is not in need of anything outside or beyond itself. And only thanks to this 'awareness' or this 'idea' are we able to recognise naive poetry as such and can we be so deeply moved by it: 'We love in it not certain objects, but the idea that they represent' (Schiller, 1867: 110).

What exactly is meant by this 'idea' may become clearer when we notice that Schiller links it *expressis verbis* to morality. Why he does so is suggested by the following comparison proposed by him. We consider the child to be 'naive' and respect its naivety because we believe a call for perfection to be present in the child's naivety. And inevitably every adult like ourselves has, each of us in a different way, failed to live up to this call for perfection. Put differently, the child embodies a promise of perfection that no adult ever succeeded in fulfilling. This is why the child confronts us with our own moral imperfections and, hence, why the child's naivety has for the adult this double significance of being a moral appeal and a sign of his own moral imperfection. Speaking more generally, the naive embodies a mode of being destined to natural perfection, which is achieved without artifice and reflection and presented to us like a gift of nature; on the one hand, it requires us to overcome our imperfections and weaknesses and to return to this natural naivety; but on the other, precisely by manifesting itself as a requirement, hence as something coming from outside ourselves and what we naturally are, it makes us deeply aware of the impossibility of ever satisfying this requirement. There is a kind of double bind in the very idea of this naive moral perfection: either we possess it, but then we are unaware of it, or we have to strive for it, and then we know that we can never achieve it.

This brings us to sentimental poetry, which is, basically, the kind of poetry originating from this awareness of the immeasurable value of naivety and of what we therefore lost forever by losing it. We now realise that we are no longer part of nature, that we belong to the world of artifice and culture. We feel unhappy about this, and therefore want to get back to nature and begin to ask ourselves how best to achieve this (impossible) goal. The result is 'sentimental' poetry. And the contrast between naive and sentimental poetry can therefore be summarised, in Schiller's own words, as follows: 'The poet, I said, either *is* nature, or he *strives* for it; the former is the naive, and the latter the sentimental poet' (Schiller, 1867: 128).

The crucial difference between the two forms of poetry is that the naive poet has no sense or consciousness of what is alien to him, for it precisely is his grace 'to be at home even after having left behind himself what is known and to *extend* nature without *moving beyond* it' (Schiller, 1867: 118). The sentimental poet is in a far less comfortable position: finding himself caught in this opposition between nature and culture, he irrevocably is part of culture and yet wants to return to nature. Reality – nature – therefore is to him as much an infinite task as an invincible barrier (Schiller, 1867: 132).

It must strike us how much Schiller's distinction between naive and sentimental poetry is in agreement with Hegel's philosophy of history: the naive is the evident analogue of Hegel's 'objective mind' and the sentimental that of the 'subjective mind'. And if we recall, next, to what extent the dialectics of the objective and the subjective mind is for Hegel the creator of all the political realities that have been realised in the course of world history, this may already give us an inkling of the political dimensions and implications of

Schiller's distinction. We therefore need not be surprised that such a distinctly political thinker as Schiller did not hesitate to translate the distinction to the domain of politics. And, indeed, he ends his essay with what is arguably one of the most interesting comments on political realism and idealism that has ever been written. Elsewhere in his essay he discusses 'naive' political personalities such as Pope Adrian VI; other examples of naive politicians proposed by Schiller are Julius Caesar and Henry IV of France because they found 'egg-of-Columbus-like' solutions for the political problems of their age. Unfortunately Schiller gave us no examples of 'sentimental' politicians. This is to be regretted because – as we shall see in a moment – political problems most often present themselves in the domain of the 'sentimental'.

But more important is the following. Transposed into the domain of politics, the naive is obviously in line with the speculations of natural law philosophy and, more generally, with the conviction that political reality is basically unambiguous and transparent and thus, in the end, completely fathomable by the naive political theorist and by naive political theory. It may not be easy to do this, and will admittedly require the greatest intellectual sophistication, but if we give our best to this important task, no impenetrable secrets necessarily need remain. In this sense almost all of political theory and contemporary political science is 'naive', as this term is understood by Schiller. For on all occasions one is convinced that a point of view, a discourse, a system, or whatever you have, can be found in terms of which the whole of political reality will become transparent to our ratio and our argument.

Compelling in Schiller's analysis, then, is that it already identifies where we should expect a fissure in this allegedly seamless web of political reality of the naive political theorist. For Schiller writes the following about the naive poetic or political genius: 'It is modest since the genius will always be a secret to himself' (Schiller, 1867: 119). The insight is that it will be impossible to adequately clarify and explain the success of the naive poet within the discourse of naivety itself – in order to do so, it will be inevitable to adopt the discourse of the sentimental. The whole of Schiller's own argument, or whatever anybody might wish to say about the poetically or the politically naive, is therefore necessarily part of the discourse of the sentimental. The naive is, hence, a category *within* the sentimental; surely, the naive as such can *exist* outside that category, but it cannot be *thought* or *conceptualised* outside the category of the sentimental.

This brings me to the essence of the argument on political style that is presented in this chapter. For the crucial implication is that the notion of poetic or of political style can have neither meaning nor content for the naive poet, politician or political theorist. They will experience their poetry, their political action or thought as a direct expression of the way the world is, as a manifestation of the nature of things, as a continuation (*Erweiterung*, as Schiller put it) of it and not as merely one of the many different ways that we may relate to reality. This they would consider an untoward concession to 'subjectivity' or even to falsehood. They can only see how nature expresses itself in self-evidence and necessity – and this is to them the sure sign of truth. Only at a later stage, when they have entered into a relationship with themselves and with the world and thereby lost their 'naivety' and naive innocence, will they realise that their 'naive' poetry and political action proceeded from merely one of the many possible perspectives that we may assume with regard to reality. Only after they have become, in a certain sense, 'an other', that is to say, a *later* self, only after they thus became able to objectify their former self, may their eyes be opened to their previous style of thinking, writing and acting (while, at the same time, necessarily remaining blind to their *present* style). And because of this most people, being little inclined to introspection and self-objectification, will remain in ignorance of the style in which they present themselves to others. In sum, as was the case with Machiavelli's perspectivism described above, our style is primarily something for the *other* to observe; we are typically blind to our own style.[2]

Obviously, all this is even more true for how we relate to others. The gap existing between our naive behaviour or self-awareness and the style that we may discern in it from a later perspective, will be the gap normally existing between ourselves and the others (we are 'naive' with regard to ourselves and 'sentimental' with regard to the others, so to speak). It is natural for the other to see me in the way that I may perhaps come to perceive myself from a later perspective – and vice versa. In short, the characterisation of personality in terms of style is what we shall opt for when we consider a personality 'from the outside' as it were; and this will be the case as long as we do not feel tempted to relate this behaviour to some hidden, deep-lying sources of the personality, and as long as we remain convinced that all that is relevant in human thought and action simply *is* this 'outside'.

For several reasons, this should not be seen as some variant of behaviourism. First, whereas behaviourism finds in publicly observable human behaviour the foundation for a science of human action, style does not (attempt to) *explain*, it *characterises*; style does not tell us *why*, but *how* individuals think or act. Second, whereas behaviourism considers human personality to be a kind of black box that will be of no use to us in our effort to explain and to predict human behaviour, human personality will be at the focus of our interest when we use the notion of style for the characterisation of human behaviour. Our conception of an individual's style will be to us a kind of *substitute, replacement* or *model* of that individual's personality, and will be of use to us precisely because it has this function for us. What we see as the person's style will be *what he is like* to us. And I also emphasise this 'to us', for when using the notion of style we thereby fully accept the 'subjectivity' that is implied by that notion. That is to say, style does not pretend to present us with some deep psychological truths about a human individual's personality that would in principle be acceptable to anybody who is able to speak the language of psychology. Style does away with this monstrous alliance of a generalised, impersonal subject of knowledge with a secret source of truth deeply hidden in some inner sanctuary of the individual – an alliance from which so much contemporary philosophy of action has originated. Style organises items of human behaviour without pretending to bring us to some deeper level allegedly lying behind these items of behaviour themselves; for it does this job of organising behaviour in the space *between* the individual human being in question and ourselves, so to speak, and not by moving *beyond* that space into the sphere of a hidden, inner self of that individual.

In this way the use of the notion of style with regard to human action strangely combines a focus on what can publicly be *seen* (as in behaviourism) with an interest in unique individual personality (with all its traditional Cartesian reminiscences). Style therefore presents us with a mix of objectivism and subjectivism in our conception of human behaviour that puts it apart from most of contemporary philosophy of action. On the one hand, style is as old as humanity, since it is the category that human individuals have always relied upon in order to make sense of each other's behaviour; but on the other, the category is new and revolutionary since philosophy of action has always shunned it on account of its unscientific nature and 'superficiality'. Admittedly, the notion of style *is* unscientific and 'superficial' in the proper sense of that word, but this is precisely why we need it so much: for in our dealings with other human beings we are interested in what goes on *between* us, so in what is on the *surface* of the behaviour of the other, so to speak. We are predominantly interested in what takes place on the *interface* between the other and myself (to use computer terminology) and not in some deep, psychological truths about the other.

This will also make clear where we should draw the boundary between what can and cannot be realised when we have had the wisdom to avail ourselves of the notion of style in our dealings with others – and in politics. With regard to what cannot be realised, where others, as we have seen, experience themselves 'naively' and *non-stylistically*, this naive experience of the self is the limit that our stylistic representation of others and their behaviour will never be able to attain. With regard to what *can* be achieved by the notion of style, it will give us access to most of what makes culture and politics of significance and of value to us. For what is truly of interest to us in culture and politics is not the objective content of what is naively given to us, is not a quasi-Kantian *an sich* of what culture and politics might mean to themselves (supposing that we could make any sense at all of this effort to reach into the *an sich* of culture and politics), but what becomes accessible to us in terms of the 'sentimental' approach of these two domains. As Schiller put it himself: 'Naivety has its value in that it may completely grasp the finite, while the other [i.e., the sentimental] has this value in the approximation of the infinite' (Schiller, 1867: 130).

We should realise that the difference between nature and the naive, on the one hand, and culture or politics and the sentimental, on the other, cannot be measured on the scale of the relative (in)adequacy of knowledge (i.e. the scale that all our present ideologies of knowledge require us to consider all-decisive). For in a certain sense there *is* no self-knowledge that could function as such an absolute measure of all knowledge and insight: naivety is not a potential object of knowledge to itself in the way that the sentimental can be. Naivety should not be seen as a kind of ideal of knowledge that can only asymptotically be approached in terms of the sentimental: for the domain of the naive *sui generis* lies outside or beyond the reach of (self-)reflection. When opposing the naive and the sentimental, Schiller assures us that 'only the latter recognises different degrees and progress', an observation that is both true and misleading. It is misleading in that it invites all these models of scientific knowledge aiming at the approximation of ultimate truth that contemporary philosophy of science has imprinted upon our minds. But here this ultimate truth – the naive – is not a goal to be approximated as much as possible. On the other hand, Schiller's statement is true in the sense that it expresses the insight that the stylistic or aesthetic understanding of the other will depend on the degree of the substitutability of our stylistic characteristisations of the other for the other's actual behaviour – at least insofar as this behaviour is seen from our *own* specific point of view.

We can summarise this as follows. All our knowledge of, grasp of, or insight into sociopolitical reality can be divided into three categories. In the first place there is 'naivety' as intended by Schiller: here the self is neither objectified nor thematised; it is experienced – if it is experienced at all – as being a mere continuation of nature and of reality. But, in the second place, the naive self may become the dominant partner in the relationship between the self and nature or reality. Then reflection about nature or reality may become a disguised form of naive self-reflection. Here we have, in Schiller's words, an 'extension' (*Erweiterung*) of the self over the non-self; and insofar as we would be prepared to use here the notions of (self)reflection, we should describe this as the peculiar kind of recognition of the self that will be given to one after one has made, unwittingly and unintentionally, the whole of reality into a mirror-image of the self. The self can here discern in reality only variants of itself – but it remains unaware of this boundless extension of the self and it can persist in this ignorance since this extension took place under the aegis of a nameless, anonymous and transcendental self. This is the world of natural law philosophy and of much, though not all, of the social sciences.

But in the third place, there is an attitude towards or an understanding of the world that respects that there is a world alien to us. This is the domain of the sentimental, of the awareness of being an outsider, of being in a relationship to nature or (political) reality without being an integral part of it (as in the naive) – and yet we wish to return to nature and (political) reality.

As soon as we enter the domain of the sentimental, we will have decentred ourselves, taken leave of naive self-awareness in both the forms that I described a moment ago. We have now left the 'egocentricity' of the naive self that is still so much urged on us by ethics, by Cartesian and Kantian philosophy of mind and all its modern successors (think, for example, of the highly characteristic 'egocentricity' of the Cartesian *cogito*). Now we no longer project ourselves on the world, but reach self-reflection and/or self-awareness via *the other*. We see ourselves as the other will see us (as we ourselves may become aware of the style of our *previous* behaviour only at a *later* phase in our life and, hence, from the perspective of that later *alter ego*). In this third, 'sentimental' paradigm, not the *self* (or some generalised intersubjective transcendental self) but the *other* is the beginning of all wisdom. This is the paradigm that we encounter in aesthetics and in the writing of history; and the most important instrument it has to offer us is the notion of *style*.

The Political Styles of Democracy

In no political system is this stylistic understanding of the other more crucial and indispensable than in representative democracy. As the concept of 'representative' democracy already clearly indicates, it is only thanks to how the state 'represents' the electorate, and in its turn, how the electorate constructs for itself a 'representation' of the state and of politics, that all the mechanisms of a representative democracy start to move and to function properly. This typically *aesthetic* notion of representation (cf. Ankersmit, 1997; 2002) suggests how the notion of democratic style could best be operationalised. For, as may be clear on the basis of the foregoing, the understanding that the electorate and the state mutually have of each other is not 'naive', not a form or derivative of socio-scientific knowledge, but essentially *stylistic*: the object of political understanding is the *style* of the other, whether of the state or of (groups within) the electorate. And the deliberate stylelessness of 'naive', economic and bureaucratic understanding that dominates contemporary political discourse – however useful these discourses may sometimes be – will ultimately result in a blockage of the mechanisms that keep the machine of representative democracy going. An economic or bureaucratic reality will then usurp the place of a political reality of an *innere Stimme* resulting from the interaction between the 'right hand' and the 'left hand' of the represented and of the representative. One of the major problems of contemporary Western democracy is that because of all the clutter of socio-scientific data – of statistics, bureaucracy and so on – the electorate and the state simply are no longer able to recognise and understand each other. Only style can guarantee this mutual recognition and understanding – and give us access to 'the other' again.

Just as either the right hand or the left hand may be the main contributor to the development of this political *innere Stimme*, so it will also be possible to indicate, on the basis of the foregoing, what must be the primary or elementary political styles in representative democracy (though I hasten to add that this does not as yet imply anything with regard to their relative merits). A distinction made by Schiller proves to be helpful here once again: I am thinking here of his distinction between the elegiac and the satirical styles. For Schiller elegiac poetry and elegiac political style correspond with the naive; they cultivate nature and what is natural at the expense of culture, art and artificiality. And, as Schiller explicitly points out, the curious paradox is that in this way the natural becomes *idealistic* and the world of art and culture *realistic*: from our present (sentimental) perspective not *culture*, but *nature* presents itself as a shaky and uncertain construction. In this way Schiller nicely and elegantly succeeds in turning Rousseau upside down. Obvious examples of this elegiac and idealistic democratic political style are the idyll[3] of natural law theory and the ideal(s) of direct democracy.

Opposite to the elegiac style Schiller places satirical poetry, which corresponds with the sentimental: 'Satirical is the poet who takes as his subject the estrangement from reality and the opposition between reality and the ideal (the effect both have on the human mind is in each case the same) (Schiller, 1867: 133). In connection to the world of politics we may think here of the political style that is ordinarily called Machiavellistic: in Machiavellism the satire of political action results from the rejection of the ideal as the highest political reality. For this reason we may agree with Robert Hariman when he writes that 'the *realist* style is the basis of Machiavelli's persuasive success, it has shaped his text's subsequent history of interpretation, and it operates as a powerful mode of comprehension and action in the modern world'. And in agreement with Schiller's notion of the satirical as a subcategory of the sentimental, he also situates Machiavelli's endeavour to bring back the idea (i.e. Machiavelli's own high-pitched republicanism) to nature, that is, to political reality (Hariman, 1995: 13). In recent analyses of the comedies that Machiavelli wrote (such as *La Mandragola*) scholars also attempt to identify in these comedies this same peculiar combination of comedy, satire and realism that is so much the outstanding feature of his political writings (for example, Fenichel-Pitkin, 1987: 110–14). Hence, where the idyll of the naive political style placed us in the universe of the citizen living in a direct democracy, the satire of the sentimental democratic style has its elective affinity with the democratic politician's dilemmas of what most prudent and effective use he should make of political power.

But more important than the style of naive idyll and that of sentimental satire is how Schiller proposes to subdivide satire. As we shall see in a moment, it is only this subdivision that will give us the style suitable for the political *innere Stimme* of democracy. The distinction that is relevant here is the one between tragic and comic satire. Tragic satire is the style proper for showing how the sheer weight of reality may reduce all human intention, whether good or bad, to dismal, tragic failure. Here the human individual is a mere plaything of social and political reality and unable to exert any autonomous influence upon it. A striking example, according to Schiller, is Tacitus' account of the brute realities of first-century Rome.

But, contrary to what one perhaps would have expected, far more interest and sympathy are displayed by Schiller for comic satire. As will become clear, this is the style that overcomes the one-sidedness of both naive idyll and sentimental satire and that best agrees with the world of political conflict in representative democracy. Schiller gives the following argument in favour of his own preference: 'This is why the tragic poet always deals with his subject matter in a practical way, and the comic poet in a theoretical way' (Schiller, 1867: 136). The idea is that the tragic poet can safely rely upon the extreme seriousness of his subject-matter to captivate the interest of the audience. The comedy writer is without this advantage; success will come in this, if at all, only thanks to the writer's wit, intelligence, inventiveness and talent to lend to fictive reality authenticity and credibility. It is the writer's handicap 'to discover everywhere chance rather than fate' and to have to create a fictive world that is believable to the audience out of the unpromising and pedestrian material that is presented by the goddess of fortune – that is, the goddess of fate and of the unforeseeable but decisive accident. Hence, the challenge the comedy writer has to meet, is 'to restore spontaneously the unity that had been taken from it by abstraction' (Schiller, 1867: 158) – a challenge that is unknown to the tragic poet since this unity is already automatically given by the sublime subject matter.

We may also observe here to what extent the logic of comedy (unlike that of tragedy) agrees with that of representation in general – and with political representation in particular. For crucial to all (political) representation is a similar substitution of the unity (of identity) of the represented for that of its representation (cf. Ankersmit, 2001: ch. 8). Even more so, this is precisely where the whole use and function of representation must be looked for: representations are 'imitations' of reality allowing us to speak about reality in terms of *them*.[4] But since it is a 'substitute reality' and not reality itself, representation may make us better aware of certain aspects of reality that remain hidden or difficult to perceive in reality – which is one of the other main merits of representation above reality itself and (true) description of reality (cf. Ankersmit, 2000). This is why representation can, in the practice of democratic politics, be so successful and even outright indispensable when we wish to listen to democracy's *innere Stimme*. In sum, Schiller's eulogy of comic satire may help us recognise in what way democracy's *innere Stimme* may present itself to our perception: we can listen to it in the political reality that is created by political representation and in the autonomy that this new reality possesses with regard to the represented.

I therefore heartily agree with the account of democracy given by Combs and Nimmo; more specifically, when they present in their book *The Comedy of Democracy* a number of arguments in favour of the view that the style of democracy is essentially comic. As is ordinarily the case when we attempt to justify stylistic characterisations, these arguments do not permit deductive or logical organisation. When we describe style(s), a web of associations is what we should expect. The following elements can be discerned in the mirror image that comedy presents to democracy. Like Schiller, Combs and Nimmo also prefer comedy to tragedy since comedy succeeds in generating its structure out of itself, while structure is effortlessly given to tragedy in its subject matter. It is both the burden and the beauty of comedy that it gives us a world without pre-existing rules; it is a world that is 'un-ruled rather than mis-ruled' (Combs and Nimmo, 1996: 16). The paradox of comedy is that its own order should suggest, as adequately as possible, the *lack* of order existing in reality itself. And Combs and Nimmo therefore also see in Machiavelli's comedies – with their satirical comments on human weakness and stupidity, with their surrender of the tragic dimensions of 'cosmic man' in favour of the imperfections of 'men in society', with their radical openness instead of the closed world of tragedy, with their recognition of the role of chance, and their inclination to the subversive and irreverent – the first announcement of the style of democracy in Western political history (Combs and Nimmo, 1996: 9). Indeed, the style of democracy is open and ironic, adverse to system and the seriousness of theory – and whoever wishes to impose on democracy a high and sublime goal will try unwittingly to exchange democracy for an aristocracy ruled by the select group of himself and his own kindred spirits.

But probably the supreme irony of this 'comedy of errors' that democracy is lies in the fact that democracy needs this kind of misconception about itself (cf. Ankersmit, 1997: 186). We need in democracy the tragic dimension of people who take themselves and their political ideals tragically seriously, along with all the misfortunes arising from this. Without this tragic self-awareness of the citizen and of the politician, there would be no material that could be fed into the machine of democratic satire. Thus the basis of democracy might well be an incompatibility of the *satire* of that political system itself with the *tragic* political inspiration of the individual citizen and politician. If this makes sense, it would follow that the future of our Western democracies will at least partly depend on our success in carefully upholding this strange and paradoxical balance between tragedy and satire.

Conclusion

In Pauline Westerman's recent study of the miseries of natural law philosophy, she gives an exposition of the conceptual inadequacies of that notion. As she convincingly makes clear, the notion of 'natural law' suggests a degree of logical coherence, of conceptual hierarchy and a reducibility to indubitable first principles that is completely at odds with the plastic and Protean character of socio-political reality. She therefore recommends that we make more use of the notion of political style than hitherto has been the case in our theorising about politics: 'An artistic style is not to be seen as a recipe for "how to paint a portrait". The term "style" rather denotes a general way of making or doing things ... For instance, the stylistic requirement of unity of time, place and action, which any successful classicist playwright had to meet, was not merely a constraint; it also opened a vast array of possibilities that would otherwise have remained unexplored. Style can be a source of creativity' (Westerman, 1997: 32).

We observed above the political creativity of democratic politics, and it seems likely that the notion of political style is ideally suited for explaining this creativity. This political creativity pre-eminently manifests itself in the creation of a new political reality, new in the sense that it transcends the more elementary and primary realities of what is in the minds of the individual participants in the domain of politics. It is a *new* political reality because it is superimposed upon the more concrete reality of already existing political desires, ideologies, administrative habits or mechanisms whose complex interaction we have tried to elucidate in terms of Schumann's *innere Stimme*. For what is true of Schumann's *innere Stimme* is true as well of this democratic extra, superimposed reality: it cannot be 'heard' but it can be 'listened to' and this can be done with the same objectivity and accuracy as what is actually 'heard'.

Precisely because we still find ourselves here in a kind of indeterminate limbo between what is already and what is not yet reality – obviously the kind of limbo in which all creativity will preferably look for its proper home – precisely for this reason, whatever ultimately solidifies into a political reality that will become recognisable to all of us in due time, will make here its first entry into the domain of politics. This political *innere Stimme* is therefore the birthplace of all the mechanisms that will keep representative democracy alive. Democracy dies when this political *innere Stimme* is smothered, or when our political ears have become unable or unwilling to listen to it anymore.

If we wish to investigate more closely the peculiar reality of this political *innere Stimme*, the notion of political style will be our best guide. For political style shares with the reality of the political *innere Stimme* the capacity to bridge this so enigmatic and Protean gap between what *is* already and what will *become* political reality. In our contemporary democracies, it is only in terms of political style that the politician may become recognisable at all to the electorate: Buffon's *le style, c'est l'homme même* is pre-eminently true of how the citizen conceives of the politician. Not political ideology, neither a political programme nor political achievement – and it is far from me to belittle these things – but political style, therefore, is the true *trait d'union* between politics and the politician on the one hand and the electorate and the citizen on the other. Political style is the category enabling all the participants of the Schillerian comedy of representative democracy to recognise each other; political style is the domain where the political party and the politician will make their first cautious efforts to redefine their relationship to the electorate or what should, in their view, be seen as beneficial and valuable future public goals.[5]

When a new political reality comes into being it always involves the birth of a new political *style*. Hence, the political theorist avoiding the notion of political style because he thinks the notion too difficult or too cumbersome to use is like somebody who decides that it would be too much of an effort to learn the language that is used by the people amongst whom he lives.

Notes

1. A Dutch version of material contained in this chapter was published in Pels and te Velde (eds) (2000); another (English) version appeared in Ankersmit (2002: 133).

2. Insofar as ethics has an affinity with our conscience, with our inner moral convictions and with what practical reason tells us that we should do, we may discern here the unbridgeable gap between the notions of ethics and of style. There could be no science of ethics for what ought to be the style of our behaviour.

3. The idyll is seen by Schiller as a subvariant of elegy: it occurs when the natural is experienced as an 'object of joy' (*Gegenstand der Freude*).

4. Which has the important implication that to representation must be granted the same ontological status as things – i.e. *not* that of reality. See for example Ankersmit (1994: 90).

5. For a number of striking illustrations of this claim, see Robertson (1995). Robertson demonstrates to what extent the evolution of Anglo-Saxon democracy found its clearest expression in evolutions of political style and rhetoric.

References

Ankersmit, F. (1994) *History and Tropology: the Rise and Fall of Metaphor*. Berkeley: University of California Press.

Ankersmit, F. (1997) *Aesthetic Politics: Political Philosophy Beyond Fact and Value*. Stanford: Stanford University Press.

Ankersmit, F. (2000) 'The Representation of Experience', *Metaphilosophy* 31(1–2): 148–69.

Ankersmit, F. (2001) *Historical Representation*. Stanford: Stanford University Press.

Ankersmit, F. (2002) *Political Representation*. Stanford: Stanford University Press.

Combs, J.E. and Nimmo, D. (1996) *The Comedy of Democracy*. Westport CT: Praeger.

Edelman, M. (1971) *Politics as Symbolic Action. Mass Arousal and Quiescence*. Chicago: Markham.

Edelman, M. (1988) *Constructing the Political Spectacle*. Chicago: University of Chicago Press.

Fenichel-Pitkin, H. (1987) *Fortune is a Woman. Gender and Politics in the Thought of Niccolò Machiavelli*. Berkeley: University of California Press.

Hariman, R. (1995) *Political Style. The Artistry of Power*. Chicago: University of Chicago Press.

Montesquieu, C. de (1973 [1748]) *De l'esprit des lois*. Paris: Garnier.

Pels, D. and te Velde, H. (eds) (2000) *Politieke stijl. Over presentatie en optreden in de politiek*. Amsterdam: Het Spinhuis.

Robertson, A.W. (1995) *The Language of Democracy. Political Rhetoric in the United States and Britain, 1790–1900*. Ithaca and London: Cornell University Press.

Rosen, C. (1996) *The Romantic Generation*. Cambridge MA: Harvard University Press.
Schiller, F. von (1867) 'Über naive und sentimentalische Dichtung', in *Schiller's Werke Band 12*. Stuttgart: Cotta. (first published in 1796.)
Westerman, P.C. (1997) *The Disintegration of Natural Law Theory. Aquinas to Finnis*. Leiden/New York: Brill.

3

Aesthetic Representation and Political Style

Re-balancing Identity and Difference in Media Democracy

DICK PELS

A Dandy in Politics

A week before national election day, on 6 May 2002, the Netherlands 'lost their political innocence', as many commentators chose to put it. Directly echoing the post-September 11 watershed sentiment, it was widely felt that Dutch democracy 'would never be the same again'. Was this still the Netherlands?, many asked in profound shock over the first political murder the country had experienced since the 1672 lynching of the De Witt brothers in The Hague. The victim of this 'un-Dutch' event, Pim Fortuyn, a millionnaire former sociology professor and flamboyant homosexual, had meteorically risen in the polls to singlehandedly embarass the self-satisfied politicians of the 'purple' Left-Liberal coalition by his unprecedented style of campy glamour, media flair, and brazen political extremism. Briefly heading a new populist party called *Leefbaar Nederland* (Liveable Netherlands), and having won an unexpected landslide victory against Labour in the municipal elections in his home base of Rotterdam, Fortuyn quickly fell out with his party after declaring that 'Holland was full' and branding Islam as a 'backward culture'. Establishing a ballot list under his own name, Fortuyn swiftly managed to mobilise large portions of the floating anti-immigration and anti-political protest vote in a remarkably personalised media blitz which took both the 'old' parties and the opinion pollers by complete surprise. Evidently heading for a major victory at the national polls, which could have turned the Lijst Pim Fortuyn into the largest political grouping and perhaps catapulted its leader into the prime ministerial seat, Fortuyn was gunned down on that fateful Monday by a crazed environmental activist when leaving a radio studio in the media town of Hilversum.

Fortuyn's brief political life and sudden death have been widely interpreted as marking a major style break in Dutch political culture. This rupture was effected as much by his success in 'saying the unsayable', especially with respect to immigration and Islam, as by his impudent and dandyesque public performances, which repeatedly scandalised a political establishment deeply sunk in the conciliatory and inclusive corporatism of the 'Polder Model'.[1] Suddenly politics in the Netherlands had turned into an exciting, 'fun' thing, whipping up unheard-of popular passions; everyone was talking politics, and everywhere Fortuyn occupied the centre of attention. A series of televised campaign debates between the major political leaders turned into a regular soap opera in which the cheeky upstart repeatedly exposed the reigning LabLib elite as a bunch of weary old men by his charming but often *ad hominem* provocations – while conspicuously failing to answer any of the disturbing questions he raised. Simultaneously, as a celebrity 'politician without party' who embodied a politics of stylish individuality and personalised trust, Fortuyn opened a dramatic rift with the established culture of party discipline and party patronage, striking a chord with an individualising electorate that was increasingly floating away from traditional partisan alignments.

Sporting a shiny bald head, flashing a trademark expensive suit with a colourful tie and pochette to match, whisking around the country in a chauffeured Daimler accompanied by two lapdogs, and receiving the press in his lavish townhouse decorated with many portraits of himself, Fortuyn consciously capitalised on his personality as a brand, radically blurring the boundaries between private life and public showtime. In his case, the 'human being' behind the politician was so immediately foregrounded as to be effectively indistinguishable from the latter. Outspoken about his existential loneliness but also about his sense of mission and even destiny ('Mind you, I will be the next prime minister of this country', he defiantly predicted after his fall from the leadership of *Leefbaar Nederland*), Fortuyn paired the arrogance of the self-proclaimed great teacher and leader to a proud openness about his sexuality (for example, regular visits to the dark rooms of gay clubs), rowdily countering his multicultural critics by saying things like: 'I have nothing against Moroccans. I've been to bed with so many of them!' Having named a ballot list after himself, Fortuyn became increasingly known on a first name basis, as 'Pim', 'Professor Pim' or by loving diminutives such as 'Pimmie' and 'Pimmetje'. After the murder, a popular weekly captioned its cover photo of Fortuyn with 'Pim is dead'. A large portion of the condolence advertisements appearing in the daily newspapers simply mentioned his first name and struck a remarkably personal tone ('Thank you Pim'; 'Pim. Foreover our Voice'; 'Dear Pim. We will miss your unique personality and the challenge of your sharp mind. Thanks for everything. Holland does not deserve you!'). In one of these advertisements, the core of what is now widely referred to as the 'spirit of Pim' was captured in another typical Fortuyn quote: 'Dear Pim. We are going to say what we think and do what we say'.

In this manner, Fortuyn's colourful appearance, narcissistic posturing and bravura lifestyle, his butler, his car, his ties and his two spaniels, entered into the same political message that also included his aggressive critique of the charmed circle of The Hague party politics (de *kaasstolp* or 'cheese cover'), of the smug consensualism of the Polder Model, of the 'Ruins' supposedly left by eight years of Purple Government (as the title of his last book maliciously proclaimed)(Fortuyn, 2002), and of a culture of political correctness that downplayed the dark sides of immigration and (Islamic) fundamentalism. In the public perception, such entertaining and expressive lifestyle elements became indistinguishable from his eclectic mish-mash of left- and right-wing ideas, in which a radical cultural libertarianism and a plea for direct democracy chafed against a curiously nostalgic nationalism and slogans about zero immigration, a clampdown on crime and street violence, severe cuts in sickness and disability benefits, and a freeze in health and education spending.

But this bricolage of disparate style elements would never have gelled so quickly into a recognisable political brand without the profuse media attention Fortuyn received from the very beginning of his brief political life. His almost presidential 'personality campaign' would have been unthinkable without the expanded visibility afforded by media technologies, which turned him into a 'household friend', blurring public and private personae, and breeding the typical 'unfamiliar familarity' or asymmetrical 'intimacy at a distance' which characterises the 'parasocial' relationship between media celebrities and their audiences (Horton and Wohl, 1986; Meyrowitz, 1985; Thompson, 2000). More than that of traditional party-based and party-raised politicians, the Fortuyn brand was made in medialand, where its exhibitionist owner played the infotainment game with freshness, gusto and brilliance. Flirting with the camera, and reliably churning out confrontational one-liners, he quickly emerged as the ideal politician for journalists, who paid back in kind by giving him considerably more attention and airtime than any other major political actor. Fortuyn was perhaps Holland's first 'mediacrat': the first politician who performed almost exclusively in an audiovisual culture, effortlessly coinciding with his televised image (Giesen, 2002; Zwaap, 2002). With dramatic appropriateness, he died on a media estate after emerging from a lengthy interview on a pop music channel; the shocking picture of his blood-strewn body stretched out on the tarmac in front of the studio made the covers of both national and international newspapers the next day.

This strange familiarity of the public persona 'in the age of mediated reproduction' could nowhere be witnessed more clearly than in the massive outpouring of popular grief and anger at Fortuyn's laying-in-state and (what virtually turned into a state) funeral. Covered live by a public TV channel, the latter event eloquently confirmed Fortuyn's speedily acquired iconic status in an extraordinary rehearsal of the rituals and pageantry of the 'new mass mourning' which had first erupted around Princess Diana's death in 1997 (see Walter, 1999). Riots broke out that briefly threatened the government centre at the Binnenhof, but people also assembled in silent commemorative marches. Massive flower tributes were laid at Rotterdam city hall, Fortuyn's home, and the Hilversum studio where he was shot, lined with candles, teddy-bears, national flags, flamboyant ties, Feyenoord football shirts, handwritten poetry, and portraits comparing him with Kennedy and Martin Luther King. Long rows of mourners queued up to sign condolence registers in city halls all over the country; flags were flying at half-mast; and Fortuyn websites were flooded with expressions of anger, sadness and fear. These spectacular events gradually built up towards the climax of a televised procession by a flower-strewn hearse followed by Fortuyn's Daimler (with lapdogs) through applauding crowds towards a pompous funeral service in Rotterdam's Roman Catholic cathedral (where the dogs were also admitted). At the close of the service, the establishment politicians ignominiously left through the back door, in order to avoid the crowd in front who were whistling and making V-signs, bursting into 'You'll never walk alone' and 'Pimmetje thanks!', but also, more threateningly, identifying the social-democratic leadership as 'murderers' and shouting 'Never again left!' Those few days of mass emotionality sealed Fortuyn's political legend as a martyr for freedom of speech and a potential saviour of the country, uncovering a talent for messiah-worship and political hysteria that few had suspected the sober Dutch were capable of. The 15 May elections partly turned into an 'open condolence register' for Fortuyn, landing his orphaned party a record number of 26 out of 150 parliamentary seats, and inflicting heavy losses on both the Labour and the Liberal parties. Still topping his own ballot list, the deceased personally gathered 1.3 million out of 9.5 million votes. In one dramatic stroke, Dutch politics was made to realise what the modern entertainment industries have known for some time: that, in a secularised society of individuals, it is no longer religion but celebrity that is the opium of the people.

The Substance of Form

Perhaps it is true that Dutch democracy will never be the same again, having been forever kicked out of its complacent smugness by this 'un-Dutch' act of political violence. What is certain is that a major threshold was crossed in the longer-term process of mediatisation and personalisation, and resultant 'aesthetic' stylisation, of Dutch political culture. Our post-ideological television age, in which a symbiotic partnership has developed between the mass media and an increasingly professionalised politics, has progressively softened the classical oppositions between left and right, interweaving political substance and political form, and replacing programmatically-based and party-aligned forms of political representation with political personalities and their *political style*. 'Style' refers to an heterogeneous ensemble of ways of speaking, acting, looking, displaying, and handling things, which merge into a symbolic whole that immediately fuses matter and manner, message and package, argument and ritual. It offers political rhetoric, posturing and instinct, the expression of sentiments (such as political fear, envy or loathing) and presentational techniques (such as face-work, gesticulation or dress codes) an equally legitimate place as political rationality, thus knitting together 'higher' and 'baser' style elements in a loosely coherent but powerful pattern of political persuasion. In this patchwork, so-called banal, vulgar or intimate details of appearance, bearing and conduct are considered equally suggestive and informative as matter-of-factness, idealistic dedication, and orientation towards substantive policy contents.[2] The intense media coverage of political performances has stripped politicians of their former aura; blurring the traditional boundaries between 'front' and 'back' regions or between public and private realms, the media have thereby 'informalised' their charisma. Electronic media reveal a whole spectrum of information that once remained confined to private interactions, breeding the typical familiarity-at-a-distance of mediated or 'parasocial' interaction (Meyrowitz, 1985: 268; Thompson, 2000). This 'style revolution' in politics expresses a more general process of 'de-institutionalisation' and personalisation of social life (Beck and Beck-Gernsheim, 2002) which is also reflected in the ever-growing intensity of the cult of public individuality or celebrity (Marshall, 1997).

Hence the Fortuyn phenomenon offers only one, albeit dramatic, episode (the more so because it occurred in a dull democracy normally bereft of high political drama) in a process of structural transformation that is already well under way. Fortuyn typically reacted to his opponents in terms of political sentiment and style, not simply listening to what they were saying but also watching *how* they said it, sensing their bodily discomfort, and mercilessly exploiting what he saw and felt.[3] Outside the Netherlands, this new politics of emotion and personality has asserted itself ever more clearly in climactic events such as the London 2000 mayoral race (Ken Livingstone the lone ranger against the Millbank machine); the USA 2000 presidential elections and its protracted cliffhanger ending; the second fall of Peter Mandelson ('one spin too far'); the second Labour election victory and the ensuing Tory leadership contest in 2001; the trial of novelist and former Tory politician Jeffrey Archer; the remarkable presence of New York mayor Rudy Giuliani in the immediate aftermath of 11 September and George Bush's equally remarkable 'absence'; and Blair's ever-more presidential and 'visionary' leadership style in the 'war against terrorism' and his political resilience ('Teflon Tony') in the face of accumulating New Labour sleaze (the Hinduja, Mittal, and Byers/Moore/Sixsmith affairs).

As is testified by the example of Giuliani in terror-stricken New York, city democracy is perhaps a privileged experimental ground for the unfolding of this theatrical personalisation of politics, especially where more or less direct elections foster new kinds of emotional resonance between representatives and represented. Fortuyn's first electoral landslide swept the city of Rotterdam, riding on the crest of a mounting protest movement of 'Liveable' parties that had emerged in cities such as Hilversum and Utrecht; his rise to national fame was perhaps facilitated by the fact that the Netherlands itself is no larger than a (large) city state. In the UK, the new style dynamics erupted most visibly in the extraordinary saga of the 2000 London mayoral election. For months, the country was transfixed by this political soap opera and the vicissitudes of its star personae, focusing especially upon the epic struggle between maverick Ken Livingstone and an anxious Labour establishment.[4] Part of the Londoners' sentiment was clearly to 'give Blair a bloody nose', to 'fart at the Emperor'. As one city slicker expressed his motives for supporting Ken: 'He's intelligent, thoughtful. He's of the far left. So what? We could do with a bit of variety. I quite like Blair, but he can't have it all his own way ... It's only four years. And, anyway, he won't be able to do too much'. Another proclaimed: 'If he goes too far, the Government will rein him in. He's a character. It'll be fun. Why not?'[5]

The notion that presentation and performance are increasingly salient in a culture saturated by image management, style consultancy, branding and design is of course very far from constituting hot news to political journalism and political science. The proximate features of what is generally described as an 'Americanisation' of political culture or as the rise of a 'designer' or an 'audience' democracy have already been hinted at: the blurring of traditional political distinctions following the demise of the politics of principle, the rise of the floating voter and the experiment-prone political consumer, the drift towards the political middle, the decline of party bureaucracies and overarching ideological programmes, and especially, the mediatisation and commercialisation of political campaigning and the political enterprise more generally (cf. Franklin, 1994; Mancini & Swanson, 1994; Scammell, 1995; Negrine, 1996: 146; Fairclough, 2000). The logic of an 'audience democracy', by introducing a more direct, media-driven form of communication between candidates and constituents that tends to bypass the legislature and party bureaucracies, induces a personalisation of electoral choice and political power. There is a concomitant change in the type of political elite, as activists and party bureaucrats are increasingly replaced by media personalities and experts in political communication. Television, more especially, confers a particular salience and vividness upon the individuality of candidates, which enhances personal trust rather than ideological principle or programmatic detail as a platform for political selection (Manin, 1997: 193). In the new relation of symbiotic dependency between media and politics, the weight thus gradually shifts towards the agenda-setting powers of the former, which implies that political discourse increasingly turns upon the personal credibility of the political players. Once again this is most evident in the case of television broadcasting which, it is widely assumed, is naturally biased towards the display of personality, the cultivation of emotion, and the whipping up of incidents and conflicts.[6]

For some, such tendencies towards political marketing and infotainment represent an acute danger, if they imply that substance is sacrificed to spin and salesmanship, if personality-mongering, image building and personal charisma are permitted to eclipse political ideas and principles, and the rhythm of political campaigning is increasingly dictated by camera-ready pseudo-events and ritual conflicts between political celebrities (cf. Ewen, 1990; Wernick, 1991: 124; Franklin, 1994; 1998; Bourdieu, 1998; Jones, 1999). Others are less disturbed by this personalisation of the political and the rise of the soundbite at the expense of sustained intellectual exposition (cf. Fiske, 1992; Brants, 1998; Van Zoonen, 1998; Street, 2001). Before the rise of Pim Fortuyn, the Dutch version of this issue for some time focused upon the worry that prime minister Kok might actually be more popular than his party or even his programme. Some marketing strategists did not lose much sleep over this: at election time Kok could still be successfully sold as a 'durable, utterly dependable A-brand' (*De Volkskrant* 15.11.97). One communication consultant even suggested that criticism of the growing importance of political appearance and presentation was 'undemocratic', 'old-fashioned', and amounted to an 'insult to the electorate'. Election returns were never exclusively determined by policy content, but by the totality of elements from which voters' perceptions were pieced together. Roughly cut concepts such as 'reason' and 'emotion' were in his view far too general to be illuminating; political perceptions rather accrued from variables that weighed differently in different issue-contexts, but which were always co-present and immediately bore upon each other (*NRC-Handelsblad* 16.6.97). For Fortuyn, of course, the spectacular in politics was never an issue: 'Politics is also play-acting, a form of theatre. People want to hear a good story and then go to sleep' (Camps, 2001).[7]

Aesthetic Politics?

But people may want to stay awake, and a story which puts them to sleep is not a very good political story. Nevertheless, in this chapter I argue for a stylish and style-conscious politics (see also Pels and te Velde, 2000), not merely as an inescapable condition for anyone who is involved in present-day political reality, but also as an attractive new medium of democratic representation and effective communication between elector and elected. The magic of political communication and political trust, which establishes a form of representative consonance between mandators and mandated, is predicated in large degree upon political style and taste (and hence upon style recognition and taste correspondence). As indicated, the notion of style usefully bridges the divide between form and content, detail and essence, presentation and principle, sentiment and reason, and hence relativises a one-sided cerebral or rationalist approach to political behaviour. It immediately interconnects more elevated, idealised principles with baser affects and interests, lavishing equal attention upon allegedly trivial details (such as sartorial appearance, competitional motives, sexual exploits or other 'private' matters) as upon those elements that the traditional image of political representation focuses as the heart of the matter (the policy issues themselves). It gives equal emphasis to subjective and emotional characteristics, to political intuitions and the political imagination, as to the more objective, matter-of-fact and formalised aspects of the political enterprise.

Political style or taste refers to the fact that judgements of persons and their programmes normally have a holistic and unarticulated character ('(s)he is not my type', 'that face does not inspire a lot of trust in me', 'I do not feel for such a view') and are distributed in terms of sweeping archetypical oppositions such as hard–soft, firm–weak, warm–cold, young–old, old-fashioned–modern, formal–informal, corrupt–honest, arrogant–modest, masculine–feminine, realistic–unrealistic, social–antisocial etc. Like the mourning for Fortuyn, the unprecedented surge of emotionality following the death of Princess Diana in the autumn of 1997 was widely interpreted as a *political* fact, i.e. as an unexpectedly massive opinion poll about the status and legitimacy of the royal house, and more generally, about how the British people wished to be represented: not so crampedly, coldly and formally as by the 'old' Windsors, but preferably in the more relaxed, warmer, modern style of 'young' Diana – and of Tony Blair who, skilfully negotiating between young and old and between formality and informality, ultimately managed to identify more visibly with the less formal, youthful and 'feminine' reach of the electoral spectrum (cf. Evans, 1999; Fairclough, 2000: 6–8).[8]

Inspiration for a serious consideration of the impact of political style and taste is initially drawn from Frank Ankersmit's articulation of an 'aesthetic' conception of political representation (Ankersmit, 1990; 1997; 2002). In Ankersmit's approach, the idea of political style is a conceptual tool that further details the phenomenon of aesthetic representation, which he regards as a core constituent of (post)modern democracies. The essence of political representation is not that voters' preferences or interests are pictured photographically, in a 'mimetic' rendering that expresses a relationship of identity; on the contrary, it presupposes a specific distance and functional difference between elector and elected, which enables them to engage in fruitful mutual interaction (cf. Pels, 1993; 2000: 1–26). As in artistic representation, the goal of political representation is not mirror-like portrayal or the creation of a perfect replica, but *autonomy* vis-a-vis that which is represented; political reality and political power only emerge in the 'hollow' or the 'gap' between representer and represented, state and citizen: 'the absence of identity of the representative and the person represented is as unavoidable in political representation as the unavoidable difference between a painted portrait and the person portrayed' (Ankersmit, 1997: 28; cf. Pitkin, 1967: 60).[9]

In Ankersmit's view, this relative representational autonomy is most accurately summarised in the theory of aesthetic *substitution* advanced by philosophers such as Gombrich and Danto. The origin of artistic representation, indeed, is not to imitate reality but to put something else in its place: all image-making is rooted in the creation of substitutes. The hobby-horse described in Gombrich's well-known essay 'Meditations on a Hobby-Horse' does not so much stand for an actual horse, but is something different that takes its place. As a consequence, the relationship between representer and represented remains indeterminate to a far greater degree than would, for example, be acceptable in traditional universalist or realist epistemology; in this respect, representation and epistemology stand at right angles to one another. Artistic representation does not copy or reflect reality but places us *in opposition to* it, and only through opposing reality are we capable of objectifying it (Ankersmit, 1994: 104–7, 113; 1997: 45, 47–48; cf. Sloterdijk, 1983: 652). In politics it is similarly not the identity but the opposition between representer and represented that provides the source of political will formation. Whereas the mimetic theory tends to erase all difference of political will, the aesthetic theory creates an opening that furnishes both representers and represented with a separate space for movement. Political power is not the property of either party to the exclusion of the other, but emerges in the force field between elector and elected. The representational gap is therefore not a *faute de mieux* for direct democracy, but the 'indispensable and only' constitutional procedure for generating political power. The idea of popular sovereignty must be rejected, since its identitarian bias conflicts with the 'nature' of representative democracy itself. The state must create sufficient distance from society in order to be capable of acting; while citizens, in their turn, can only effectively exercise their rights of citizenship if the roles of representer and represented are clearly demarcated from each other.

Political style is the concept that simultaneously marks this representative gap and bridges it in a novel fashion. Since aesthetic representation puts citizens and politicians at a distance and brings them in dynamic equilibrium, politicians are no longer required to be 'at one' with their electorate, but acquire a distinct professional profile and a larger area of discretion over and against those whom they represent. Conversely, citizens are no longer required to submit to high-strung ideals of participation and competence, but may in good conscience decide to leave the political enterprise largely to the professionals (the right to political indifference).[10] As a result of this mutual demarcation and protective shielding off of political positions, citizens acquire a measure of freedom of thought and action over and against ideological and programmatic forms of politics, which are often a politics 'of and for politicians', in the sense of being supported by rationalistic presumptions and overstrained expectations with regard to the average citizen's propensity to political commitment and participation. Citizens no longer need to be educated to the level of ideological competence and personal commitment of the politician, but savour their independence and preserve a healthy distance from professional politics. But they simultaneously retain their capacity for political judgement, because the style of political conduct, precisely in its accidental and contingent detail, includes ample opportunities for trustful recognition and identification (or their opposites), supplying criteria that enable citizens to judge, without mastering technical details or specialist expertise, whether a particular person, party or policy does or does not 'speak' or appeal to them.

Political style hence enables citizens to regain their grip on a complex political reality by restoring mundane political experience to the centre of democratic practice (cf. Ankersmit, 1997: 54, 157–9). This idea is interestingly supported by the Jungian psychoanalyst Samuels, who has argued for a political psychology that affords new legitimacy to emotional, bodily and subjective reactions in politics: 'the personal should become once again political' (Samuels, 1993; 2001). Samuels likewise advocates a new social or political aesthetics, and similarly links the revaluation of subjectivity and emotional expression to the idea of greater accessibility of the political process to ordinary citizens. Such a rehabiliation of affect, bodily sensation and fantasy, of feelings of disgust, fear, discomfort, anger or sympathy supports a form of political analysis that breaks the rationalistic limitations of much current political theorising. According to Samuels, people are much more political than they think: they possess a hidden political wisdom that lies concealed in personal, deep-lying, somatic reactions to what happens in the political world. Taking such a somatic subjectivity seriously enhances a style of political engagement that is still considered invalid and illegitimate in our political system, which tends to discount emotional reactions as irrational, prejudiced, unreliable, unsound, or 'feminine'. Over and against this 'constricting privileging of the rational', the body must be reappraised as an organ of political information, as the foundation of a somatic world of representation that can be further articulated and clarified. This goes beyond the mere recognition that objectivity in politics is impossible; it confirms the legitimacy of a personal, emotional, fantasy-laden way of doing politics, which once again releases the force of subjectivity in the political world and recreates a place for the affective and the irrational (Samuels, 1993: 21, 33, 41; Marshall, 1997: 240; Coward, 2001; Goodwin, Jasper and Polletta, 2001).

In Ankersmit's analysis, therefore, style display simultaneously creates a political gap and bridges it. However, one drawback of his rather abstract philosophical approach (or intellectual style) is the absence of sociological references to the crucially generative impact of media technologies on the development of personality politics and aesthetic representation, which has the effect of underplaying the *audiovisual* and *parasocial* nature of what he calls 'mundane political experience'. As a result, his analysis of political style tends to (over) emphasise autonomy and distance and to underplay the novel forms of identification that are enabled by the quasi-proximity and quasi-intimacy of electronically mediated interaction. In similar fashion, Samuels fails to centrally link his rehabilitation of emotional expression and personalised trust to the new expanded visibility of mediated politics. Of course, any form of political representation is required to balance the dimensions of distinction and similarity, or those of difference and identity. In an age of mediated interaction, however, the difference that representation makes is balanced out and compensated for by the quasi-familiarity that is generated by the continuous and intimate exposure of political personalities. The intervention of new technologies of visibility generates a need for aestheticised, stylish conduct that 'rarefies' the politician, as it does any celebrity over and against the mass of nameless consumers. But it simultaneously turns the political actor into a 'media friend' (or enemy) with whom political audiences cultivate a relationship of parasocial intimacy-at-a-distance. In this sense, a televisual 'audience democracy' offers more direct channels of communication and a more continuous interplay between political professionals and citizens (or rather: journalists who pose as the people's true spokespersons) than is afforded by more traditional forms of political representation. Still, these new media-facilitated forms of 'direct democracy' do not reinstate a traditional ideal of 'mimetic' or unmediated political identity or popular sovereignty. Televisual mediation accentuates the representative gap (which is also a gap between the visible few and the invisible many – or, in actress Liz Hurley's suggestive terms, between celebrities and 'civilians'). However, while forcing political players to adopt more stylish and personalised forms of self-display, it simultaneously promotes aesthetic, style-bound forms of identification on the part of their audiences, which are based upon more intuitive, expressive and holistic forms of political information.

This tensionful balance between stylish difference and mediated identity may go some way towards explaining, for example, how a political dandy such as Pim Fortuyn, whose flashy appearance, *nouveau riche* lifestyle and unconventional morality put him at some distance from the cultural experience of ordinary Dutch citizens, could still be seen as 'one of us', who 'spoke our language' and indeed 'said what we were not allowed to say'. Fortuyn was conspicously different, not merely from run-of-the-mill politicians (he was definitely not one of *them*), but in a more immediate existential sense; nevertheless, this very difference appeared to generate forms of trustful identification on the part of citizens who themselves felt excluded and politically homeless (Schuyt, 2002). In a personalised democracy, it is perceived *authenticity* rather than 'mimetic' resemblance that bridges the representative gap.[11] In a culture of individualisation, a cultivated eccentric such as Fortuyn, who was visibly and loudly 'unlike anybody else', easily turned into a role model for individuals who all desperately want to be 'an original' (as the cigarette advertisement has it), and who are increasingly bored by grey apparatchiks and predictable party men. Identifying with 'the people' against the political establishment, and wanting to 'give society back to the citizens themselves', Fortuyn nevertheless rejected all accusations of populism, projecting a missionary sense of the great leader as a 'good shepherd' who was not afraid to lead the way: 'In my campaign not only politics get a whipping; I also come down hard on the citizen. Worthless politicians but also worthless citizens'. The enigma of the charismatic outsider who captures the feelings of ordinary people precisely as a result of his extraordinary qualities, also found a curious expression in his view that 'someone who is able to show the way, automatically becomes the incarnation of the people' (Camps, 2001).

Right-wing Political Artistry

Both Ankersmit and Samuels therefore distance themselves from forms of political objectivism and intellectualism (as exemplified by rational choice models, Habermasian theories of deliberative democracy, or normative–universalist conceptions of citizenship) in order to reappraise political taste, intuition, emotion, and experience as channelling new forms of political energy, and as enabling new forms of democratic participation and control. Naturally, such a redefinition of political competence as emotional power of judgement ('the body of the political analyst leads in a spontaneous political analysis', [Samuels, 1993: 33]) is not devoid of intellectual and political risks. It can plausibly be interpreted as a democratic rehabilitation and appropriation of the Romantic aestheticisation of the political, which has for some time enjoyed a rather bad press as a consequence of its association with the fatal disasters that 'political artistry' has wrought in the shape of Fascism and National Socialism during the past century. Indeed, right-radical political ideologies are still routinely dismissed as sub- and anti-intellectual phenomena, as forms of unprincipled opportunism that were dominated by a perfidious lust for power and a brainless dedication to activism. Fascism and National Socialism, in this customary view, embodied an irrationalist 'spirit of revolt' that privileged action and spectacle above content and emphatically subordinated political reason to the dictate of political will and political energy (cf. Pels, 1993; 2000: 110).

However, it is an important implication of my present argument that we cannot leave the aestheticisation of politics to the (historical) right, but may incorporate and rework some of its elements in order to promote a further 'democratisation of democracy' (cf. Simons, 1999; 2001). This project requires us to keep our distance from facile dismissals of right-radical political traditions and political styles, while attempting to assess them more carefully in their own context and on their own terms. In contrast to well-entrenched judgemental reflexes that tend to associate the political Enlightenment with progress, emancipation and democracy and political Romanticism with the opposite values of decadence, elitism and totalitarianism, we need to acknowledge that both traditions are Janus-faced and have left behind a complex and morally ambiguous political heritage. The notorious 'dialectic of the Enlightenment' is matched and mirrored by an equally intrinsic 'dialectic of Romanticism'; both the lineage of thinking about the 'scientific state' and that which has focused upon the 'aesthetic state' have a long history that has left both democratic and totalitarian sediments (cf. Chytry, 1989).

As a critical expression, the notion of the 'aestheticisation of the political' probably originated in Walter Benjamin's 1930 review of *Krieg und Krieger*, a programmatic anthology of conservative–revolutionary writings edited by Ernst Jünger, which celebrated the cult of struggle and war as metaphysical forces that subordinated everything to a relentless drive for 'total mobilisation'. In the epilogue to his 1936 essay on 'The Work of Art in an Age of Mechanical Reproduction', Benjamin repeated his view that this cult of total war should be seen as an uninhibited translation of the principles of *l'art pour l'art* to the theatre of war itself (Benjamin, 1930; 1992: 234–5).[12] The notion of an 'aesthetic totalitarianism' or 'political expressionism' can also be traced to the turn-of-the-century nationalist writings of Maurice Barrès (Sternhell, 1972; Carroll, 1995: 19), whose decisive influence on the generation of German intellectuals who were formed during the First World War was not only noted by Benjamin but also acknowledged by Jünger himself. In an early (1921) book on Barrès, Ernst Robert Curtius already described how his political will was governed by the same law as his relationship to art, which was not oriented to formal beauty but to the expression of spiritual and meta-political values. Barrès himself intriguingly defined politics as 'emotional energy, directed by an expressive will' (cit. Hillach, 1979: 105–6).

Close to Barrès, Maurras' nationalist *Action Française* offered a similar example of political stylisation in which doctrine, organisation, and leadership impulse constituted a closely knit framework, the originality of which was found in – as Maurras himself suggested – a 'judicious combination of brain and brawn' (Nolte, 1965: 135–8; Carroll, 1995: 71ff).[13] A similar political aesthetics was cultivated in the Sorelian movement and in Italian proto-Fascism, where especially Marinetti's Futurist movement enthusiastically propagated metapolitical values such as dynamism, speed, hardness, violence, technological beauty and action for action's sake (Mosse, 1993: 91). After the First World War, the new totalitarian aesthetic was adopted by Spengler, Jünger and other intellectuals who sympathised with the Conservative Revolution – such as Schmitt, who perhaps provided the most formal philosophical theoretisation of this form of political expressionism (Schmitt, 1996). As political movements, both Fascism and National Socialism saw themselves as preparing not so much for a class war as for a cultural revolution, which would shape the national community as a *Gesamtkunstwerk*, being energised by the leadership of the Schillerian *Staatskünstler* or Wagnerian poetic genius (Chytry, 1989). Inspired by D'Annunzio's experiment in spectacular and 'poetic' politics at Fiume during 1919–1920, Mussolini posed as a political artist who would bring back 'style' to Italian political life, which it had been deprived of by liberal democracy (Falasca-Zamponi, 1997: 15, 89–90, 100–1). Modelling his own political style after that of Mussolini, Hitler similarly emphasised the essential unity between his aesthetic and political conceptions, repeating that his regime had finally succeeded in reconciling politics with what was perhaps the highest form of art: the reshaping of German character out of a formless human mass. Not accidentally, the Nazi elite itself featured a disproportionate number of would-be, frustrated or failed semi-artists, who besides Hitler himself also included Eckhart, Goebbels, Rosenberg, von Schirach, Frank, Funk, and Speer (cf. Fest, 1977: 566–8, 1127).[14]

Nevertheless, it is arguable that the conjunction between an aesthetic and a totalitarian politics is not a necessary or 'essential' one. Mosse has, for example, traced the aestheticisation of politics even further back to the French Revolution, which he views as the true incubator of modern revolutionary nationalism and modern populist dictatorship or, following Talmon's familiar expression, of 'totalitarian democracy' (Talmon, 1970). In the new age of mass politics inaugurated by the Revolution, the written word not only progressively receded before the spoken word, but words themselves also increasingly had to compete with visual images, which rendered the phenomenon of political style equally as important as traditional political theory. Mosse goes so far as to suggest that the new style of totalitarian democracy, in establishing direct forms of mediation between government and people, constitutes an integral feature of mass politics, is not definitionally tied to totalitarian forms, and hence also necessarily intrudes upon the paradigm of liberal representative government (Mosse, 1993: 2–3, 60ff).

Mosse's attempt to relocate political aesthetics and political style in the mainstream of political culture and to dislodge it from the historical context of autocracy and totalitarianism appears to run parallel to Ankersmit's 'romantic' approach; even though Mosse fails to clarify how totalitarian democracy can credibly be de-totalitarianised if one of its defining characteristics, i.e. the mimetic or identitarian mediation between government and people, remains in place (Mosse, 1993: 62–3). It bears repeating at this point that in all of the political currents traced above, from revolutionary Jacobinism via the integral nationalism of Barrès, Maurras, Spengler, or Schmitt up to Fascism and National Socialism, leadership claims were predicated upon an identitarian theory that guaranteed the immediate self-presentation or self-expression of the nation through a spokesperson who was simultaneously present and absent (the leadership group, the party, the charismatic or prophetic genius). According to Gentile and Mussolini, state and individual constituted the inseparable terms of an essential synthesis; the Fascist state was a popular state, the pinnacle of democracy, even if the nation manifested itself as the conscience and will of a few, or even of a single man (Mussolini and Gentile, 1973: 42–5). The mimetic conception was elaborated with particular force by Carl Schmitt, who specified that *homogeneity* was the essential characteristic of democracy. It ideally established the 'identity between rulers and ruled, governors and governed, those who command and those who obey' and hence also implied the exclusion and even annihilation of heterogeneous elements, of the cultural and political stranger. This democratic identity between state and society did not permit qualitative differences to arise between the two poles of the political process: in democracy the *Volk* was simply identical with itself (Schmitt, 1988: 9, 13–17, 30).

We can only begin to extricate the notions of aesthetic politics and political style from this dark genealogy by dismissing all lingering presumptions of this (literally unmediated) form of representative identity, and by firmly embracing a liberal conception of political difference. However, we also need to remain acutely aware that, as Talmon has classically demonstrated, the political Enlightenment has itself been captured by the logic of totalitarian democracy, and that ideals of resemblance and identity still residually define current conceptions about popular sovereignty and the mandatory function of spokespersons for the people in both politics and the media. From Hobbes to the English Puritans and the American revolutionary democrats, from the French *philosophes* to Marx, Lenin, and the communists, the theory of political identity has also taken an intellectualist or scientist rather than aesthetic turn – suggesting a surreptitious affinity between rationalism and Romanticism, and between the radical left and the radical right, which has been anxiously repressed on both sides of the political spectrum. In these terms, it is therefore not so much the void or the gap between representers and represented (between elite and mass) itself that endangers democratic practice, but rather the opposite identitarian ideal that dreams of closing it, and which thereby renders the representative elite invisible and unaccountable to public judgement.

Political democracy is therefore equally rooted in the Romantic as in the Enlightenment tradition, and it is precisely the former that enables us to correct the rationalist dogmatism of the latter. Despite its inner ambiguities, the history of political Romanticism accentuates those twin elements that appear conducive to a democratic conception of political style: a closer recognition of the role of emotional expression and political will, and a more conscious demarcation of the representative distinction between 'elite' and 'mass'. The concept of political style neither delivers us to an unbounded political expressionism, nor does it usher in authoritarian elitism. It rather envisages a new equilibrium between reason and sentiment, while its demarcation between political professionals and laypersons does not place the weight of political representation exclusively with one category or the other. It does not reverse rationalist prejudices by prioritising spectacle and form over argument and content, but denies their separability in the dynamics of modern media-sensitive political persuasion. The style concept appeals to the capacity for discernment of citizens without placing excessive weight upon their political competence and their propensity for political action. It strikes a proper balance between indifference and involvement, between political distance and political contact. It enables politicians to 'stick their necks out' and profile themselves, while rendering it less easy for them to hide their personal or group interests behind the broad back of the electorate. As a result, both representers and represented may acquire a more articulated understanding of the autonomy of the political game, while recognising that the resultant gap between professionals and laypersons does not necessarily represent a democratic deficit but constitutes an important prerequisite for their democratic interaction (cf. Manin, 1997: 232–4).

Restyling Political Identity and Difference

What can be distilled from the above considerations for outlining an interesting conception of stylish democratic politics? A first conclusion might underline some of the affinities (or style correspondences) between an emphasis on the aesthetic character of political representation and a radical view of the role of thought styles in the formation of scientific knowledge.[15] Although I have touched upon it before, this analogy between epistemology and politics, or between the patterns and mechanisms of scientific and political representation, cannot be pursued in any detail here (White, 1987; cf. Lang, 1990; Latour, 1993). Suffice it to say that in both domains a critical contrast arises with the absence of style (or rather 'style ingenuousness') that characterises traditional objectivistic performances of science and politics. While aesthetic or performative politics focuses the difference between spokesperson and constituency, and no longer pretends that the popular will, the general interest, or the needs of the whole can be represented in immediate and neutral fashion, new rhetorical and reflexive approaches in science studies similarly emphasise perspectivism, partiality, and the constructivist difference between word and world (cf. Gilbert and Mulkay, 1984; Ashmore, 1989; Gross, 1996). Over and against 'mimetic' epistemology, which seeks a maximum of resemblance between the description and the object described, rhetoric and style precisely affirm the *autonomy* of the narrative over and against what is narrated. In both the field of science and that of politics, therefore, a logic of identity or resemblance that banks upon epistemological security and scientific groundedness is contrasted with a logic of difference and figurative expression, which celebrates the uncertainty of perspectival narratives and contingent decisions.

The style-bound perspective that emerges here at least stimulates a greater sensitivity to the performative, reality-constituting effects of political language and imagery, which do not operate according to the logic of neutral observation and description, but follow the far more intricate one of the *self-fulfilling prophecy*. Discursive and symbolic activity, and the making and breaking of reputations, more than ever before constitute the heart of doing politics (Bourdieu, 1991; Fairclough, 2000; Thompson, 2000). Image-making and reputational work have always been paramount features of political behaviour; but in a mediated culture the increased visibility of the political game crucially destabilises the political credit of persons, positions, and institutions, and creates a new fickleness of political fame. The capital of name and fame is more fragile than other forms of credit; it circulates much faster than ever before and needs to be maintained with greater frequency and care in order to preserve its relative value. The never-ceasing opinion ratings about the electoral standing of political parties and the popular appeal of individual politicians exercise a circular, self-fulfilling 'reality effect'. They may set loose an unstoppable snowball that realises precisely what they apparently report about in neutrally descriptive terms (an impending electoral defeat, the sinking popularity of a government, the 'damaging' of a party leader, an individual minister who has 'lost the plot'). This unprecedented reputational sensitivity and need for public recognition, which is forced upon politics by its friendly–inimical alliance with the media, whips up the anxiety of politicians about their appearance and presentation, and transforms the upkeep of credibility (of their honour, dignity and good name) into a matter of life or death. Increasingly, positions of political power are dependent upon public trust, belief and confidence (and upon those who are able to manipulate these volatile variables), and hence upon a recognisable political style that weaves together matter and manner, principle and presentation, in an attractively coherent and credible political performance.

Resistance against objectivism in politics thus implies resistance against an overly rigorous separation between person and cause, as well as a double plea for 'personal knowledge' and a more personalised politics. Samuels already argued for a reappraisal of pre-reflexive political emotions and subjective gut reactions that do not need to wait for intellectual articulation and systematisation in order to be admitted to political reality. This is not a sell-out to irrationalism, but favours a redefinition of the domain of political rationality, which is broadened in order to encompass the emotional political intelligence (EPI) of ordinary citizens. As a result, fragmented, irregular, issue-specific and 'extra-parliamentary' activities, which are not supported by well-rounded argument or analysis, can be revalued as significant political facts; as can citizens' widespread political 'indifference' and 'anti-political' discomforts about the functioning of the political class as a whole. On the side of the political professionals, a more personal profile that is nurtured through the audiovisual media may lead to more rounded and varied information about their political trustworthiness. Highlighting the 'human being' behind the politician in a media presentation which not only transmits *what* is said but simultaneously visualises *how* it is said and *who* says it, supplies not only cognitive but also affective information about the authenticity and credibility of individuals and groups that strengthens the capacity for judgement of the citizenry – whereas more traditional media such as newspapers, pamphlets and radio necessarily maintain a certain level of separation between programme, person, and presentation. As in the broader society, where a neo-romantic sensibility and emotional expressivity have come to fulfil important functions of recognition and identification, introducing new forms of 'emotional democracy' (van Stokkom, 1997), political trust and distrust are likewise increasingly attributed and distributed on the basis of a broader and more realistic package of information than that of the distanced, purely intellectual message.[16]

In this manner, auratic and heroic politics (the politics of great men, big words, and high-strung ideals) shares the fate of auratic science (the science of foundational security and universalist appeal) in being levelled down to a more ordinary enterprise. Both science and politics participate in a more general de-auraticisation of high culture which, in its closer approximation to the popular, is also a process of de-rationalisation, contextualisation and emotionalisation. Analogous to the levelling of the epistemological hierarchy between expert and lay forms of rationality, the loss of aura of 'high' politics tends to diminish the distance between political professionals and ordinary citizens. Benjamin was among the first to connect this fading of cultural halo to the spread of technologies of reproduction, even though his guardedly optimistic conclusions about the popularisation of art were offset by a rather negative view about the emotionalisation and aestheticisation of politics. As a result of the enhanced visibility introduced by media technologies, *presentation* had become paramount in politics; a change that affected both actors and rulers, depleting both theatres and parliaments in a new 'selection before the equipment from which the star and the dictator emerge victorious' (Benjamin, 1992: 240n).

In contrast with Benjamin's misgivings about the undemocratic consequences of this technological 'selection', authors such as Meyrowitz have instead suggested that celebrity politicians lose their aura of greatness precisely as a result of the familiarising, even banalising effect of continuous media exposure. While the traditional image of the great leader and helmsman depended upon mystification and aloofness, and required a large arena in which to project his superhuman persona, the new electronic media tend to erode the barriers between politicians' traditional back and front regions. The camera and the close-up minimise the distance between audience and performer, revealing so much expressive and personal detail that the distant image of the politician is replaced by something resembling 'an encounter with an intimate acquaintance' (Meyrowitz, 1985: 273). The daily TV news, current affairs programmes and chat shows turn political actors into media regulars whose familiar personae are developed in a continuous soap-like narrative (Marshall, 1997: 229; van Zoonen, this volume). Their charisma is routinised (albeit not in a Weberian sense) and informalised; by presenting themselves as 'ordinary people', they are levelled down to the 'household' dimensions of the modern media celebrity as (s)he is consumed by a distracted and zapping television audience.

This new staging of the political as parasocial intimacy-at-a-distance alters the form and re-balances the dimensions of identity and difference in political representation, undercutting the parameters that have traditionally framed the dilemma of elitism *vs.* populism. As we have seen, a representative or spokesperson is always a *different* person who takes the place of (and in this sense *silences*) the represented in order to be able to mediate their views and interests. There is always a fault line in representation: only through distance is the representer able to represent. But representation simultaneously implies resemblance and proximity, since the representer embodies the represented and speaks in their name. Parasocial or mediated interaction, I have argued, changes the terms and conditions of political proximity and political distance (cf. also Corner, this volume). 'Old-style' political identity implied a literal unity in which the individual coincided with the collective and the collective spoke in a single voice through a single spokesperson. Such an *essentialist* or mimetic resemblance differs from the logic of parasocial identification insofar as the latter stages a proximity (and even intimacy) that remains virtual and asymmetrical, since it comes with a structural sociological gap between celebrities and 'civilians', or between the Big Names and the great Anonymous. Parasocial recognition is less interested in identity than in *authenticity*, which is more respectful of difference and does not deny the gap. The trustful recognition of self in a public individual is therefore more like an encounter with a family member with whom one acknowledges a *family resemblance* in the Wittgensteinian sense: one that is always partial, distributed, and actively constructed. On the one hand, political leaders shed their elitist aura and try to become 'one of us'. On the other hand, distance is reasserted by the remoteness of the star who, while dwelling constantly in the public eye, is still seen as untouchable and as 'living in a different world'. In this sense, politicians increasingly share in the 'extraordinary ordinariness' which characterises the modern democratic celebrity.[17]

This is not to dissimulate the dark side of parasocial interaction, which always generates the risk of 'false intimacy' and obsessive identification, as is displayed in pathological forms of fan behaviour such as stalking, hooliganism and other forms of individual or collective hysteria. The democratic ideology that governs the celebrity system suggests that stars are not that different from ordinary people, that everybody can rise from the plebs, and that talent and hard work are the only legitimate distributors of social privilege. The reality, of course, is that the capital of visibility and reputation is very unequally divided and commands unheard-of perks, privileges and powers. The star-struck individual or group easily forgets about the virtuality and asymmetry of the relationship in order to feel 'at one' with the political hero, while the hero may in turn delude himself into thinking that he immediately coincides with his following.[18] Indeed, such pathological forms of identification were generated to excess in the mass adulation that was received by the murdered Pim Fortuyn, who was obsessively seen as 'one of us', and who himself claimed to be on a divine mission to embody the true soul of the Dutch people. Normally, however, an 'audience democracy' positions the viewer not as a participant of the political process but as a witness (or perhaps a *voyeur*), who recognises the inability of crossing into the text as a political actor (Marshall, 1997: 229). In accentuating this structural gap between 'passive' audience and 'active' players, it strikes a new balance between representers and represented that is based on aesthetic stylisation and the personalisation of political trust.

In this new constellation, media professionals increasingly play the part of the 'rational citizen' (always a mythical figure) as controllers of the political elite, tendentially bypassing formal representative institutions such as parties and parliaments. Current political debate is much more a game that is played between professionals who entertain simultaneously diverging and converging interests, than a 'power-free' dialogue between equals in a mysteriously levelled public sphere. It is questionable, however, whether the routine complaint about the alleged passivity of the 'zapping' citizen is in all respects justified. The reach of public debate has also been extended, resulting in a greater information density that has enhanced the capacity for judgement of the average citizen. This capacity must not be represented in a one-sided cognitivist or intellectualist manner, but rather in terms of richness of imagination, intuitive experience and emotional intelligence. Without formal expertise, ordinary citizens are quite capable of realistically judging what is performed on the media-political stage. Soaps and talk shows enact an incessant discussion about and experimentation with modern relational morality, while news shows and reality TV are confronting us with images of war, disease, love, sex, and violence that previously did not touch us so directly. In this chapter, I have tried to argue that the media show that is called 'politics' similarly promotes forms of emotional realism, which enable ordinary citizens, in spite of their political 'passivity' and even 'indifference', to react adequately and competently to whatever their political representatives are putting on.

Notes

1. The Netherlands' widely admired 'Polder Model' has institutionalised a form of democratic corporatism which features tripartite consultations between employers, unions and government that seek consensual agreement and workable compromises on all major issues of economic and social policy. The two 'purple' coalition governments led by Wim Kok from 1994 until 2002, which squeezed out the Christian Democratic centre and spanned the former extremes of the left–right political spectrum, can be seen as a dramatic exemplification of this institutionalised consensualism. Fortuyn heavily criticised the Polder Model's shady backroom dealing, its exclusionism, and its technocratic aloofness, proclaiming that 'we have to change from the Polder model to a conflict model'. For a critical discussion, see Peet (2002).

2. In Fairclough's specification, communicative style is a matter of language in the broadest sense – certainly verbal language (words), but also all other aspects of the complex bodily performance that constitutes political style, such as gestures, facial expressions, how people hold themselves and move, dress, hairstyle etc. Style thus also captures the somatic aspect of performativity: wagging your finger, peremptory looks, a firmly set jaw, emphatic gestures, assertivity in tone of speech (Fairclough, 2000: 4; cf. 6–8, 95.). Thrift notes that style is a package of disparate elements that are together modulated as significant, even while displaying considerable ambiguity; indeed, this ambiguity is a crucial part of the power of style (2002: 202).

3. No doubt Fortuyn's ability to respond to his opponents as (male) *bodies* rather than 'talking heads' was another advantage of his gayness. At least some of his opponents were clearly apprehensive of the emotional tricks this malicious queen might play on them.

4. As represented by the unfortunate Frank Dobson. One humorous but also telling incident from this campaign was the grave matter of Dobson's *beard*. Labour spin doctors, drawing on psychological evidence that bearded men are generally regarded as untrustworthy, advised Dobson to 'jazz himself up' in order to face up more successfully to clean-shaven Ken. However, Dobson kept the beard, which is of course directly associated with historical socialism (see Marx and Engels), and which is more generally interpreted as an old-fashioned signifier of age, experience and trustworthiness. New Labourites such as Mandelson, Hoon, Darling and Byers had all shaved off their facial hair with their socialism, including formerly 'Red' Ken. Dobson defiantly proclaimed that the electorate should consider his policies rather than his facial furniture: 'I told them to get stuffed because, quite frankly, I'm not in the image business. With me, what you see is what you get. If you don't like what you see, don't vote for me but listen to what I've got to say' (The *Guardian*, 13.3.2000). Ken Livingstone's unique sartorial appearance, including his famous one-suit wardrobe (in wrinkled beige), was the subject of a dedicated article in The *Guardian*'s Style section, where it was described as exuding an 'innate, unshakeable air of devil-may-care scruffiness ... to look careless, or clueless, in the style stakes gives the air of a true rebel. Simply by stuffing things in his pockets and ruining the line of his coat and suit, Ken marks himself out as a man of the people' (Cartner-Morley, 2000).

5. The *Observer* 12.3.2000. The examples of Fortuyn and the London mayoral contest clearly suggest that personalisation and spectacle do not kill popular interest in politics, but instead tend to reverse the 'apathy' that was again so widely deplored at the UK general election of June 2001. In the same vein, sleaze and scandal may well serve to increase rather than decrease voter interest (Little, 2002).

6. Bourdieu, (1998: 1–9, 17–19, 51–2) for example, deplores the 'particularly pernicious form of symbolic violence' which is exercised by television which, by broadcasting non-events and *faits divers*, is only capable of displaying the most anecdotal, sensationalist and ritualised aspects of political life, and accordingly offers a 'superficial information spice' which depoliticises and reduces public life to gossip and mindless chatter. In my view, Bourdieu remains constricted by an intellectualist ideal of citizenship and of the origins of political (dis)trust that insufficiently accounts for the democratic effects of emotional political 'interpellation' and style recognition. A more balanced (though still critical) assessment of the art of political packaging

is provided by Franklin (1994; 1998), who likewise appears to take his normative bearings from an 'Athenian' image of a broad participatory democracy (cf. 1994: 11–12).

7. 'It seems ages ago that one collectively bemoaned the greyness of Dutch politics. With the rise of Pim Fortuyn, the theatre entered in its most flamboyant form. First as farce, with 'At Your Service' (Fortuyn's mock military greeting at his election as leader of *Leefbaar Nederland* – DP), then as operetta, in the debate between political leaders, and finally as nineteenth century Italian opera at Fortuyn's death' (Groot, 2002).

8. Evans effectively describes how, in the 1997 election campaign, different cultural styles created a massive gap between the Tories and Labour. An 'anxious masculinity', which was frightened of 'women, foreigners and gays and any human or abstract phenomenon that does not come packaged in a tight collar and a formal sentence structure', clashed with an emotionally literate and 'feminised' public culture that constructed the world 'less through the denial of the private than through the increasing valorisation and prioritisation of the private'. Labour's relation to the world was generally perceived as more feminine: less rigid, less socially hierarchical and more rooted in ordinary experience, also its public language emphasised schools, health and transport, which represented specifically female concerns related to the caring functions (Evans 1999: 232). Cf. also Fortuyn's 'feminine' aura *vs*. the impersonal macho politics that was attributed to the Purple Professionals.

9. Ankersmit's notion of 'aesthetic' politics is strictly speaking a misnomer, since art itself has of course always demonstrated inner divisions and tensions between realist and anti-realist currents. See Alpers' (1983) familiar argument about the polarity between the Dutch 'art of describing' and Italian narrative and symbolic art in the sixteenth and seventeenth centuries; White's (1987) account of literary and historical realism in Flaubert and Marx; or Lepenies' (1985) description of 'horizontal' correspondences between a right-radical 'artistic' style and a left-democratic 'scientific' style that cut across 'vertical' separations between the domains of politics, literature and science. This tension is also captured in a quote from John Adams, who famously stated that the political representation should be 'an exact portrait, in miniature, of the people at large, as it should think, feel, reason, and act like them'. For Ankersmit, Adams perfectly expresses the 'mimetic' idea of representation that his own 'aesthetic' view is meant to counter; but Adams himself adds that 'in a representative assembly, *as in art*, the perfection of the portrait consists in its likeness' (cit. Pitkin, 1967: 61, cf. 66).

10. Cf. Pels (1993: 172). Ankersmit similarly defends political indifference: it is 'not necessarily the sand in the political machine but rather the indispensable oil for making it function' (1997: 102–3). Political representatives may enjoy great political freedom, on the crucial condition that power remains *visible*. Indifference creates the gap or distance from which citizens can acquire a proper grasp of the political game. Indifference (which normally finds its basis in trust [1997: 154]) creates the necessary distance or 'alienation' between people and rulers that precisely makes power visible and accountable.

11. In contrast to the widely perceived 'hypocrisy' of the ruling (especially left-wing) elite, Fortuyn was seen as authentic precisely because he clearly was 'not a man of the street', but then 'did not act as if he was'.

12. According to Benjamin, the Fascist aestheticisation of politics is the logical result of giving the masses a means of expression and a grandiose aim (national war), deflecting attention from and thereby preserving the capitalist property structure. In utter self-alienation, 'mankind' experiences its own destruction as an aesthetic pleasure of the first order (1992: 234–35). However, this Marxist interpretation of Fascism underestimates the revolutionary seriousness of the Fascist movements, and implausibly views the aestheticisation of the political as a consummation of bourgeois *l'art pour l'art*. But Fascism precisely denies the auratic nature of art and the autonomy of aesthetics, blurring the boundaries between culture, media and politics in much the same way as the communist politicisation of art that is recommended by Benjamin as a counterstrategy. Further critical discussions of Benjamin's claims are provided by Hewitt (1992; 1993: 23–4, 164–8), Carroll (1995: 5) and Falasca-Zamponi (1997: 9–14).

13. Nolte describes style as 'the visible essence' of a political phenomenon, not merely a composite of discrete elements, but its 'living past', which cannot be set apart merely as one component. Style, he adds, may be manifest in a single photograph, while in thousands of speeches it may only be present in vague outline (1965: 135).

14. A Bohemian political 'artist' such as Fortuyn cannot be readily positioned in terms of the traditional left–right political spectrum. In earlier writings, I have defended a 'horseshoe model' of political positioning that adds a 'vertical' dimension of political sentiment and expressivity to the traditional 'wing model' of left and right. The ideological extremes 'touch each other' in the realm of radical political Bohemia (where the aestheticisation of politics finds its true cradle) (Pels, 1993; 2000). In this rather darkly-lit spot, where radicals and revolutionaries of all stripes stand in sharp opposition to the quietly reformist bourgeois–liberal centre, we encounter 'crossover intellectuals' such as Sorel, Mussolini, De Man and De Kadt, who came up with various mixtures and combinations of socialism, liberalism and nationalism. It seems that Fortuyn's unelaborated and eclectic mix of libertarianism and nationalism is closer to this particular 'third way' tradition than to any other ideological combination.

15. Though usually traced to Fleck's 1935 classic (Fleck, 1980), the concept of *Denkstil* is already encountered in some early essays by Mannheim from the 1920s (cf. Barnes, 1994; Pels, 1996). A thought style, in Mannheim's conceptualisation, refers to a dimension of pre-theoretical intuition and experience residing 'below' the specific content and form of individual cultural expressions, which produces an encompassing 'will to think' that organises the stylistic unity of various cultural utterances (1982: 35–7, 86–8). As such, the concept is only an alternative expression for the central preoccupation of the Mannheimian sociology of knowledge: the 'existential' or 'volitional' determination of thought.

16. Marshall (1997) similarly emphasises the affective function of (political) celebrities. Celebrities function as cultural signs that simultaneously embody certain conceptions of individuality and offer a focus for collective identification by groups or audiences that are continually reorganised, assembled and disbanded in an increasingly 'classless', individualised and volatile mass culture. This system of celebrity power and fleeting audience formation, which functions by means of affective recognition and the selective imitation of elements from the lifestyles of famous people, is convertible to a wide variety of social domains, being progressively translated from the entertainment industries towards more 'serious' fields such as business, politics, and science (1997: xiii, 76, 203).

17. Marshall (1997: 214) has developed a differential theory of celebrity culture that makes the same point about the apparently contradictory nature of political legitimation. Politics amalgamates three 'codes of subjectivity', which originate from the entertainment industries and define three forms of affective association. It balances the construction of *familiarity*, which is informed by television culture (for example, the literal staging of the politician's family), the construction of *solidarity* with and immersion in the crowd, which copies the spectacular performance culture of popular music (for example, the political convention and the fan behaviour of political supporters), and the simultaneous construction of an auratic *distance*, which is modelled after the film celebrity (for example, the filmic construction of a political character in campaign advertisements), and legitimates their differentiation from the crowd.

18. Cf. Hitler's words: 'I know that everything you are, you are through me; and everything I am, I am through you alone'.

References

Alpers, S. (1983) *The Art of Describing. Dutch Art in the Seventeenth Century*. London: Penguin.

Ankersmit, F. (1990) *De navel van de geschiedenis*. Groningen: Historische Uitgeverij.

Ankersmit, F. (1994) *History and Tropology. The Rise and Fall of Metaphor*. Berkeley: University of California Press.

Ankersmit, F. (1997) *Aesthetic Politics. Political Philosophy Beyond Fact and Value*. Stanford: Stanford University Press.

Ankersmit, F. (2002) *Political Representation*. Stanford: Stanford University Press.

Ashmore, M. (1989) *The Reflexive Thesis*. Chicago: The University of Chicago Press.

Barnes, B. (1994) 'Cultural Change – The Thought Styles of Mannheim and Kuhn', *Common Knowledge* 3(2): 65–78.

Beck, U. and Beck-Gernsheim, E. (2002) *Individualization*. London: Sage.

Benjamin, W. (1930) 'Theorien des deutschen Faschismus', *Die Gesellschaft* 7(2): 32–41 (English tr. 1979, *New German Critique* 17: 120–8).

Benjamin, W. (1992) *Illuminations*. Ed. H. Arendt. London: Fontana.

Bourdieu, P. (1991) *Language and Symbolic Power*. Cambridge: Polity Press.

Bourdieu, P. (1998) *On Television and Journalism*. London: Pluto Press.

Brants, K. (1998) 'Who's Afraid of Infotainment?', *European Journal of Communication* 13(3): 315–35.

Camps, H. (2001) 'Ik ga vanuit het Catshuis regeren (interview with Pim Fortuyn)', *Elsevier*, 1 September.

Carroll, D. (1995) *French Literary Fascism. Nationalism, Anti-Semitism, and the Ideology of Culture*. Princeton: Princeton University Press.

Cartner-Morley, J. (2000) 'Here's looking at you, Ken', The *Guardian*, 30 June.

Chytry, J. (1989) *The Aesthetic State. A Quest in Modern German Thought*. Berkeley: University of California Press.

Corner, J. (2003) 'Mediated Persona and Political Culture', this volume.

Coward, R. (2001) 'Passion in politics', The *Guardian*, 5 June.

Evans, M. (1999) 'The Culture Did It: Comment on the 1997 British General Election', pp. 229–45 in L. Ray and A. Sayer (eds) *Culture and Economy After the Cultural Turn*. London: Sage.

Ewen, S. (1990) 'Marketing Dreams. The Political Elements of Style', pp. 41–56 in A. Tomlinson (ed.) *Consumption, Identity and Style. Marketing, Meanings, and the Packaging of Pleasure*. London & New York: Routledge.

Fairclough, N. (2000) *New Labour, New Language?* London: Routledge.

Falasca-Zamponi, S. (1997) *Fascist Spectacle. The Aesthetics of Power in Mussolini's Italy*. Berkeley: University of California Press.

Fest, J.C. (1977) *Hitler*. Harmondsworth: Penguin Books.

Fiske, J. (1992) 'Popularity and the Politics of Information', pp. 45–63 in P. Dahlgren and C. Sparks (eds) *Journalism as Popular Culture*. London: Sage.

Fleck, L. (1980 [1935]) *Entstehung und Entwicklung einer wissenschaftlichen Tatsache*. Frankfurt: Suhrkamp.

Fortuyn, P. (2002) *De puinhopen van acht jaar Paars*. Uithoorn: Karakter Uitgevers.

Franklin, B. (1994) *Packaging Politics. Political Communications in Britain's Media Democracy*. London: Edward Arnold.

Franklin, B. (1998) *Tough on Soundbites, Tough on the Causes of Soundbites. New Labour and News Management*. London: The Catalyst Trust.

Giesen, P. (2002) 'Mediamagneet', pp. 70–72 in *Het fenomeen Fortuyn*. Amsterdam: De Volkskrant/Meulenhoff.

Gilbert, G.N. and Mulkay M. (1984) *Opening Pandora's Box. A Sociological Analysis of Scientists' Discourse*. Cambridge: Cambridge University Press.

Goodwin, J., Jasper, J.M. and Polletta F. (eds) (2001) *Passionate Politics. Emotions and Social Movements*. Chicago & London: University of Chicago Press.

Groot, G. (2002) 'Nederland moet terugkeren tot de realiteit', *NRC-Handelsblad*, 10 May 2002.

Gross, A.G. (1996) *The Rhetoric of Science*. 2nd ed. Cambridge MA: Harvard University Press.

Hewitt, A. (1992) 'Fascist Modernism, Futurism, and "Post-Modernity"', pp. 38–55 in R.J. Golsan (ed.) *Fascism, Aesthetics, and Culture*. Hanover and London: University Press of New England.

Hewitt, A. (1993) *Fascist Modernism. Aesthetics, Politics, and the Avant-Garde*. Stanford: Stanford University Press.

Hillach, A. (1979) 'The Aesthetics of Politics: Walter Benjamin's "Theories of German Fascism", *New German Critique* 17: 99–119.

Horton, D. and Wohl, R. (1986 [1956]) 'Mass Communication and Para-social Interaction: Observation on Intimacy at a Distance', pp. 185–206 in G. Gumpert and R. Cathcart (eds) *Inter/Media. Interpersonal Communication in a Media World*. New York & Oxford: Oxford University Press.
Jones, N. (1999) *Sultans of Spin. The Media and the New Labour Government*. London: Victor Gollancz.
Lang, B. (1990) *The Anatomy of Philosophical Style*. Oxford: Blackwell.
Latour, B. (1993) *We Have Never Been Modern*. Cambridge MA: Harvard University Press.
Lepenies, W. (1985) *Die drei Kulturen. Soziologie zwischen Literatur und Wissenschaft*. München: Hanser.
Little, R. (2002) 'Don't knock sleaze – it pulls in the voters', The *Guardian*, 27 February.
Manin, B. (1997) *The Principles of Representative Government*. Cambridge: Cambridge University Press.
Mancini, P. and Swanson, D. (eds) (1994) *Politics, Media and Democracy*. New York: Praeger.
Mannheim, K. (1982 [1922–23]) *Structures of Thinking*. London: Routledge.
Marshall, P.D. (1997) *Celebrity and Power. Fame in Contemporary Culture*. Minneapolis & London: University of Minnesota Press.
Meyrowitz, J. (1985) *No Sense of Place. The Impact of Electronic Media on Social Behaviour*. New York and Oxford: Oxford University Press.
Mosse, G.L. (1993) *Confronting the Nation. Jewish and Western Nationalism*. Hanover & London: Brandeis University Press.
Mussolini, B. and Gentile, G. (1973 [1932]) 'The Doctrine of Fascism', pp. 43–57 in A. Lyttleton (ed.) *Italian Fascisms: From Pareto to Gentile*. New York: Harper & Row.
Negrine, R. (1996) *The Communication of Politics*. London: Sage.
Nolte, E. (1965) *Three Faces of Fascism*. New York: Holt, Rinehart and Winston.
Peet, J. (2002) 'Model makers, A survey of the Netherlands', *The Economist*, 4 May.
Pels, D. (1993) *Het democratisch verschil. Jacques de Kadt en de nieuwe elite*. Amsterdam: Van Gennep.
Pels, D. (1996) 'Karl Mannheim and the Sociology of Scientific Knowledge: Toward a New Agenda', *Sociological Theory* 14(1): 30–48.
Pels, D. (2000) *The Intellectual as Stranger. Studies in Spokespersonship*. London & New York: Routledge.
Pels, D. and H. te Velde (2000) *Politieke stijl. Over presentatie en optreden in de politiek*. Amsterdam: Het Spinhuis.
Pitkin, H.F. (1967) *The Concept of Representation*. Berkeley: University of California Press.
Rawnsley, A. (2001) 'Ready to go to the people', The *Observer*, 6 May.
Samuels, A. (1993) *The Political Psyche*. New York & London: Routledge.
Samuels, A. (2001) *Politics on the Couch. Citizenship and the Internal Life*. London: Profile Books.
Scammell, M. (1995) *Designer Politics*. London: Macmillan.
Schmitt, C. (1988 [1926]) *The Crisis of Parliamentary Democracy*. Cambridge MA: The MIT Press.
Schmitt, C. (1996 [1932]) *The Concept of the Political*. Chicago & London: University of Chicago Press.
Schuyt, K. (2002) 'De man die nergens bij hoort', pp. 67–69 in *Het fenomeen Fortuyn*. Amsterdam: De Volkskrant/Meulenhoff.
Simons, J. (1999) 'The Aestheticization of Politics: An Alternative to Left-Modernist Critiques', *Strategies* 12(3): 173–90.
Simons, J. (2001) 'Aesthetic Political Technologies', *Intertexts* 6(1): 74–97.
Sloterdijk, P. (1983) *Kritik der zynischen Vernunft*. 2 vols. Frankfurt: Suhrkamp.
Sternhell, Z. (1972) *Maurice Barrès et le nationalisme français*. Paris: Éditions Complexe.
Stokkom, B. van (1997) *Emotionele democratie*. Amsterdam: Van Gennep.
Street, J. (2001) *Mass Media, Politics and Democracy*. Basingstoke: Palgrave.
Talmon, J.L. (1970) *The Origins of Totalitarian Democracy*. London: Sphere Books.
Thompson, J.B. (2000) *Political Scandal. Power and Visibility in the Media Age*. Cambridge: Polity.

Thrift, N. (2002) 'Performing Cultures in the New Economy', pp. 201–33 in P. du Gay and M. Pryke (eds) *Cultural Economy. Cultural Analysis and Commercial Life*. London: Sage.
Walter, T. (ed.)(1999) *The Mourning for Diana*. New York: Berg.
Wernick, A. (1991) *Promotional Culture*. London: Sage.
White, H. (1987) 'The Problem of Style in Realistic Representation: Marx and Flaubert', pp. 279–98 in B. Lang (ed.) *The Concept of Style*. Ithaca & London: Cornell University Press.
Zoonen, L. van (1998) 'A Day at the Zoo: Political Communication, Pigs and Popular Culture', *Media, Culture and Society* 20: 183–200.
Zoonen, L. van (2003) '"After Dallas and Dynasty we have … Democracy": Articulating Soap, Politics and Gender', this volume.
Zwaap, R. (2002) 'Media Culpa? Bij de dood van een mediacraat', *De Groene Amsterdammer*, 11 May.

4

Mediated Persona and Political Culture

JOHN CORNER

First, an historical instance:

Leo Braudy's brilliant, scholarly study of the history of celebrity and fame (Braudy, 1986) contains a photograph of Theodore Roosevelt taken in 1886, when he was on the edge of the political career that would lead to the Presidency. Clad in buckskin and wearing a hunting hat, Roosevelt is sitting on a rock, holding a rifle to cover three, rough-looking men gathered forlornly under a tree. The setting is a lakeside. Braudy's caption reads that Roosevelt:

> ... is here photographed after successfully tracking some men who had stolen a boat from his North Dakota farm. At least that was the story up until a few years ago, when it was discovered that the photograph had been restaged with some of Roosevelt's own men 'playing' the thieves ... (Braudy, 1986)

This is perhaps one of the earliest examples of the political photograph in its full, self-conscious and strategic inauthenticity, combining the mythic resonance of emblematic painting with the documentary claims of the lens.

More broadly, it is an example of the use of mediated persona as part of political performance. Although varieties of performance are ancient requirements of political elites, with royalty constituting a special subclass, it is widely noted that the introduction of technologies of media has radically changed their nature.

There is an established subspecialism of political studies that has for some time been concerned with the changing conventions of political marketing and campaigning and the personal 'branding' that this involves (recent examples would be Franklin, 1994; Kavanagh, 1995: Maarek, 1995; Scammell, 1995; Jamieson, 1996; Swanson and Mancini, 1996). A revised perspective on general media-political relations, as these are seen to be changing, has sometimes provided the framing for the latest studies (see, for instance, Bennett and Entman, 2001, Axford and Huggins, 2001 and the synoptic account of Street, 2001). Such work provides one important route for asking questions about mediation and persona, including the tracking of candidate profiles in campaigns. However, my chief concern here is with an agenda of issues to do with the location of political performance within the culture of mediated democracy, which has received less attention than it deserves. This agenda presents an apt challenge to the interdisciplinary imagination and to a growing concern for identifying the work of the symbolic within the everyday. It also locates the formal and narrow field of the 'political' within those broader settings of public and private life that are its resources and, frequently, its strategic targets.

Any analysis of political persona must recognise that performance, involving varying degrees of self-consciousness and calculated deceit, is a constituent factor of social life, including the realm of 'private life'. Goffman's classic work on the 'presentation of self' (Goffman, 1959) highlighted this within the framework of social psychology and provided what has become an influential vocabulary for its analysis. The self-presentation of politicians, however, is widely seen to be distinctive as a result of the scale of its projection (in political leaders this becomes national and possibly global), the degree of self-conscious strategy attending its planning and performance, the intensity of its interaction with media systems and the degree to which certain personal qualities are seen not merely to enhance but to *underwrite* political values.

We need to keep in mind, too, the extent to which the strategic management of the self, playing off the 'outer' against the 'inner', was considered as one of the accomplishments of statecraft long before the availability of mediations based on recording technologies. The indispensable reference here is, undoubtedly, the early-sixteenth century commentary of Machiavelli in *The Prince*. Its celebrated tone is well indicated in the following passage:

> Therefore it is unnecessary for a prince to have all the good qualities I have enumerated, but it is very necessary to appear to have them. And I shall dare to say this also, that to have them and always to observe them is injurious, and that to appear to have them is useful; to appear merciful, faithful, humane, religious, upright, and to be so, but with a mind so framed that should you require not to be so, you may be able and know how to change to the opposite. (*The Prince*, trans. H. Butterfield, 1958: 99).

The sustaining of the appearance of virtue, together perhaps with a reputation among rivals and enemies for ruthlessness, is here complementary to the exercising of powers which place the majority of people as subjects, open finally to direct coercion. When this majority is the electorate and also thereby a 'public', political performance and 'political theatre' are a major element in securing, or failing to secure, consent and a popular sense of representative adequacy in politicians. Modern democracy therefore requires specific kinds of political persona as the focus of the political system, at the same time as terms of its mediation introduce new levels of scale and flexibility into the performance. There have been different ways of assessing the consequences of these new conditions of political distance and proximity. Predominantly, they have been judged as deficit, as the introduction of yet more opportunity for deceit and manipulation and an undermining of democratic process. Yet some accounts have been more positive. For instance, Ankersmit's (1996) comprehensive review of theories of political representation sees the widening gap between representatives and the represented (a gap in which elaborated forms of political style have developed) as providing the essential grounds of democratic culture. Such a gap, he thinks, allows a politics in which the differences between the aims and perspectives of the professional political class itself and those of the 'people' are routinely and openly recognised, rather than being denied by a rhetoric of political mimesis.

Mediations can be seen to project political personhood in three broad modes. First of all, *iconically*, following the developing conventions of painting and then photography in displaying the demeanour, posture and associative contexts of the political self. Political publicity attempts to extract maximum benefit from this by means of symbolic management (as in the photo opportunity) but it also has to be wary of the kind of journalistic opportunism that threatens the off-guard politician with the wrong sort of visibility, both in terms of literal depiction and broader resonances.

Second, they mediate *vocally*, as recording technologies and conventions have allowed an increasing informality of public address such that the significance of *what* is said becomes more interfused with *how* it is said and the political and the personal are thus more closely articulated. This has brought about a political culture of strong 'secondary orality' (Ong, 1982) in which a 'theatre of voices' has partly displaced the written accounts of the press, with consequences not always fully acknowledged in writing on media-political relations.

Third, they have introduced a *kinetic* element to depiction – the political self in action and interaction (for example, the 'high politics' of the international conference, the 'low politics' of the visit to the factory) which, certainly for television, requires a choreographic attention.

Combined, the performative requirements made on political subjectivity have reached an intensity from which it is hard to imagine them ever declining (the development of websites into fully performative spaces is the next likely extension of the repertoire). Joshua Meyrowitz (1985) drew attention to general features of this reconfiguration in his suggestive study of media and social change, and John B. Thompson (1995) included them within his influential account of the new terms of interaction within modernity.

Although any detailed historical account is well beyond my scope here, it is worth noting how valuable a study of the relationships between changes in political culture and emerging forms of media (photography, film, radio and television) would be. National accounts would be welcome, although international comparisons could clearly offer a major contribution to our understanding.

With these points in mind, I want to turn first to an example from British political culture in order to establish better the kinds of structures and processes at issue.

The Archer Affair

In Britain, the most notable, recent instance of the media–politics–persona dynamic is undoubtedly provided by the case of Lord Archer, in his candidature for Mayor of London. Jeffrey Archer's distinctive political profile within the Conservative Party, the assets and vulnerabilities of his projected personal identity and his close relationship with the press have all been factors in the circumstances which, in November 1999, caused him to make a shock withdrawal from the Mayoral elections.

Forced to resign as a Member of Parliament in 1974, when he became bankrupt due to a company collapse, Archer came to full public prominence only on his return to politics in the 1980s. The return occurred within the distinctive political culture of Margaret Thatcher's Conservative Government. This was a culture which, while it continued to support most of the traditional class privileges of British society, saw itself as nevertheless committed to a new spirit of 'Enterprise', drawing on American models of entrepreneurial vigour.

Within these terms, Archer's unrestrained style of self-promotion, his lavish entertaining, his show-business approach to publicity, his attempts to be seen as a 'fun politician' (the smile and the joke a key part of his presentation) contrasted strongly with the more inhibited and muted masculine modes of demeanour and address then prominent among senior politicians in his party. His attainment of a distinctive personal style was helped enormously by the fact that, following his investment disaster in the 1970s, he had attempted to recover financially by writing melodramatic blockbuster novels about ambition, money, love and betrayal in the worlds of politics and business. Titles like *Not A Penny More, Not A Penny Less, Kane and Abel* and *First Among Equals* became best-sellers (120 million sold worldwide) providing him with great wealth, a kind of second identity as a self-made success that usefully overlaid his earlier career, and a strong association with political fiction of a kind that was increasingly interwoven with his own activities and milieu. Few politicians have managed their own publicity alongside such resources of narrative and characterisation and from such a base *within* commercial popular culture.

The wealth brought both a degree of independence from institutional support and the chance to ingratiate himself with senior officials and 'gatekeepers' by substantial donations to the Party and by what quickly became famous levels of hospitality. The Party's and the Government's ideological project was seen to be enhanced by such a highly visible and energetic advocate, able to transfer the popular touch of his novels to party campaigning and party identity. He helped 'front' the Party to the nation at large, without the disadvantages of too narrowly political an identity that other senior figures might have brought to the task. His was a good persona – amiable, blandly inclusive within existing inequalities, grounded in a self-making through talent – for a politics seeking 'to go beyond politics'. Moreover, his degree of routine social contact with senior media figures surpassed that of most other politicians in any of the parties. Success in this role of political showman overcame the doubts of many party officials as to his safeness when judged by the more established criteria for political advancement that might otherwise have ruled him out. Nevertheless, stories about his inventive freedom with the details of his family background, his educational qualifications and his previous jobs were circulating among political journalists in a way that, over the years, became legendary (his most recent biography (Crick, 1996) has the subtitle *Stranger Than Fiction*).

In the mid-1980s, Archer became Deputy Chairman of the Conservative Party but was quite soon forced to resign when allegations from a prostitute appeared in the popular press and generated a very British kind of 'scandal'. Although he protested his innocence, Archer's position was considerably damaged by the revelation that before the first stories had been published he had, through an aide, paid the woman in question £2,000. In his own account, this was an act of generosity implying no guilt – it was to help her evade growing press attention stimulated by rumours rather than to secure her silence. Either way, it was an attempt to intervene in the money–publicity dynamic, this time to protect rather than to project persona. However, negative press and public assumptions were too strong for him to remain in office, despite his subsequently winning a libel case against the newspaper that had run the first story. Like many male politicians in trouble, particularly sexual trouble, Archer strongly projected the happiness of his married life and he was helped here by the support of his wife in the attempt to counter adverse personal publicity. Indeed, in a remarkable departure from convention, the Judge at the libel trial saw fit to make Mary Archer's own persona a matter of explicit comment in summing up to the jury. He noted to them that 'your vision of her probably will never disappear. Has she elegance? Has she fragrance? Would she have, without the strain of this trial, radiance?' and asked them to consider whether a man married to such a woman would be likely to seek the services of a prostitute.

Despite this second career crisis, in the 1990s Archer managed yet another comeback, with a Life Peerage gained largely for his services to the Party. Established in the House of Lords, he once again set about developing his role as showman, and routine apologist, for Government and Party.

However, in 1999, the circumstances of the mid-80s events returned to public attention, causing further trouble just as Archer was again on the political stage as a candidate for the newly-created post of elected Mayor of London. A TV producer friend revealed to a Sunday newspaper that he had been asked by Archer to produce a false alibi in court during the 1980s libel action. This was not because Archer had been with the prostitute, but for another 'private' reason – because he had been dining with a ladyfriend and wished to keep this from his wife. Even though the friend's evidence was not actually required in the libel trial (the newspaper's allegations were shifted to the day before), the public implications of contriving to mislead a court made it impossible for Archer to remain a contender for public office.

The Archer case shows strong elements of that kind of publicity–scandal dynamic that is now a structural feature of populist political presentation within an intensively mediated celebrity culture. In Archer's case, 'revelations' have often been prompted by the cash rewards offered by newspapers and sometimes by political rivalry or by a claimed political conscience (in the latest incident, the former friend gave the grounds for his breach of private trust as the public good of stopping Archer being appointed to an office he was unfit to hold).

Archer's deep inter-articulation of public and personal codings are nowhere more graphically revealed than in the large photograph on the front page of the British broadsheet newspaper, The *Guardian*, on November 26, 1999, a few days after he resigned. He and his wife Mary are seen in mid-close-up having coffee at their kitchen table, with a cat on the wife's lap. Mary looks at her husband, who appears to be gazing reflectively at the cat. The caption reads "'Oh Jeffrey: I am cross with you". Mary Archer, with Stan the cat, yesterday summed up the week that wrecked her husband's career.' Thus a major political development becomes re-worked (if with more than a touch of irony) as a domestic upset, with a named cat into the bargain! In a subsequent, even more dramatic, twist of the story, Archer appeared before the courts in 2001 charged with perjury in relation to the events described above. He was found guilty and sentenced to a term in prison, where he is currently finding the time to make progress on further fictional work.

Not all questions to do with political persona connect with such a marked pursuit of celebrity but the 'celebrity frame' is now increasingly needed to make sense of political role-playing, particularly at national level. Marshall (1997) very usefully explores how politicians figure in a broader contemporary star-system that includes actors, models and successful people from the world of music, sport and business in its scope. Neither is scandal a routine accompaniment to persona strategies (see Lull and Hinerman (1997) and Thompson (2000) for useful studies into this aspect of mediated public life[1]). But these are the poles between which a great deal of political persona-work now positions itself. I think that a diagram can go some way towards bringing out more sharply the relationships involved (see Figure 4.1).

Political Persona and Spheres of Action

Politicians can be seen to work within two different spheres of political action. First, there is the sphere of political institutions and processes within which they establish their identity as politicians and enjoy career development,

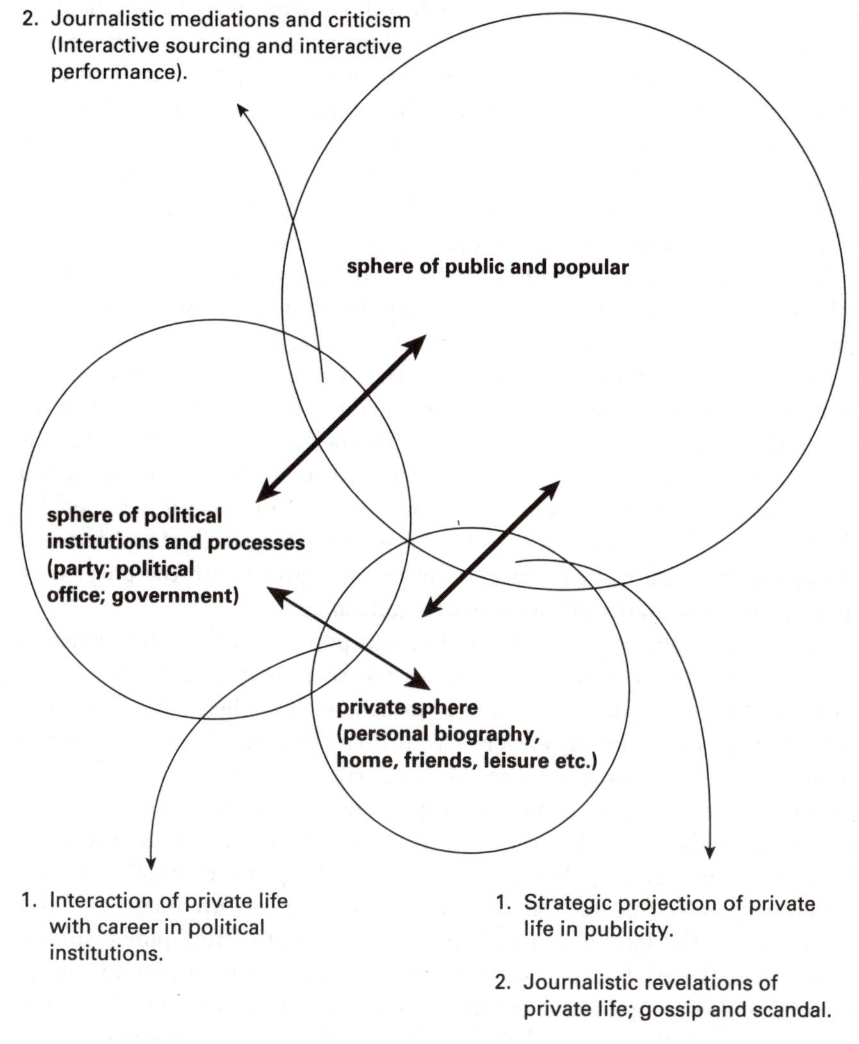

Figure 4.1 *Political Persona and Spheres of Action.*

taking on various posts and duties. These duties may relate to political party organisation and involve the development of political programmes and specific policies. In many cases, they will also involve the real duties of public office, the exercising of powers at various levels of administration, including perhaps that of national government. The extent to which politicians are now a professional grouping comparable in many ways with other public sector managers will vary nationally, but it is an interesting point in relation both to their conduct to each other and to the perceptions of them held by the public. Insofar as political practice has become an exercise in managerial competence within broadly consensual frameworks of action, the status of politicians as part of an administrative elite rather than as agents of debate about principle and value is a significant shift. It reinforces a tendency towards an internalist (specialist, self-referencing) rather than public-oriented culture, the latter relationship being seen as increasingly the realm of auxiliary specialists, public and press relations advisors.

As well as requiring different kinds of competent action in relation to substantive tasks, activity in the sphere of political institutions and processes also includes a requirement to 'perform the self' agreeably to others within the political and administrative culture. This is a performance which might well, for instance, involve ways of being ingratiating, of admitting error, of asserting superiority or of being 'tough'. Self-performance in this sphere is not usually subject to direct media projection. It tends to become mediated only indirectly, either as a supportive 'back story' to publicity designed for the sphere of the public and popular, or as a negative 'back story' fed into this sphere through party political or journalistic gossip with the purpose of undercutting the status of someone of significance.

The second sphere, that of the public and popular, is the fully mediated complex of settings in which politicians are seen as 'public figures'. I am using the two terms in combination to designate this sphere while recognising that they are often in tension. I return to the point later, but I would want to note here how politicians need to have reach into the wider parameters of the popular, simultaneously using 'public' as a term both of normative validation for this reach and also of implicit exclusion for that which falls outside of a given political project and its due sense of publicness, and which may indeed be seen as a threat. In this respect, my diagram makes connection with Habermas' much discussed concept of the 'public sphere' (Habermas, 1989) but in this chapter it is not my intention to engage directly with the arguments and assumptions about the broader changes in the character of the state and civil society entailed by his more comprehensive, critical usage. My primary reference here is to the realms of mediated political performance not to the historical conditions of democratic discourse, even though I am aware that, finally, the two are mutually implicated and that study of the one will inexorably lead to study of the other.

The sphere of the public and the popular is the realm of the visibly 'public', the space of a *demonstrable* representativeness, whatever the public values informing less accessible behaviour. It constitutes the stage where, for instance, politicians develop reputations, draw varying levels of support, are judged as good or bad, undergo meteoric or steady advancement, decline, resign or are sacked. The performance requirements here might be seen as *largely* presentational ones, with the Archer example above providing an extreme case of this. It is the substantive business achieved within the sphere of political institutions and processes which then, in this second sphere, becomes the subject of strategic publicity. One might see the first sphere as the 'political workplace' and the second as the 'political shop', although the degree to which activity in the sphere of the public and the popular also includes real deliberation and exchange as well as presentation and marketing will be a matter of dispute among both politicians and political analysts. It will also be a key focus of debate about the true participatory character of any given, nominally democratic, system and therefore, finally, about the relationship between the 'production' and 'consumption' of politics as the two terms indicate relative moments in a system that necessarily involves both reproduction *and* change, structure *and* agency. Election periods will clearly produce phases of more intensive and more openly adversarial competition between personae and between policies as the significance of the broader sphere in relation to the narrower one increases (the 'shop' temporarily becomes both primary and crucial).

The criteria of popular political appraisal that operate in this broader sphere are likely to be different from those that are active in the 'inner appraisals' of the political and administrative class itself, notwithstanding some impact of the one upon the other. It is in this sphere that the identity of the politician as a *person of qualities* is most emphatically and strategically put forward, with inflections towards what are perceived as the contours of popular sentiment or sectional value (for example, the youthful, the ordinary, the thoughtful, the cultured, the funny). These contours will frequently, of course, have strong national features as well as ones with a more international character. The projection of an optimal political self will often require careful attention to popular values in the light of the range of possible projections that any given politician has available to them. These limitations will very likely include factors of age, ethnic origin and gender and in many countries they will also include factors of wealth, social class and education. It is clear that the strength and nature of the media-performative criteria now seen to operate in this broader sphere are often such as to disqualify certain candidates either from becoming public political figures at all or at least from competing for high office, while at the same time this helps to advance the careers of others. Primary physical characteristics are implicated here – for instance, Meyrowitz (1985: 280) looks at the height and build of presidential candidates in relation to indicators of esteem, and Rees (1992) offers a useful commentary on the 'look of the leader'.

A third sphere depicted in my crude diagram is the private one. Clearly, the private realm and personal background of a political figure will feature in the formation of their identity and career in political institutions as well as in their more public projections. For instance, in Britain a high level of biographical clustering in relation to education and previous profession is easily demonstrable in the political class, with variations across parties. In the development of a successful political career, institutional assessments as to how a promising person might 'play' in a more visible role will be made. These assessments will draw on the known personal biography and be additional to (though confusable with) judgements about practical political abilities in a promoted role. Again, the Archer example shows such processes at work across diverse and conflicting data.

In relation to the realm of the public and popular, there is ample evidence that the private sphere of politicians is now more than ever being used as a resource in the manufacture of political identity and in its repair following misadventure. Such use attempts to engage 'human' more than 'political' values, or rather it frequently attempts to achieve a beneficial alignment of the latter with the former. Liesbet van Zoonen (1998a and 1998b) has drawn on examples from Dutch public life in charting some of the cultural factors in play here and the precise mode of their deployment. 'Going personal' is often considered a strong option by politicians, but there are hazards in this venture, clearly. In recognising them, we should note that the private sphere is not only connected to the public and popular as a resource for self-projection. Indeed, for many politicians the primary form of the connection is registered as *risk*. The risk of details about private life (sexual, financial etc.) producing counter-publicity is an ever-present threat to the political self, even when it is judged that there are no good grounds for scandal. Where such grounds exist, risk-management may become a continuing concern, one overtly recognised within the sphere of political institutions itself. As Thompson argues (1995), and van Zoonen illustrates (1998a), this placing of the 'private' both as political opportunity and political risk is an important aspect of modern media–political dynamics, reflecting that broader playoff between the media as agencies of disclosure and transparency and as agencies of concealment and opacity widely commented on in contemporary media analysis. The opportunity–risk couplet is clearly demonstrated in all its volatility in the Archer example.

I realise that my three-circle model might be seen to beg some questions about clarity of differentiation and firmness of borders. My view, however, is that its distortive potential in this regard is exceeded by its analytic suggestiveness at the present stage of developing a research agenda around process and transition in political culture.

I want to turn now to the specific functions of media in the interconnection of all these activities.

Media Functions

There is now a growing literature on media–political relations. See, for instance, the synoptic accounts of McNair (1995), Negrine (1996) Blumler and Kavanagh (1999) (a detailed review based on a strong sense of recent political history) and Street (2001), together with the edited collections of Bennet and Entman (2001) and Axford and Huggins (2001). Here, however, it is useful to consider these relations as they bear directly on the essentially cultural and performative dimensions of mediated persona. The mediation of the specialist sphere of political institutions and processes to the general sphere of the public and the popular is accomplished by what we can see as three broad types of mediation. First of all, there is *political publicity*, which projects politicians within the most favourable or unfavourable light depending on its party origins. Second, and shading away from this, there is the spectrum of *interactive news-making* where with differing degrees of involvement, both politicians (with their aides) cooperate in the production of news and comment, often for pre-selected outlets. This will include news about how specific politicians are performing their duties. Such cooperation has its routine procedures and conventions of story origin and development, taking on a more hectic and covert character during periods of perceived crisis or public discontent.

Third, there is what might be called *journalistic revelation*, in which in some cases without any political cooperation at all and in others with support from sectors of the political establishment at points (a classic instance being the leaked document), stories are developed that are critical of particular politicians. These stories can be exclusively to do with the execution of professional duties or exclusively a matter of private affairs. Quite often, they will be a mixture of the two, the one tending to generate the other if the news visibility of the politician passes (as it did for Archer) beyond a certain threshold across the array of press and broadcasting outlets.

Keeping these three categories cleanly apart may sometimes prove difficult, of course. A personalised political story may start as publicity but effectively re-energise itself as something else, perhaps revelation, drawing in new resources and addressing itself to new audiences. Nevertheless, I think the above classifications help analysis.

Alongside these modes of intercommunication, there are the less news-based opportunities for politicians to project themselves on the public stage. I am thinking here, for instance, of their appearance in quiz shows and within various entertainment formats as special guests (again, Marshall (1997) presents a perceptive review).

Interactive news-making is regarded by Meyrowitz (1985) as a key strand of development. It is certainly a strand that political communications researchers have frequently focused on – see particularly Blumler and Gurevitch (1995). Here, we can usefully distinguish further between *interactive sourcing* and *interactive performance*. Interactive sourcing involves the provision of information, including that by personal contact. Interactive performance, however, is a primary element of broadcast political reporting and involves the politician in direct self-presentation before the microphone and the camera, most often within the format of the interview. The interview can be regarded as a primary source of political knowledge in many modern societies, whether it is focused around a specific issue or (as at election times) a direct inquiry into an individual's political identity and qualities (for a good general account see Watts (1997)). Other contexts for political performance in which there is at least partial interaction with journalists and with media producers would include the photo opportunity and its televisual equivalents. In all these various media fora, some more choreographed than others, the political persona is performing, at times to its maximum possible audience, under what may be the most flattering or the most hostile of conditions.

What of the private realm? No established conventions of mediation govern the linkages here. Within the realm of the public and the popular, it may even be espoused as a principle that politicians' private lives are their own business. However, this is unlikely to stop the extensive use of private materials in the construction and maintenance of public, political identity. Once again, Archer offers a high-definition instance. In its *post-facto* form, such a strategy can also be seen in the established and highly successful genre of the political autobiography and diary. Conventionally published after leaving high office, among other things this typically inscribes a positive rendering of the author's private qualities and private life into a narrative of public events.

Protestations about the borders of privateness are even less likely to stop the journalistic surveillance of all politicians of standing in the quest for 'human', 'revelatory' and, best of all, 'shocking' stories about the character and conduct of their off-duty selves.

Having laid out something of the broad configuration of factors involved, I now want to look more closely at how they relate to two salient and interconnected issues in contemporary public life – the integrity of politicians and popular investment in democratic politics.

The Uses of Deceit

A level of deceit seems to be widely recognised, and to some degree accepted, as an endemic element of all political discourse. Why should this be? First of all, because there is a widespread perception of politicians as being involved in virtually continuous strategies of assertion and denial, reassurance and expressed alarm, against competing claims concerning policy and practice from within the professional political realm. Political speech is extensively a pragmatic discourse, with party interests, and perhaps the preservation of consensus across diverse sectorial groupings, often asserting primacy over the requirement of honesty or 'truth'. In a recent review of commentaries on the Clinton/Lewinsky affair, Martin Jay (1999) remarks how it may be useful to see 'political lying' as a necessary constituent of the very practice of politics rather than as some gross and fundamental deformation of its nature. In support of his claim, he cites Arendt's (1973) essay, on the subtle and close relationship between what might well be categorised in specific contexts as 'lying' (particularly, over-promising benefits and under-recognising problems) and the political imagination, as well as noting more generally the bounding pragmatic conditions of political speech acts. This is, I think, a welcome recognition, serving to place the scrutiny of political discourse within a more productively realist framework as an institutionalised cultural practice, without thereby disabling the terms of political *critique* or the advocacy of alternative, more 'honest', modes of address[2].

Although within the sphere of political institutions and processes, political discourse may show itself to be highly self-reflexive, alert to its own latent contradictions and openly self-critical, in its connection with the public and the popular its tendency, in much modern experience, is towards a distinctive language of publicity. This is shaped largely as a monologic tool rather than as the means of dialogue (see Mayhew (1997) for a recent general commentary on the resemblance between politics and advertising). For instance, it often incorporates strategic under-definition (with emphasis falling on values and goals that are not contentious in order to counteract critical focus on those that are), a systematic bad faith in assessing outcomes and a level of evasiveness and deniability that allows for subsequent upsets and/or reversals of policy. In an illuminating study, Norman Fairclough (2000) provides a detailed scrutiny of the particular discursive devices by which the project of 'New Labour' has been advanced in Britain, chiefly around the pronouncements of Tony Blair.

Broadcast interviews, especially those done 'live', frequently present the strongest test both to the promotional tactics and the persona stability of politicians, although methods for responding to this challenge are well established (see, for instance, the discussions in Jones (1993) and Watts (1997)). Here, as I noted earlier, shifts to a more personalised level of response can create problems for promotional aims, since while deceit may be tolerated as a professional political vice when a politician is fully 'in role', this will not necessarily stretch such as to legitimise deception or evasion performed in what are perceived as more 'out of role' modes. For instance, it may be allowed by both interviewer and audience that a politician is obliged to speak the party line at points in an exchange and that there is thus some permissible distance between message and messenger. Once a politician becomes more personalised and 'frank', however, appearing temporarily to step aside from their institutional obligations, such allowability may disappear.

A compounding difficulty here is the shifting and often uncertain nature of present media distinctions between 'in role' and 'out of role' performance, with the stronger element of confession and disclosure of many popular print and broadcast genres now reconfiguring the opportunity–risk calculus. Making 'out of role' indications (for instance, by grounding a political claim in recounted personal experience) may seem a good way to provide political claims-making with integrity, but it may also direct attention to matters of biographical detail and consistency (perhaps attracting counter-testimony, as my earlier example showed) which thwart the attainment of primary objectives. A distinctive feature of the Archer case is the way in which the sequence of deceit almost entirely concerns matters in the private sphere, matters that Archer did not seek to employ directly to further his political career. His specific acts of duplicity are thus not easily assessable through that combination of resigned familiarity and cynicism that routinely helps to frame responses to 'professional political lying'. By a process of inference as to his essential character they lead to an assessment of 'unfitness for office'.

The interplay between public and private deceit, and between deceit that counts as significant on substantive grounds (its specific conditions, scale and consequences) and that which is significant for what it reveals of true character, is an interesting and highly variable one within the new terms of publicity and revelation.

Persona and Democratic Sentiment

The 'personalisation' of politics is often criticised for detracting attention from questions of principle and policy and from the real complexity of political events. Such distraction is often seen to be slowly undermining political literacy and creating a (variously cynical) expectation of personalised spectacle in what then becomes a vicious circle of mediation. Yet it is clear that the *figure of the politician* has long been at the centre of political culture even if it has frequently been neglected in political theory. What might the dominant modes of mediated political persona mean for the kinds of representation and consent obtaining at present and for popular perceptions of, and investment in, politics?

Political figures serve to condense 'the political', both for the subjects of sovereign or totalitarian rule and the represented citizens of democracy. Agents of political choice and action, they are nevertheless foci for political values and ideas in a way that goes beyond the limits of their sphere of *practice*. There is a symbolic excess at work in the figure of the politician, a relationship between person and political system, and often between person and nation, which exceeds rationalistic commitments to particular programmes and even perceived levels of competence in the performance of public office (Novak (1974) explores this well in relation to the US presidency). Empathy, attraction and even an erotics of political personhood are to be found alongside the conventional spectrum of respect through to contempt.

In making sense of certain instances, as my diagram suggests, we might view the realm of the popular/symbolic as one already securely 'captured' for the extension and enhancement of political management by increasingly clever forms of media strategy. This is the view underpinning the continuing alarm in Britain about the character and consequence of 'spin'. Yet it is also possible that emerging dynamics of mediation are helping to undercut the effectiveness of personae fabricated entirely according to the relentlessly top-down recipes of modernist political marketing (a lively debate about just how different kinds of marketing relate to ideas of the democratic has developed in Britain, see the positive account in Lees-Marshment (2001) and Scammell in this volume). On this account, alongside what else is happening, space is being created for more direct terms of accountability for political action. Van Zoonen (1998a) emerges from her own case-study of political talk with this possibility in view. Mulgan (1994: 33) notes how, where there is a loosening of party affiliations, the positions taken by politicians will 'become more personal, more obviously tied to the personalities they may project' and he regards this as having ethical benefits. There are no good reasons for abandoning the critical idea that one strong tendency is for contemporary mediated politics to be *displaced* on to the terms of personality, thereby working to create a degree of opacity regarding the system as a whole. But a popular engagement with the changing conditions of personal belief and action in professional politics, an engagement still interested in seeking a representational adequacy but almost terminally cynical about current conventions for providing this, could have the reverse effect. It could contribute to a political culture that was in important ways more *transparent* about causes and consequences and about the linkage between personal and systemic factors.

In his suggestive discussion of the 'secret life of politics', the psychoanalytic scholar Andrew Samuels (2001) cites the work of Donald Winnicott on parental roles in talking of the 'good enough' leader. For Samuels, the 'good enough' leader is positioned between idealisations of leadership on the one hand and wholesale denigration of it on the other. Acceptance of 'good enough' leadership is a product of recognising the *inevitability of failure*. Samuels believes that the greater recognition, and more open handling, of failure, limitation and uncertainty by politicians could be a decisive step in moving away from the 'heroic' models of political persona towards more democratic ones. These would entail the development of images of leadership that might:

> infuse into bottom-up, networked, collaborative, organisational models the same kinds of energic charge that we can see all too clearly at work in top-down, heroically led, organisations such as the modern state. (Samuels, 2001: 82)

For my argument, it is important to note that Samuels is not talking here about any overall reduction in the cultural role of persona within politics. Nor, unlike much critical writing from within political studies, does he underplay the affective dynamics of inspiration, affiliation and investment. An 'energic charge' is still generated around leader figures, but it now has a different character and it facilitates different forms of the political imagination as well as of political practice. As I suggested in my previous section, we should expect that what we might quickly view in other contexts to be objectionable forms of insincerity will still play a role in this kind of politics. Naive projections of a direct, interpersonal honesty on to the political realm, failing to take account of the complex institutionality of the relationships involved will, as always, be beside the point. No utopian promises are implied, but the conditions both of what is expected from, and what is offered by, the professionalised political self could nevertheless change significantly.

It is likely that, in many countries, versions of the 'good enough' idea are already present at the level of popular perceptions of politics, albeit in contradiction with a continuing residual idealism about what politics and politicians can achieve and the manner in which they should *claim* to do this.

I am suggesting, then, that at least some routes to the stronger inflection of the personal in politics seem to be moving us nearer (even if this is not intended) to 'good enough' terms both of political claims-making and popular engagement. They also seem to carry the possibility of a change in the gendering of political persona. Gender discrimination in politics has a number of roots – legislative, economic and cultural – but the projection, across several variants, of a dominant model of political leadership and claims-making, and a dominant and confident form of the play-off between public and private self, have undoubtedly been instrumental in its perpetuation (see the studies in Sreberny and van Zoonen (1998)). A political culture better able to handle uncertainty and unpredictability might be a great aid to progress here.

Conclusion

It has been my aim to put forward an agenda of critical points about mediated political persona. These points are framed by the broader relations, and tensions, between the political and the popular and, as I hope to have shown, they open out on to questions about current and likely changes in the culture of democracy.

Some recent analyses of the media style of contemporary politicians, while they might not have been directly concerned with persona, have gone beyond an emphasis simply on marketing to make connection with the kind of points I have tried to raise. Such work includes studies within Norwegian (Johansen, 1999), Dutch (van Zoonen, 1998a) and Australian (Deutchman and Ellison, 1999) political systems. What the commentaries also point to is the considerable scope for future inquiry, including historical approaches.

Clearly, the President Clinton/Monica Lewinsky affair has taken the public apprehension of the private to new levels of sexual explicitness; never before has a major political figure been subject to such a forensically intensive form of personalisation (see Thompson (2000) for a brief but suggestive commentary on this case). Yet, at the same time, opinion polling has shown the significance of the gap between assessments of political direction and competence and assessment of personal value, with Clinton benefiting from consistently high ratings for the former, whatever the slump in the latter. (By contrast, Meyrowitz, (1985: 103) notes how in the early 1980s Reagan's rating as a person was much higher than his competence rating as President.) More data on the nature of popular political knowledge, in particular on perceptions of political character and on the various criteria for judging and re-judging this, would be a valuable complement to the analysis of performance itself. Hacker (1995) on US presidential campaigns provides an example, but the area could benefit from approaches of a more ethnographic and discursively-aware kind (here, the work of Gamson (1992) and Neuman, Just and Crigler (1992) remains instructive).

The resources and recipes drawn on in constructing political personae reflect in part the institutional features and the representative machinery of a given political system. Yet the terms of persona also reflect and then help shape the norms of political life and, indeed, what 'politics' popularly means. They help regulate the way in which the personal is related to the political, providing a focus for democratic engagement and investment, a resource for political imagination and implicit criteria for judging both the ends and means of political practice. By exploring these terms, we are moved further away from an easy media-centricity or a general dismissal of 'virtual politics'. Instead, we are brought closer to that increasingly volatile interplay of terms upon which national and international political culture is sustained, both as knowledge and as feelings, around the careers of elite persons.

Notes

1. Thompson's book was published after the completion of the first version of this study. Its implications for the analysis of political scandal in relation to political communications and culture as well as political theory are considerable.
2. The extent to which alternative practices can make headway here in the absence of alternative structures is clearly a recurring issue. Building the optimum conditions for greater political honesty is always going to involve a good deal more than individual moral commitment.

Acknowledgement

I would like to acknowledge the helpful comments made by Liesbet van Zoonen and anonymous readers on an earlier draft of this chapter, published in the *European Journal of Cultural Studies*. I also acknowledge the general encouragement given by the editors of that journal.

References

Ankersmit, F. (1996) *Aesthetic Politics*. Stanford: Stanford University Press.
Arendt, H. (1973) 'Lying in Politics', pp. 9–42 in *Crises of the Republic*. Harmondsworth: Penguin Books.
Axford, B. and Huggins, R. (eds) (2001) *New Media and Politics*. London: Sage.
Bennett, L. and Entman, R. (eds) (2001) *Mediated Politics*. Cambridge: Cambridge University Press.

Blumler, J. and Gurevitch, M. (1995) *The Crisis of Public Communication* (chapter 3, 'Politicians and the Press'). London: Routledge.
Blumler, J. and Kavanagh, D. (1999). 'The Third Age of Political Communication: Influences and Features', *Political Communication* 16, 209–30.
Braudy, L. (1986) *The Frenzy of Renown*. New York: Oxford University Press.
Crick, M. (1996) *Jeffrey Archer: Stranger Than Fiction* (revised edition). London: Hamish Hamilton.
Deutchman, I.E. and Ellison, A. (1999) 'A Star is Born: the Roller Coaster Ride of Pauline Hanson in the News', *Media, Culture and Society*. 21(1): 33–50.
Fairclough, N. (2000) *New Labour: New Language?* London: Routledge.
Franklin, B. (1994) *Packaging Politics*. London: Arnold.
Gamson, W. (1992) *Talking Politics*. Cambridge: Cambridge University Press.
Goffman, E. (1959) *The Presentation of Self in Everyday Life*. New York: Anchor Books.
Habermas, J. (1989) *The Structural Transformation of the Public Sphere*. Cambridge: Polity.
Hacker, K. (ed.) (1995) *Candidate Images in Presidential Elections*. New York: Praeger.
Jay, Martin (1999) 'Mendacious Flowers', *London Review of Books*. 21(15): 16–17.
Jamieson, K. (1996) *Packaging the Presidency: A History and Criticism of Presidential Campaign Advertising*. New York: Oxford University Press.
Johansen, A. (1999) 'Credibility and Media Development' in J. Gripsrud (ed.) *Television and Common Knowledge*. London: Routledge.
Jones, B. (1993) 'The Pitiless Probing Eye: Politicians and the Broadcast Political Interview', *Parliamentary Affairs* 46(1): 66–90.
Kavanagh, D. (1995) *Election Campaigning: The New Marketing of Politics*. Oxford: Blackwell.
Lees-Marshment, J. (2001). *Political Marketing and British Political Parties*. Manchester: Manchester University Press.
Lull, J. and Hinerman, S. (eds) (1997) *Media Scandals*. Cambridge: Polity.
McNair, B. (1995) *An Introduction to Political Communication*. London: Routledge.
Machiavelli, N. (1958) *The Prince*. London: Everyman's Library.
Maarek, P.J. (1995) *Communication and Political Marketing*. London: John Libbey.
Marshall, P.D. (1997) *Celebrity and Power*. Minneapolis: University of Minnesota Press.
Mayhew, L. (1997) *The New Public*. Cambridge: Cambridge University Press.
Meyrowitz, J. (1985) *No Sense of Place*. New York: Oxford University Press.
Mulgan, G. (1994) *Politics in an Anti-Political Age*. London: Polity Press.
Neuman, R., Just, M. and Crigler, A. (1992) *Common Knowledge*. Chicago: University of Chicago Press.
Negrine, R. (1996) *The Communication of Politics*. London: Sage.
Nimmo, D. and Swanson, D. (eds) (1990). *New Directions in Political Communication*. Beverly Hills CA.: Sage.
Novak, M. (1974) *Choosing Our King: Powerful Symbols in Presidential Politics*. New York: Macmillan.
Ong, W. (1982) *Orality and Literacy*. London: Methuen.
Rees, L. (1992) *The Myth of the Leader*. London: BBC Books.
Samuels, A. (2001) *Politics on the Couch*. London and New York: Profile Books.
Scammell, M. (1995) *Designer Politics*. London: Macmillan.
Sreberny, A. and Van Zoonen, L. (eds) (1998) *Women's Politics and Communication*. New York: Hampton Press.
Street, J. (2001) *Mass Media, Politics and Democracy*. London: Palgrave.
Swanson, D. and Mancini, P. (1996) *Politics, Media and Modern Democracy*. New York: Praeger.
Thompson, J. (1995) *The Media and Modernity*, Cambridge: Polity.
Thompson, J. (2000) *Political Scandal*. Cambridge: Polity.
van Zoonen, L. (1998a) '"Finally I Have My Mother Back": Politicians and their Families in Popular Culture', *Harvard Journal of Press/Politics*, 3(1): 48–64.
van Zoonen, L. (1998b) 'A Day at the Zoo: Political Communication, Pigs and Popular Culture', *Media, Culture and Society* 20(2): 183–200.
Watts, D. (1997) *Political Communication Today*. Manchester: Manchester University Press.

5

The Celebrity Politician

Political Style and Popular Culture

JOHN STREET

> Arlette Laguiller, candidate for extreme left Lutte Ouvrière (Worker's Struggle) and surprise third favourite [in the 2002 French Presidential campaign], has a team of media finesse merchants who are driving political journalists crazy. *Le Monde*'s Caroline Monnot rails against the Trotskyists: 'Lutte Ouvrière is borrowing the tactics from movie stars' agents. Accreditations have to be applied for, there are waiting lists and you only get three timed questions with the star. It's as though you were interviewing Julia Roberts or Andie MacDowell.' (Stuart Jeffries, 'How the French lost their cleavage', The *Guardian*, 14 April 2002)

This report on the 2002 French Presidential contest suggests that politicians – even those on the far left – now act like film stars. It prompts a question that this chapter tries to answer: do we gain anything in our understanding of modern politics and of modern political communications by making this comparison between politics and show-business? In a world in which pop stars increasingly are portrayed as, or behave like, politicians does it make equal sense to think of politicians as pop or film stars? When Bono, lead singer of the rock band U2 and tireless campaigner for an end to third world debt, is granted an audience with the Pope or is invited to spend time with the US President in the White House, it certainly *seems* as if the worlds of politics and popular culture are almost inseparable.

Over half a century ago, the economist Joseph Schumpeter wrote *Capitalism, Socialism and Democracy* (1976; first published 1943) in which he drew a different analogy. He focused on the similarity between the world of commerce and the world of politics. Just as the business person dealt in oil, he suggested, so the politician dealt in votes. Both were governed by the operation of the market, by the law of supply and demand. Success in business and success in politics were just a matter of producing a product that customers wanted. Competition ensured that the best won.

Were he alive to survey the modern world, Schumpeter might feel a certain pride or vindication in the way that his insight has become the norm of political practice. Parties and politicians use the language of, and experts in, market research. Policies are advertised and citizens targeted; parties are branded and politicians hone their image. As if to confirm the wisdom of Schumpeter's argument, political scientists now devote considerable time and energy to the ideas and practices of political marketing (see Scammell (1999), for an overview of the field).

But before we slip too easily into the embrace of this conventional wisdom, it is important to look carefully at both the argument that underlies it and the implications of it. The two are connected by a concern about democracy. Familiarly, the development of political marketing has been the focus of complaints about the trivialisation of politics (the substitution of the substantial by the superficial), by the spread of cynicism (politics as appearance and presentation), and by the failure of accountability (the management of news/political coverage) (for example, Franklin, 1994; Hart, 1999; Meyrowitz, 1986). Paradoxically, though, the intellectual move that Schumpeter made, and which involved the comparison between business and politics, was inspired by a desire to *rescue* democracy and to give it a firmer grounding in a world in which its rhetoric and many of its practices had been systematically abused by the great dictators of the twentieth century.

What I want to do in this chapter is, first, to look more closely at the intellectual heritage provided by Schumpeter and others who belong to the 'economic theories of democracy' school, to draw attention to the assumptions (about both politics generally and democracy in particular) that are incorporated within the analogy between politics and business and which help ground 'political marketing'. Second, I want to turn to the way in which the notion of political marketing is being used to make sense of modern political communications – and the limits to this approach. While the notion of marketing does provide an insight into the strategies and practices of political agents, it also obscures other aspects. Finally, the chapter ends by drawing out some of the neglected aspects of modern forms of political communication. Put simply, rather than seeing political communication as a branch or application of commercial marketing, we should see it as a branch of a rather different business: show-business. Here the currency is celebrity and fame, and the products are stars and performances. Politicians' concern with how they look and sound, the techniques of self-projection/promotion that they use, and the associations they exploit, might be best understood as analogous with the practices of popular culture. The thought is that understanding politicians as 'celebrities' or 'stars' calls for a different story to be told about what is going on than that which draws on the traditional marketing model. Pushed to its extreme, this argument suggests not just that politics is *like* a soap opera, but that it *is* a soap opera. If this is the case, the way politics is understood and analysed is changed too. Sting, Bono and Warren Beatty cease to be isolated cases of politically ambitious or engaged stars; instead they become political role models (and the 'art' of politics takes on a new meaning). When Schumpeter wrote *Capitalism, Socialism and Democracy*, he was doing more than introducing a simile; he was not just saying that the two realms – politics and the market – were like each other. He was offering an analogy; our understanding of how firms and markets operate could help us understand how politicians and politics operate. This chapter adopts a similar stance by asking whether politicians do, in fact, act like stars or artists.

Selling policies, buying power

The idea that politics is 'marketed', with pointers to the accompanying political marketing literature, has become a conventional wisdom of much contemporary comment. Whether as the source of complaint or innovation, it is suggested that we need to understand political communication as 'marketing'. But in the rush to embrace this idea, there has been relatively little attention paid to the assumptions and theories that animate it. These, I have noted above, can be found in a particular school of thought. Much of the thinking about what modern politicians do and how they must be understood derives, explicitly or implicitly, from what have become known as economic theories of democracy. In the 1940s and 1950s, writers like Schumpeter and Anthony Downs (1957) argued that politics could (and should) be understood through the insights generated from within economics. Their arguments added force to the ideas that Max Weber (1991; first published 1919) had voiced in his essay 'Politics as a Vocation'. In doing this, the economic theorists created the intellectual basis for viewing politics as a form of marketing.

What is a politician? Schumpeter's answer is that it is someone who seeks power, and who achieves it by 'selling' the public a product that it wants and/or that it rates above alternative products. Schumpeter's argument derives from his rejection of 'classical democracy', by which he means a system intended to realise some notion of the 'common good' (1976: 250). For Schumpeter, democracy cannot involve the imposition of something that is 'believed' to be good, but which the people 'do not actually want – even though they may be expected to like it when they experience its results' (1976: 237). Undemocratic means cannot be justified by 'democratic' ends, and democracy must be defined, insists Schumpeter (1976: 242) as a 'method'. Democracy is a system for *reaching* decisions and has nothing to say about the decisions themselves. Democracy is an instrument, not an end.

In asking what method is appropriate, he rejects the idea that it can be based on the 'will of the people'. Not only is he sceptical about whether the people do indeed possess a 'will' (i.e. not just a 'indeterminate bundle of vague impulses loosely playing about given slogans and mistaken impressions' (1976: 253)), but even if they do have independent and rational thoughts, the aggregation of these would not necessarily result in coherent policy choices (1976: 254). This scepticism has subsequently been reinforced by Arrow's Impossibility Theorem, which demonstrates that there is no logically consistent method of aggregating preferences. Schumpeter himself makes this case, not via formal logic, but by reference to human nature. He argues that there are two conflicting forces at work. First, there is the capacity for people to be manipulated. He is drawing here on Gustav Le Bon and the idea of 'crowd psychology'. When gathered together, people are easily worked into 'a state of excitement' in which 'primitive impulses', 'infantilisms and criminal propensities' replace 'moral restraints and civilised modes of thinking' (1976: 257). The agglomeration of people deprives them of their capacity to reflect rationally. They become a 'rabble', and this is the case whether or not they are 'physically gathered together'; it applies equally to 'newspaper readers' and 'radio audiences' (1976: 257).

The counter-force to which Schumpeter refers is people's capacity to develop rational expertise in relation to matters of direct relevance to them. While people may be seduced by the messages of advertisers, repeated experience of the products advertised teaches consumers about their actual worth. Direct experience of things 'which are familiar to him [the voter] independently of what his newspaper tells him' will be more likely to induce 'definiteness and rationality in thought and action' (1976: 259). As he famously remarks: 'The picture of the prettiest girl that ever lived will in the long run prove powerless to maintain the sales of a bad cigarette' (1976: 263). Applying this logic to politics, Schumpeter argues that local politicians and local politics are more likely to be judged rationally than national ones, and at the national level, it is those issues that directly affect citizens that will receive rational attention. This is not a matter of intelligence versus stupidity, but of rationality and experience (1976: 260–1). Equally, without the equivalent of the 'bad cigarette' test, political decisions lack the 'rationalising influence of personal experience' (1976: 263).

Out of these arguments emerges Schumpeter's revised form of democracy in which the decision making is allocated to others, not the 'people'. The latter are confined to the role of deciding between competing decision-makers (1976: 270–3). Leaders compete for votes in the same way that business people compete for customers.

Subsequent application of economic theory to politics reached similar, if not identical, conclusions. Downs (1957), for example, drew attention to the impact of imperfect information on political behaviour in a democracy. In a situation where the views of voters are not immediately transparent to parties, and party policy is unclear to voters, each has to incur costs in finding out such information. Such costs have to be weighed against the benefits of the vote cast. And given that no single vote is likely to be decisive, the incentives for voters to be informed are weak. In such circumstances, it pays parties to produce information in easily (i.e. in relatively costless) forms. 'Ideology', by this logic, is less an indicator of political principle, and more a 'brand', a device for identifying the general character of the party. Once again, the idea and the practice of marketing and commerce are placed at the heart of the democratic process.

What is important to note, however, is that Schumpeter and Downs are both concerned with showing how democracy develops (or needs) a form of politics that is analogous to business practice. This argument is based on two important assumptions: the first is about what is meant by democracy (the competitive struggle for power, decided by the popular vote), and the second is the motivation of agents within democracy (as actors operating with bounded-rationality). These assumptions give weight to the notion of marketing as a legitimate and appropriate form of political practice, which establishes the connection between the world of commodities and the world of politics.

Schumpeter and Downs might be seen as explaining the emergence of political marketing. They are offering reasons for rational actors to adopt a marketing approach. But my concern here is not so much with the explanatory power of their theories, but rather with the way their view of politics as a form of marketing is prevalent throughout the discussion of politics. The language of marketing shapes accounts of politics generally, and is not confined to a particular aspect of political life, namely political communications and electioneering.

What started with Schumpeter and Downs as a set of reflections on the development of modern democracy has become a political practice. Or at least, it is now interpreted as such. Political marketing is treated as a fact of life, and the point is (for politicians) to use it better and (for political scientists) to understand it better. It seems that much understanding of contemporary politics implicitly and explicitly works with the insights produced by Schumpeter and Downs, not just in the emergence and application of rational choice theory (for example, McLean, 1987), but in the political science and sociology of voting behaviour. The dealignment thesis of Ivor Crewe and Bo Sarlvik (1983) suggested that voters choose between parties on the basis of policy preferences, like consumers in a market. Just as Anthony Heath and his colleagues (1991) explained the Labour Party's electoral defeats in the 1980s in terms of their failure to offer a credible product to their natural constituency.

The way political marketing, and the assumptions it incorporates, is being integrated within political science is best illustrated by Jennifer Lees-Marshment (2001) who talks of the 'marriage' of marketing and political science (see also Scammell, 1999). She argues that political science should not just recognise that politics is marketed, but that it should draw on the approaches and literature generated within the study and practice of marketing.

She notes the ways in which political science already thinks in terms of marketing in accounting for the behaviour of parties, but she goes on to argue that 'marketing' is not one thing. She distinguishes, for instance, between different marketing orientations: product-oriented, sales-oriented, and market-oriented (2001: 695). She also draws attention to the different dimensions of marketing – product, pricing, promotion and place (the 4Ps) (2001: 695). The particular orientations of a party affect its behaviour. A product-oriented party is to be seen as one in which its ideas (its 'product') take precedence over all else, and will not be sacrificed or modified, whatever their electoral consequences. Whereas a sales-oriented party aims to persuade. It uses 'the latest advertising and communication techniques to persuade voters that it is right.' (2001: 696) With each orientation a different marketing mix – a different balance of the 4Ps – is adopted. Lees-Marshment contends that her differentiated approach better explains the behaviour of parties (2001: 709). In other words, in understanding the kind of business parties are in, and the marketing strategy they adopt, we can explain their behaviour. Political marketing does not just *describe* an aspect of party practice; it *explains* how parties operate.

But while the marketing analogy, and Lees-Marshment's refinement of it, may help us to understand a key dimension to the character of modern political communications, there is a danger that it may obscure other, equally important dimensions. Marketing – or the way marketing is discussed in the political science literature – tends to think in terms of products and brands. The point is that this understanding is not simply the product of objective, innocent observation. Rather, it is a consequence of an economic approach to politics (incorporating a particular account of economics) that necessarily casts politics in terms in terms of goods and markets. But what if the business of politics is not commercial business (i.e. selling oil) so much as show-business (selling people and performances)? What if politics is not understood as purely instrumental, but expressive, as a cultural relationship rather than a market one? It is this thought that I want to pursue in the next part of this chapter.

Selling performances, buying reputations

The idea of politics as a particular form of marketing belongs to a distinct tradition, one, as I have suggested, that can take sustenance from Schumpeter's claims about modern democracy. But there is another element to Schumpeter's argument, one that is implicated in his argument for democratic elitism, but which gets lost in the discussion of marketing. This is the capacity for the people to act 'irrationally', to become a 'rabble', to be manipulated. These are the responses that Schumpeter wants to guard against and that cause him to be critical of 'classical' notions of democracy. But such responses cannot be eliminated, merely curbed. Indeed, we might argue that they are still present in the ways in which people are invited to judge between competing politicians or party brands. We are responding to the images, rather than to actions or experiences. This suggests that politics is about more than the instrumental means for achieving prior ends. Politics, in F.R. Ankersmit's (1996) distinction, is about aesthetics, rather than ethics; it celebrates and depends on the gap between representative and represented, and it is about the imagined bridging of this gap.

Although there are important insights to be garnered from the study of political marketing and the approach to political communications derived from it, it does not provide a complete or adequate picture. There are two (related) criticisms to be made. First, economic theories of democracy, and the logic with which they invest political marketing, derive from a particular account of political rationality. Politics is driven by instrumentality, with rational action being viewed as the mechanistic matching of means and ends. This is to privilege, though, one version of rationality and politics, one which is committed to what Habermas (1971) once described as the scientisation of politics. The application of marketing to politics follows the same logic as did the application of 'science' to management (Braverman, 1974). What critics of this process have argued is that there is another rationality available that is premised, not on instrumentality, but on expressivity based around the recognition and realisation of some concept of the 'good life' (Fay, 1975; Hargeaves-Heap, 1989; Sandel, 1996).

The second criticism of the emphasis on political communication as marketing and politics as consumption is that this entails an ideological perspective, rather than hard-headed realism. Political marketing does not emerge simply from the 'realities' of modern politics, but rather it is a discourse that shapes or constitutes those realities. Schumpeter's 'irrational' citizen is not an insurmountable fact of life but the product of a political order that makes rational engagement (as defined by Schumpeter) impossible. If these criticisms are valid, then the question arises as to how political communication should better be understood?

One answer is to adopt a better analogy. This is the strategy suggested by David Marshall (1997) who argues that we need to incorporate into our account of politics the 'irrationality' of the emotions that inspire political life. We find this 'irrationality', suggests Marshall, in the world of entertainment, and the relationship established between celebrities and their audience. Political parties and politicians are not mere instruments. They *represent*, and this means more than offering a conduit for prior preferences. They have instead to give expression to inchoate thoughts and feelings. As Marshall writes (1997: 203): 'In politics, a leader must somehow embody the sentiments of the party, the people, and the state. In the realm of entertainment, a celebrity must somehow embody the sentiments of an audience.' These two imperatives draw, suggests Marshall, from similar sources. The linkage is provided by the fact that both sets of relationships (politician–people, celebrity–audience) are built around the 'affective function' (1997: 204). This refers to the emotive response that is generated by these relationships – the feelings and meanings that constitute them and motivate the actions that follow from them. The rational calculations of Downsian or Schumpeterian citizens would not generate the required response, any more than 'need' explains why people buy particular cars, records or clothes.

Marshall argues that the construction of politicians *as celebrities* has to be understood as part of this process of filling out political rationality. The business of political communication is about turning politicians into celebrities in order to organise the sentiments they want to represent. Spin doctors are the equivalent of PR people in film and record companies, managing the image of, and access to, their stars. Celebrity status is a matter of managing access and output. It is about deciding on what interviews, with whom, when and managing the supply to coincide with the release of the latest record/policy initiative. Managing access is also about insuring that it reaches its target audience – *Smash Hits* or *NME* or *The Face*; *Today* or David Frost or Des O'Connor. And just like pop stars and football clubs, parties have their own merchandising. The Labour Party sells merchandise coffee mugs, T-shirts and cuff-links branded with its logo. Sometimes they even use the same support personnel. It was reported, for instance, that Ann Widdecombe, the prominent Conservative politician, hired a former manager of Shaun Ryder's group Black Grape as her House of Commons' secretary (*The Independent*, 17.11.2000). Politicians may be commodities, just like pop and film stars are commodities, but the way they are sold does not fit into the pattern set by consumer goods. Instead, they belong to the field of cultural goods, which are significantly different in kind and character from other consumer products. Their value lies in their meaning as texts, rather than their use as commodities. Marshall writes (1997: 214): 'The political leader, in terms of function and as a form of political legitimation, is constructed in a manner that resembles other public personalities that have emerged from a variety of cultural activities ... Entertainment celebrities, like political leaders, work to establish a form of cultural hegemony.'

By focusing on politicians as celebrities, rather than as traditional commodities, our account of political communication can be enriched in a way that enables us to make sense of, and accord prominence to, what might otherwise appear trivial and irrelevant (from a traditional political perspective). A politician's dress sense, for instance, may be read politically. Maria Pia Pozzato (2001: 292) describes how a previously anonymous Italian politician 'repositioned' himself in the political realm through his choice of dress and venue. He was, Pozzato reports, 'increasingly seen at social events in smart evening dress – or, at the opposite extreme, in shorts, a fishing hat and gumboots while pottering about the olive trees at his country home.'

In the UK, *The Mirror* revealed (6.6.2001) that Tony Blair wears Calvin Klein underpants. On the front page, it reported: 'Tony Blair has let his guard slip – and revealed that he wears the world's trendiest underpants.' Chancellor Gerhard Schröder, it was announced (*The Observer*, 7.4.2002) was taking action to prevent the German media from discussing whether or not he dyes his hair. The point here is not whether indeed the Chancellor is going grey, but that it matters what people think about his hair.

Marshall's analogy between the world of politics and celebrities, just as Schumpeter's between dealing in oil and votes, is revealing of the processes at work. But although Marshall supplements and extends Schumpeter's insight, he still leaves some questions unanswered. Marshall says, for instance, relatively little about the politicians themselves, about how they differ in the way they play out their 'celebrity' status. Marshall's focus, like Schumpeter's, is on the structural dimensions of the process, and so says little about the individuals who occupy their roles as celebrities. For this, I want to suggest, we need a new analogy, one that takes yet more seriously the link between politics and culture. This means seeing politicians as 'artists' or 'performers', or in David Hesmondhalgh's (2002: 5) more neutral language 'symbol creators'. We cannot hope to understand the ways in which political communication works (or fails to work) without acknowledging the activities of a key intermediary. Just as cultural life cannot be understood simply in terms of the industry and the audience, so political life cannot be understood in terms of system and citizens. In focusing on politicians, and in thinking of them as 'symbol creators', the focus is shifted from commodities and marketing to art and style.

By way of illustration, consider how Simonetta Falasca-Zamponi (1997) analyses and accounts for the rise of Mussolini in Italy in the 1920s. Where Schumpeter's answer to the question 'what is a politician?' is someone who trades in votes the same way that business people deal in oil, Falasca-Zamponi's answer is that a politician is an 'artist' (1997: 7) and that the people are their 'work of art'.

This argument derives from a general assumption about the way political reality is produced through narrative: 'we make sense of our experience by telling stories that draw upon a common stock of knowledge, a cultural tradition that is inter-subjectively shared.' (1997: 3) These narratives are not simply expressions of a pre-existing social world; they constitute that world: they 'produce power while representing it' (1997: 3). One way in which narratives come to constitute political reality is by giving an identity to the 'people'. The suggestion is that who 'we' are is created via, among other things, the rhetoric of those who seek political power. This is not marketing as selling to an established market or 'demographic'; this is about *creating* an identity (that may subsequently be exploited by marketing strategies). Creating an identity depends on the use of the symbols and devices of poetry, song, processions and the like. This is exactly what the early Fascists did to create an emotional response and identity in the people that served the Fascist cause. Hence, Falasca-Zamponi's discussion of how Mussolini worked with the 'conception of the "masses" as a passive material for the leader-artist to carve', but that this 'was counterpoised by his belief in people's active, symbolic participation in politics.' (1997: 7–8). Mussolini himself is quoted as saying: 'That politics is an art there is no doubt.... In order to give wise laws to a people it is also necessary to be something of an artist' (quoted in Falasca-Zamponi, 1997: 15). As Falasca-Zamponi explains:

'Guided by an aesthetic, desensitized approach to politics, Mussolini conceived the world as a canvas upon which to create a work of art' (1997: 13) Falasca-Zamponi not only argues that Fascism has to be understood as an artistic project by which the people are fashioned, but also that this fashioning has a particular character because of who is doing it.

Central to this process of fashioning the people is giving them 'style'. Again Falasca-Zamponi quotes Mussolini himself: 'Democracy has deprived people's lives of "style". Fascism brings back "style" in people's lives...' (1997: 26). The point was to create a sense of what it was to be an 'Italian', but this was not simply encoded in the language of political ideology, but rather within a way of being, a 'structure of feelings' (in Raymond Williams' formulation).

This argument is not exclusive to the peculiarities of Fascism. Pozzato, writing of contemporary European politics, claims that style is fundamental to what is being communicated. The person responsible for 'branding' François Mitterrand in the 1980s admitted that 'However brilliant a candidate, he cannot allow himself to neglect his image' (Pozzato, 2001: 288). Pozzato (2001: 295) goes onto to observe that 'The political star is liked, much in the way that singers or actors are liked.' They both deal in 'authenticity'.

The cultural approach to politics generates ideas that are similar to those generated by the economic approach in that they are about image and emotional responses, but there are also important differences too. The economic approach talks of *products*, while the cultural approach offers *performances*. And in doing so it invites a different literature and approach. While Lees-Marshment's attempt to marry marketing and politics is entirely appropriate to the former, it has little to say about the latter. The question becomes, then, how we might make sense of, and assess, political performance.

Performing Politics

If political communication is to be understood as a work of art or a performance, the issue is: what kind of art, what kind of performance? Who or what are politicians trying to be and say? There is clearly not one answer to these questions. First, there is a general distinction to be made between the kind of performance, and associated aesthetics, required by different political ideologies. The populism of Fascism, and its particular evocation of the 'people', is different from the democratic elitism of representative politics. And within democratic politics, political communication is performed through different dress codes and lifestyle choices as much as by political ideology or policy decisions. Second, it will also matter what the context is and who is being addressed. Performing grief at the death of a member of the Royal Family involves a different set of criteria to performing to a party conference, which is, in turn, different to the performance given in an interview (which will vary depending on whether it is for a chat show or a current affairs programme). These aspects have a strongly political character: they represent competing notions of the people and establish a variety of relations to them. They also have a cultural dimension. The way they are performed is dependent upon generic conventions deriving from the cultural resources upon which they draw. When political leaders appear on chat shows, they have a clear political agenda (they may want to be seen as 'human', as 'like us'), but the way they convey their 'human-ness' and the 'us' they address are defined through the generic conventions of the chat show – the anecdotes, the jokes, the banter with the host, etc. Cristina Giorgetti (2001: 279) makes this point in relation to styles of dress: 'Clothing has always been a vehicle of political communication in societies where conflicting ideologies exist. Having to live with, and be compared with, political opponents generates the need to diversify one's language and proclaim – through posture, gesture, rhetorical style and clothing – the validity of one's own proposals.' What is being created in these performances is political capital, the resources by which politicians are enabled to act. As with any profession, politicians have to acquire appropriate skills. Traditionally, these have been learnt via activisim within political parties or other cognate careers. Whatever their apprenticeship, skills of political performance are essential to their armoury. It was, therefore, to be expected perhaps that, in Britain, the Royal Academy of Dramatic Art, the country's leading drama school, was reported (*Today*, BBC Radio 4, 5.3.2002) to be training local councillors in performance skills ('If you don't breathe', one tutor advised, 'neither can your audience'). Skills of performance are skills in self-presentation, in style. Style matters to politics, just as it does to other cultural forms. But if style is an important component of political performance, how should it be understood and analysed?

Within cultural studies, it is widely assumed that style is significant. The very idea of cultural studies is premised on claims about the centrality of style. But what cultural studies has represented, at least when it first emerged in the 1960s and 1970s, was that style was 'political'. For Dick Hebdige, Paul Willis and other members of the Birmingham Centre for Contemporary Cultural Studies, style was political, even when it appeared to have no direct connection to the conventional political realm (see Gelder and Thornton (1997), for a good overview). Dress codes and musical tastes, among other things, gave form to political attitudes and ideas. These claims were focused on the subcultures of punk, skinheads, bikers and their ilk, who, it was suggested, challenged the hegemonic conventions of the dominant order. While cultural studies was subject to criticism, its critics, for the most part, did not attack the underlying assumption that style was politically significant. If anything, they tended to confirm this assumption. Their criticism focused as much on the Birmingham CCCS's tendency to privilege the radical politics of subcultures, ignoring the politics of other cultures, and even to overlook the conventional politics of the subcultures (i.e. their attitude to, and treatment of, women, for example). Despite the prominence of the style-as-political approach within cultural studies, it remained confined to that discipline (and to sociology). Political studies have, for the most part, ignored it. The exception to this general rule is to be found in work on new social movements (NSM), where cultural forms and practices have been incorporated into accounts of NSM politics (see Eyerman and Jamison, 1998; Martin, 2002). But if traditional politics are to be understood as a form of popular culture in their dependence on style and performance, then the methods and concerns of cultural studies need also to be applied to traditional politics.

Cool Politics

By way of illustration, let us consider one particular stylistic convention that is deployed by representative politicians. One, but by no means the only, way in which politicians try to present themselves is as 'cool'. This is not just a matter of being popular, but of being popular in a particular way. They want to be stylish in the way that stars of popular culture are stylishly cool. We need only to think of Tony Blair with Bono or Noel Gallagher or with a Fender Stratocaster.

The reasons politicians want these associations derives from the general cultural value placed on cool, and the notion of 'authenticity' associated with it. 'Cool' represents being in charge *and* in touch. Dick Pountain and David Robins (2000: 9) quote Norman Mailer's definition of cool: 'to be cool, to be in control of a situation because you have swung where the Square has not ...'. This sense of being in charge and in touch chimes with criteria that define someone as authentically representative.

But while the notion of 'cool' links to the discourses of representation, the idea itself derives from popular culture, and is dependent on the meanings that it acquires from this field. As a result, political aspirations to coolness cannot be guaranteed to succeed. First, as Dick Pountain and David Robins (2000) illustrate, the historical roots of 'cool' can be found in opposition to the very authority that politicians seek. 'Cool' has entailed challenging authority (think of James Dean or Marlon Brando). Second, contemporary notions of 'cool' have typically been associated with indifference to, or transcendence of, politics (think of John Travolta in *Pulp Fiction*). Pountain and Robins (2000: 26) locate 'cool' in persons, not things, and define it as displaying 'three core personality traits, namely narcissism, ironic detachment and hedonism.' Each would seem to capture exactly what politicians are not, indeed what they cannot afford to be. 'Cool is never directly political, and politics, almost by definition, can never be Cool,' write Pountain and Robins (2000: 171): 'To get anywhere in politics you need to care passionately about something, whether it is a cause or merely the achievement of personal power, and you need to sacrifice present pleasures to the long and tedious process of campaigning and party organisation.' And while it may be that some politicians can be deemed 'cool' (for example, J.F. Kennedy), most are not, and all – including Kennedy – inevitably enact policies that are deemed 'uncool'. Despite New Labour's associations with 'cool' (as in the use of the slogan 'Cool Britannia'), their attitudes belie the adjective (Pountain and Robins, 2000: 174–5). This tension between the 'cool' and the 'political' works in reverse. It represents one of the obstacles faced by stars of popular culture when they try to engage with conventional politics.

'Coolness' is just one of the possible aspects of contemporary political style. It has been used here to illustrate a facet of political communication that might otherwise be missed if the focus were exclusively on marketing and economistic accounts of political relations. Many other forms of self-representation – as caring and compassionate, as tough and decisive – could be treated in the same way. The point is to analyse them through the repertoire and conventions of the popular culture upon which they draw and through which they are articulated.

Conclusion

In discussing the way certain styles translate into politics, it does not follow that style is all that matters. Rather, it draws attention to one important dimension of political communication. Nor should it be concluded that, by focusing on style, we are dealing with the product of individual 'genius' or 'inadequacy'. The style is part of a process, just as is marketing and branding. Styles are manufactured too, but in analysing this process we need to appreciate the appropriate analogy – not commerce but celebrity, not business but show-business. Too much attention on the marketing model will cause us to lose sight of the aesthetics of politics. In focusing on the style in which politics is represented, we need to go beyond mere description of the gestures and images. We need to assess them, to think about them as *performances* and to apply a critical language appropriate to this. In what and how successfully do Bono or Blair evoke feelings and passions that are acted upon? These are questions about the politics of popular culture itself.

What I have been trying to do is to reveal another analogy to political communication, one not drawn from commerce but from entertainment. This analogy, like Schumpeter's, is intended to reveal the actual nature of a relationship, not just to find a metaphor. To see politics as coterminus with popular culture is not to assume automatically that it is diminished, any more than associations with marketing necessarily diminish it. The point is to use this approach to discover the appropriate critical language with which to analyse it. Just as there are good and bad performances in popular culture, so there are good or bad political performances. Just as cultural critics assess cultural performance in terms of its fidelity to democratic ideals, so political performances may be assessed on similar lines. Disillusionment with politics has, by this account, less to do with some inevitable social trend or structural change, and instead has more to do with the performances given by politicians. Just as Schumpeter's competing parties may lose elections because they fail to win customers in the (political) market place, so competing politicians may also lose because they fail to evoke symbols and styles that their audience responds to.

References

Ankersmit, F.R. (1996) *Aesthetic Politics*, Stanford, Cal: Stanford University Press.

Braverman, H. (1974) *Labor and Monopoly Capital*, New York: Monthly Review Press.

Crewe, I. and Sarlvik, B. (1983) *The Decade of Dealignment*, Cambridge: Cambridge University Press.

Downs, A. (1957) *An Economic Theory of Democracy*, New York: Harper and Row.

Eyerman, R. and Jamison, A. (1998) *Music and Social Movements: Mobilizing Traditions in the Twentieth Century*, Cambridge: Cambridge University Press.

Falasca-Zamponi, S. (1997) *Fascist Spectacle: The Aesthetics of Power in Mussolini's Italy*, Berkeley, University of California Press.

Fay, B. (1975) *Social Theory and Political Practice*, London: Allen and Unwin.

Franklin, B. (1994) *Packaging Politics: Political Communications in Britain's Media Democracy*, London: Edward Arnold.

Gelder, K. and Thornton, S. (1997) *The Subcultures Reader*, London: Routledge.

Giorgetti, C. (2001) 'Dress, Politics and Fashion, 1960–80', pp. 278–85 in L. Cheles and L. Sponza (eds) *The Art of Persuasion: Political Communication in Italy from 1945 to the 1990s*, Manchester: Manchester University Press.

Habermas, J. (1971) *Towards a Rational Society*, London: Heinemann.

Hargreaves-Heap, S. (1989) *Rationality in Economics*, Oxford: Basil Blackwell.

Hart, R. (1999) *Seducing America: How Television Charms the Modern Voter*, Oxford: Oxford Univerity Press.

Heath, A., Curtice, J., Jowell, R., Evans, G., Field, J. and Witherspoon, S. (1991) *Understanding Political Change*, Oxford: Pergamon.

Hesmondhalgh, D. (2002) *The Culture Industries*, London: Sage.

Lees-Marshment, J. (2001) 'The Marriage of Politics and Marketing', *Political Studies*, 49(4), pp. 692–713.

McLean, I. (1987) *Public Choice*, Oxford: Basil Blackwell.

Marshall, P.D. (1997) *Celebrity and Power: Fame in Contemporary Culture*, Minneapolis and London: University of Minnesota Press.

Martin, G. (2002) 'Conceptualizing Cultural Politics in Subcultural and Social Movement Studies', *Social Movement Studies*, 1(1), pp. 73–88.

Meyrowitz, J. (1986) *No Sense of Place: The Effect of Electronic Media on Social Behaviour*, Oxford: Oxford University Press.

Pountain, D. and Robins, D. (2000) *Cool Rules: Anatomy of an Attitude*, London: Reaktion.

Pozzato, M.P. (2001) 'Fashion and Political Communication in the 1980s and 1990s', pp. 286–98 in L. Cheles and L. Sponza (eds) *The Art of Persuasion: Political Communication in Italy from 1945 to the 1990s*, Manchester: Manchester University Press.

Sandel, M. (1996) *Democracy's Discontent*, Cambridge, Mass: Harvard University Press.

Scammell, M. (1999) 'Political Marketing: Lessons for Political Science', *Political Studies*, 47(4), pp. 718–39.

Schumpeter, J. (1976) *Capitalism, Socialism and Democracy*, London: George Allen & Unwin.

Weber, M. (1991) 'Politics as a Vocation', pp. 77–128 in H.H. Gerth and C. Wright Mills (eds) *From Max Weber: Essays in Sociology*, London: Routledge.

6

'After *Dallas* and *Dynasty* we have ... Democracy'

Articulating Soap, Politics and Gender

LIESBET VAN ZOONEN

In January 1999, the Labour government in Britain issued a statement denouncing the obsession of national newspapers with 'trivia, travel expenses, comment and soap opera', and condemned their reluctance to report on matters of political substance (Wintour, 1999). The government announced that it would therefore seek other media outlets for its messages, such as the women's and ethnic press, regional media and foreign news agencies. Tony Blair's official spokesman, Alastair Campbell, a former tabloid journalist himself, warned that 'the papers' agenda of gossip, Concorde flights, soap opera and instant judgement', would inevitably produce 'delusion [which] leads to disappointment which leads to cynicism about politics which finally results in the pessimistic sense that change is not possible' (White, 1999). Labour leader Tony Blair himself had already likewise scorned the national press for its alleged shallow political reporting (White, 1999).

Only some months later, in a perfect mirror of Labour's complaints, the leader of the Conservative opposition William Hague took on the Blair regime when he told *The Independent*: 'I think the Government is actually in the business of promoting indifference to politics. It is systematically trying to diminish the substance of debate and conduct politics as soap opera and photo-calls' (Grice and Macintyre, 1999). He repeated his accusation at his address to the Conservative Party conference of 2000, saying that the Labour government had only been an act, with Tony Blair 'the biggest actor in town' (Smith, J. 2000). He added: 'We saw them last week, divided, arrogant and out of touch. What a bunch they are – this soap opera of a government. No ministers in recent times have lost touch so rapidly with the people who elected them' (Hague, 2000).

The media keep their end up in these quarrels and regularly charge both the government and its opposition with 'soaping' politics: 'Stop acting like a soap star, Mr. Blair and start acting like a prime minister again', *The Independent* commented on the occasion of a leaked government memo about ways to sell the government's achievements to the public (*The Independent*, 18.7.2000). The Conservative Shadow Chancellor of the Exchequer, Michael Portillo, was warned by the press not to turn his own future into a soap opera, when publicly hesitating about his possible succession to the leadership after the expected defeat of the Tories at the coming elections (Macintyre, 2000b).

Simultaneous to all these disparaging comments on the soaping of politics, Labour, the Conservatives and the media alike, have eagerly incorporated the soap format and its actors into their political campaigns and coverage. The Conservative party produced soap opera style election broadcasts featuring an ordinary couple discussing 'issues' at their kitchen table (Ward, 1999a). The Labour government has turned its attention to existing soaps, trying to convince their producers to insert story lines about government policies in the scripts (Smith, A. 2000). The Labour campaign was backed by a whole range of celebrities, among them soap actors from *EastEnders*, *Crossroads*, *Hollyoaks* and *Emmerdale* (Dillon, 2001; Landale, 2001). The online edition of The *Guardian* made up 'a new election soap running non-stop on all terrestrial and satellite channels until June 7.' Tongue in cheek – admittedly – the newspaper revealed a storyline in which main actor Tony B. worries about the body of Old Labour: 'Tony and pals know it's securely buried under the patio at Number 10. But their enemies, headed by bungling Wee Willy Hague, are intent on rooting out the evidence' (Brooks, 2001).

What we see in these examples is the ubiquitous presence of the soap opera as a frame of reference both for presenting and understanding politics. This is by no means an exclusively British phenomenon. The story of Bill Clinton's escapades with Monica Lewinsky and his other alleged affairs have repeatedly been told in terms of a soap opera, with the President appearing as the 'entertainer in chief' – as one of his former aides said (Stephanopoulos, 2000). More generally, the use of film and television celebrities to endorse candidates and parties has always been part and parcel of American politics, with occasional actors becoming politicians, and politicians becoming actors or talk show hosts (Brownstein, 1992). Likewise politicians and parliamentary journalists from such diverse countries as Canada, Germany, The Netherlands or Indonesia – and likely a whole range of other countries as well – have applied the soap frame (respectively: Troost, 2001; Zippert, 2001; Hoedeman and Nicolasen, 2000; Soetjipto, 2000).

Such use of the soap opera in constructing politics testifies to the fact that television culture has become a dominant if not *the* dominant means for interpreting social and political life. Whereas in previous times the theatre may have provided a more common figure of speech to mould political life, with, for instance, regular evocations of Shakespearian tragedy, nowadays, politics is more easily described in terms of television genres, *Big Brother* providing the latest variety: 'I do at least know why *Big Brother* is so popular this summer. It's because the Labour Cabinet is on holiday and *Big Brother* is its natural replacement' (Kington, 2000). This, in fact, goes much further than simply saying that television has become the primary and unavoidable means of political communication and information. Television is indeed our prime source for learning about politics and it provides the instruments for understanding, evaluating and appreciating it. This generally shared acknowledgment – whether appreciated or criticised – is usually built on analyses of news, current affairs and some infotainment programmes (Iyengar and Kinder, 1987). The popularity of soap metaphors and symbols shows, however, that television culture has another, as yet unexplored relevance: through its entertainment genres in particular, possibly much more than through its informative programming, it provides narratives and perspectives that express and make sense of politics, which may replace or transform the existing ones evoked through more traditional channels of political communication.

At present, as the examples given earlier show, the outlook of politicians and journalists on this prospect is rather schizophrenic: the soap simultaneously provides the metaphor with which to criticise the political behaviour of opponents – be it politicians, parties or media – and the symbols with which to create affirmative ties between candidates, constituencies and possible voters. As I have argued elsewhere (van Zoonen, 1998a), this tension is typical for contemporary politics and has its roots in the contradictory social roots of politics on the one hand, and popular culture on the other. 'The folkloric world of popular culture ruled by coincidence and marked by suspicion and sensation seems to be thoroughly at odds with the modern tradition of contemporary political institutions and culture, which is distinguished by a belief in rationality, progress and the capacity of people to take control over their own destinies' (van Zoonen, 1998a: 187). This contradiction in itself does not explain why politicians or journalists who evoke the soap metaphor to frame political conflicts, usually do so to express criticism and derision, neither does it account for the simultaneous, decided incorporation of soap narratives and soap actors in the political campaign. That paradox can only be understood by reading the gendered subtexts in the articulation of soap and politics.

Gender, Soap and Politics

As several authors have shown, the most common metaphors and symbols in politics are those associated with masculinity. Karen Wahl-Jorgensen (2000) uses the 1992 US presidential campaign to show how metaphors and symbols perpetuate masculine hegemony in American politics. Candidates drew images and language from the domains of sports, the military and the family to represent themselves and their issues and these were readily taken over by journalists. In addition to the central terminology of 'the running mate', a discursive forum is produced, according to Wahl-Jorgensen (p. 63), 'in which male intimacy and power are closely linked. Engaging in publicly glorified male bonding, these men make decisions about the future of the country, and their decisions are guided by the very exclusivity and intimacy of their man–man relationships.' On the subject of the 1993 elections in Canada, Gidengill and Everett (1998) contend that such 'macho metaphors' conjure up an atmosphere of aggression, especially when it comes to the 'struggle' between candidates for political leadership. Both candidates and journalists frequently used metaphors of warfare, sports, games and general violence, whereas metaphors to do with the theatre and show business, nature, occupations and movements were marginal. Only one metaphor linked a traditional female domain – cooking – to politics.

In the context of the dominance of masculine metaphors and symbols, the emerging symbolic and metaphoric articulation of soap with politics becomes all the more interesting. The soap is a genre usually considered to appeal to women. In van Zoonen (1994:121) the different factors that explain the popularity of soaps among women are summed up: the particular gendered pleasures of soaps are seen to originate from the centrality of themes and values associated with the private sphere. These themes are experienced and processed by the protagonists through extensive and never-ending conversations, showing different emotions and involvements at length; physical or immediate action is rare in soaps. The focus on women as protagonists, on their rational and calculated behaviour and the mischievous attitude towards male power form some of the sources of pleasure for the female audience. Further pleasures stem from the ability of soaps to evoke a mode of reception that is simultaneously critical and involved. The particular scheduling of daytime soaps ensures that the audience tends to consist of housewives and others working outside the nine-to-five labour market. In addition, there is the cyclical narrative of soap: story lines never have a definitive ending, resolution of conflict is always only temporary; even death is not always the final word in soaps, for deceased characters can return from the grave. Some authors have made much-contested claims that these cyclical narratives accord particularly well with women. Modleski (1984), for instance, argues that they are in line with the 'rhythms of women's work in the home' whereas Mattelart (1986:15) contends that the repetitions and eternity in soap narratives are linked to women's experience of time. This brief listing shows that the generic features of soaps seem fundamentally at odds with the generic features of politics: soaps are about the private sphere, whereas politics is about the public sphere; soaps are about emotional involvement while politics is about rational debate; the soap narrative centres around conversation, politics contrarily is focused on planned action; soap solutions are always temporary whereas political solutions are supposed to last. These oppositions are gender specific and within the confines of dominant gender codes, the soap cannot take centre stage in the masculine encoded domain of politics. When political problems, debate and conflicts are framed as resembling a soap opera, politics implicitly receives an accusation of feminisation, of being effeminate and unmanly. As feminist political philosophers have repeatedly shown, the incorporation of 'the feminine' into the political domain has been seen by otherwise clearly opposed authors as undermining its rational and universal basis (for example, Elshtain, 1981; Kennedy and Mendus, 1987). In the form of an explicit treatment of the nature of politics, such views have disappeared from the public arena. However, when reviewing the experience of women in politics, their struggle with the dominant codes of conduct (Norris, 1996) and their representation in various media (Sreberny and van Zoonen, 2000), it is clear that as a practice, politics is still very much constructed as male territory. The only self-evident, unproblematic position that territory allows for women is one of support; support of the female colleague for the male leader or support of the wife for the husband in politics (van Zoonen, 1998b). Those are the gender arrangements that make it possible for the soap to be simultaneously mobilised as an inspiration to political campaigns and exploited as an instrument with which to condemn political acts and behaviour. The position of the soap in politics is thus very much like the one of the First Lady: accepted when being supportive to her husband, expelled when entering the field herself (Brown and Gardetto, 2000).

The naturalness of the discourse in which soap and politics are articulated is rooted in the modernist conception of politics as ideologically informed conflicts and negotiations between rational actors who have no personal stakes in political issues, about the best organisation of society. An informed citizenry, which relies on information, facts and rational argumentation for its political sense-making, is considered a prerequisite for modern politics and society (Habermas, 1989). In the modernist discourse of politics, the only legitimate place for popular culture, and for qualities traditionally associated with women (private life, emotional commitment, intuition or care) is located outside the political domain, as sources of support rather than as part of the process itself. Whereas the soap metaphor is obviously one means of accomplishing that exclusion, its sheer existence and regularity is simultaneously a sign of the perceived crisis in modernist politics. As the usual critical comment claims: information has been replaced by entertainment, political stature by personal appeal, ideology by technicalities, political constituencies by taste communities, substantial campaigning by elegant marketing, political preference by consumer choice and reproducible political deliberations by melodramatic personal combat (for example, Hart, 1994; Postman, 1985). Such criticism testifies more to a nostalgia for an ideal form of politics and citizenship that has never existed (for example, Calhoun, 1992; Schudson, 1998) than to providing a means of understanding and improving contemporary politics and of reconciling the antagonistic requirements of popular culture and representative democracy (van Zoonen, 1998a). The soap metaphor, apart from reconstructing modernist political discourse and ringing its predicaments, may also provide a way of exploring such a reconciliation. I have looked therefore in more detail at how soap metaphors have been applied to politics in a variety of newspapers from the UK, US, Germany and The Netherlands.[1]

A consistent result of research on soap texts and audiences is that the genre simultaneously evokes critical and referential modes of reception. The critical mode constitutes a more or less detached way of viewing in which the audience recognises and criticises the construction of the storyline and the quality of acting. Audiences bring all kinds of intertextual knowledge to their speculation on future developments. When watching referentially audiences tend to identify with storylines and characters and use them to make sense of their own experience (cf. Hobson, 1989 in Seiter et al., 1989; Geraghty, 1990; Liebes and Katz, 1990). We will examine whether a similar double-edged reaction is prompted by the soap metaphor in politics, assuming that in modernist discourse the soap metaphor will mainly invite readers to review the acts and behaviour of politicians in a critical and detached way, whereas in a more hybrid understanding of contemporary politics the soap metaphor would enable readers to identify and connect with politics in ways that – like the soap opera – 'often act as a catalyst for wide-ranging and open discussions' (Hobson, 1989: 166).

Modernist Discourse

Scandal, conflict and incompetence, both personal and political, provide one set of core ingredients for the soap metaphor in modernist discourse. With an occasional exception, all these stories contain distancing mechanisms, estranging readers from politics and politicians, rather than involving them.

Scandal

Bill Clinton's affair with Monica Lewinsky, which brought him close to impeachment, has become the quintessential political soap story, constituting a predictable frame of reference for other similar stories about the sexual misdemeanours of politicians. New York's mayor Rudy Giuliani went publicly through adultery and divorce in May 2000, with the newspapers referring to the 'Rudy-Judi-Donna-Cristyne soap opera' (Rich, 2000); a 'weeper [that] has everything: politics, stymied ambition, a marriage on the rocks, a bitter wife, whispers of an old love affair, a new girlfriend and a cancer menace' (Haberman, 2000). A Mississippi governor who seriously criticised Clinton's conduct in the Lewinsky affair, found himself the subject of 'soap' when journalists found him vacationing in France with a woman who was not his wife (Ayres, 1999). Californian congressman Gary Condit topped his colleagues when it was alleged he was responsible for the disappearance of intern Chandra Levy and became 'embroiled in a tragicomic soap opera involving multiple secret girlfriends, allegations that he made unsavoury efforts to keep them quiet, lie-detector tests, DNA blood traces, and more' (Gumbel, 2001). This list could easily be expanded with other politicians presented as actors in their self-invoked personal melodramas. When the soap metaphor is used it usually contains an inventory of the story's ingredients, as the examples above show, pointing at the construction of the story and creating distance among the readers, rather than inviting involvement or empathy with the characters. In the numerous marital scandals that journalists framed as soaps, only once was the common pragmatics turned around: 'This whole soap opera is in some ways a public service, since Mr. Giuliani, intentionally or not, helped uncover one of the most common traumas of modern America – divorce. ... For those of us who've been through divorce, there is cathartic value in seeing that the high, mighty and normally self-possessed can behave as childishly and be hurt as badly as the rest of us at that tragic moment when a marriage dies' (Rich, 2000).

The soap metaphor regularly encapsulates a wider range of scandals than just the sexual or marital: 'The drama that has been unfolding here has all the ingredients of the convoluted soap operas that Brazilians love to watch: a power struggle, betrayal, sexual intrigue, jealousy, revenge. But most of all it's money, lots and lots of money, that has brought about the downfall of Celso Pitta, mayor of Sao Paulo' (Rother, 2000). Similarly, Peruvian presidential candidate Alejandro Toledo was said to have got caught up in affairs of soap quality: 'It has also been heavy soap opera, rich in personal scandal that has obscured Mr. Toledo's campaign message and damaged his credibility ... a story of sex with prostitutes, cocaine use, abandonment of an illegitimate daughter, domestic violence and laundering campaign money' (Krauss, 2001). It is no coincidence that in these cases the soap metaphor was applied particularly to politics in new or deficient democracies in Latin American countries (Krauss, 2000), Russia (Gordon, 1999) or Asia (Hagedorn, 2001). These exotic locations place the reader as a distant, superior observer who frowns in benign surprise. Nevertheless, corruption occurs in Western democracies as well. Political corruption in the US (Chen, 2000), France (Lichfield, 2001) and England (Blackhurst, 2001), has also been framed in soap terms. Again, the Clinton presidency provides an easy target for journalists: 'An opulent mansion drenched in sex and money, where business and bedroom adventures abound, the over-the-top saga of a twisted dysfunctional family. It's not Titans ... its "Clintons in DC" (Dowd, 2000). Journalists, even from the serious newspapers, seem to revel in the sheer deviance of it all, reporting sensational details: 'a former ally videotapes two women engaged in lesbian trysts at a water-pumping station, later asks one to murder the other, according to the other, then tries to commit suicide himself' (Chen, 2000). Here, the distance is created by constructing the politician's behaviour as completely beyond any kind of ordinary reality or moral standards. Whereas the involved mode of watching the soap depends on the quality of its emotional realism (cf. Ang, 1985), the soap metaphor for sex and corruption scandals in politics creates bewilderment and distance.

Conflict

While the 'soaps' that went on in the US government in the last decade centred on the sexual escapades of the President and the couple's alleged loose financial mores, Tony Blair's soaps – according to the press metaphors – are about strife in his cabinet. *The Independent* compared the Labour cabinet with real life soap: 'The greater part of the fascination of the Labour cabinet ... comes from wondering who is for the chop next at the hands of Tony "Big Brother" Blair' (Kington, 2000). Rivalry and conflict within the cabinet opened the way for the Conservative opposition to apply the soap opera metaphor for 'a government whose leading lights fight each other like rats in a sack' (The *Guardian*, 17.10.2000). Another comment was that 'the feuding has grabbed the headlines although the schemers knife each other in a virtually policy-free vacuum' (Richards, 2000). Apparently, the soap framing of personal conflicts was convincing enough to seduce German newspapers to repeat it in an analysis of tensions in the Labour cabinet (Kielinger, 2000). The occasions for the metaphor may differ, but the soap frame itself seems to have become an inescapable one for every conflict among Tony Blair's ministers and advisors: 'This is politics as soap opera: a Downing Street tale of broken friendship, betrayal and revenge that would not be out of place on BBC1 or ITV. Peter Mandelson and Alastair Campbell are now bitter enemies after one of the most spectacular Westminster falling-outs in living memory' (Maguire, 2001). Evidently, the Labour government is not the only one to suffer from personal conflicts of (seemingly) soap quality. Different American primaries have witnessed 'soap opera-like drama' (Hicks, 2000a); 'scripts for a soap opera' (Hicks, 2000b); Gerhard Schröder's German cabinet has been typified as 'Die Leute vom Reichstag – Die politische Daily Soap' (Zippert, 2001); the Dutch Labour party saw its chairwoman withdraw because of internal feuds in soap style (Hoedeman and Nicolasen, 2000), etcetera.

Wherever they come from, all these stories make great reading and must be fun to write.[2] However, the authors all apply the soap metaphor in a somewhat abridged way, by forgetting that in real soaps, personal conflicts always have a substantial base. Sometimes the sources of conflict are so far in the past, that only the most devoted viewers remember, nevertheless conflicts in soaps are never simply irrational feuds based only on likes and dislikes. They have good reasons, just as the political conflicts must have a substantial logic, but they tend to get buried in the metaphor. I found a soap metaphor applied substantially only once, when the Dutch *De Volkskrant* paraphrased a rather complicated tax discussion between the Minister of Finance and the president of the national bank, as 'a lovely soap', and presented the different arguments in terms of daily episodes (Kalshoven, 1999). This exception notwithstanding, when the soap metaphor is used to frame conflicts between politicians, it constructs them as personal rather than political. As journalists themselves acknowledge, this creates at best a distance and at worst evokes cynicism among the electorate (Macintyre, 2001). However, they tend to blame politicians ('do you think it is demeaning to treat the Labour cabinet as if it were a TV show?', 'but that is how we have been taught to treat it') (Kington, 2000) rather than their own incomplete use of the metaphor.

Incompetence

Although it is not my intention to make cross-cultural comparisons, it is striking that in the Dutch applications of the soap metaphor, incompetence of local, regional and national governments was mostly the prompt: 'One could write a soap opera about Council politics, which would make Peyton Place fade away' (*Algemeen Dagblad*, 2001). The soap metaphor is used to point at unexpected and incomprehensible changes of conviction and policy. 'In the soap about the Study House,[3] it seems that secretary of Education, Karin Adelmund, plays the part of fidgeter' (Hageman, 2000). On account of provincial elections, an observer criticises regional policies as 'episodes of the soap: "A shameless spectacle"' (Godschalk, 1999). An enduring debate about an unfinished flyover is typified as a regional soap (Van den Broek, 2000). In the Dutch cases, these typifications are applied rather superficially and sometimes a little incoherently, for instance when a commentator wrote of the political aftermath of the Srebrenica drama as being 'an unmitigated soap' as well as 'a fascinating farce' (Faber, 2000). Such undeveloped notions of soap are likely to be caused by the short history of soaps in The Netherlands' consciousness, much unlike the British and American soaps.[4]

The Americas, both North and South, had a soap of political incompetence in the story of the Cuban boy stranded in Miami (Lanting, 2000). In England, it was the inability of the Tories to come up with a new leader after William Hague's election defeat. Some journalists used the soap metaphor to claim that no one would be interested in the battle for the Tory leadership. It is hardly the most complex exercise in history, McElvoy (2001) claims, nor the most interesting one: 'As brutal a shock as it must be to the main characters involved, there is precious little enthusiasm for an omnibus-length leadership opera.' Other journalists equally put down the Tory party: 'Before our very eyes, the Conservatives have become the party to hate itself', but saw much more excitement in it: 'Tory Story has had it all: betrayal, hatred, even that time-honoured staple of soap – the queeny matriarch loved by a few and condemned as a dragon by everyone else' (Freedland, 2001).

Spin Control

The soap metaphor is applied in a rather different way in stories that try to analyse the current state of the art in politics, calling it postmodern, personalised, Clintonised, popularised, artificial, spin controlled, celebrity politics or whatever. At the heart of these analyses is the supposed lack of authentic political drive among politicians: 'Politicians speak like performers in a Karaoke bar, mouthing the words of other people, and taking no responsibility for those words, once their performance has ended' (McLaren, 1999). Politicians are presented as the characters in a script that is written sometimes by themselves, but more often by their advisers, the infamous spin-doctors. The champions of spin control, as many journalists remind us, were of course part of Bill Clinton's administration (Joseph, 2000; Wintour, 1999). However, in the most recent period it is the Blair government that especially faces this kind of charge: 'So was this the beginning of the end of the Blair soap opera? Will the events of the past week finally force the real Blair to stand up, free of spin doctors and advisers who have created such cynicism among traditional voters' (Ahmed, 2000; also *The Independent*, 2000; Rawnsley, 2000). As noted in the very beginning of this chapter, journalists blame Blair and his advisers for the current obsession with image, style and polls, but Blair's advisers accuse the press: 'He believes that he is more spinned against than spinning' (Hoge, 2000). A third party in this unhappy marriage between politicians and journalists is the public, who receive their blows from journalists and politicians alike. It is claimed, for instance, that they expect 'their daily fix of soap opera' from politicians (Dowd, 2000), or that they see politics as 'just another open-ended, pointless soap opera, complete with artificial crisis, all of which are meaningless within a week' (Joseph, 2000), or that they are 'riveted by the soap operas of public lives' (Dowd, 2000). Slightly more sophisticated analyses move away from the persons and the public, and point at the lack of real political disagreements and the loss of ideologies as the main source behind soap opera politics: 'When real politics lacks life and death drama, the punters search for alternative entertainment' (Rawnsley, 2000). When politics lacks an ideological basis, says a Dutch observer, it descends to the level of personal relations and becomes a soap (Kleinrensink, 2001). The German newspaper *Die Welt* particularly ascribes the lack of ideological conflict to the 'third way politics' introduced, among others, by Clinton, Blair and Schröder, resulting in supermarket logic, in which every social democratic opportunist can select his own mix of products. '*Eklektiker und Schauspieler sind die Prototypen postmoderner Demokratie*' (Weimer, 2001).

The stories of scandal, conflict, incompetence and spin control that journalists have framed as soap opera indeed contain many classic elements of the genre. A crucial part of many of the stories reviewed here is an inventory of these elements to prove one is witnessing something like a soap. In addition, the unfolding of the narratives in these stories also parallels the conventions of the soaps, with stories and characters coming back to haunt each other, and political death sometimes being – like death in real soaps – only temporary, as the many resurrections of, for instance, the come-back-kid Bill Clinton, attest to. Nevertheless, the metaphor is also used in an extremely limited and biased way. Characters in these political soaps are invariably portrayed as immoral and spoiled (scandals), or petty and vindictive (conflicts), or silly and incoherent (incompetence). All of them are continually scheming to cover up their wrongdoings and polish their own image (spin control). It is unclear whether, apart from a hunger for sex, money and power, something more elevating motivates them. The political soaps thus feature wicked, self-centred people, mainly men, with despicable or incomprehensible motives. No channel manager in his right mind would accept such a scenario for prime time soap, for audiences would be appalled by it, as appalled as they are often said to be by politics. In these modernist applications of the soap metaphor, there are no sympathetic characters one can identify with, as there are in real soaps; they are not driven by experiences we can understand on the basis of our own lives, as we can in real soaps; there are no storylines that we can recognise or sympathise with because we or our fellow-(wo)men have 'been through it'. In short, the soap metaphor in these contexts positions the reader at a critical, superior distance, looking down on politicians and the political process as an extraterrestrial species that is primarily busy with itself. The resulting alienation is as much a product of occurring political abuse, as it is a result of the limited way journalists apply the soap metaphor, only evoking its critical and detached mode of reception and failing to exploit its capacity to involve and connect people to characters and stories, and thus – maybe – to politics.

Are there particular ways in which the engaging qualities of soap could raise politics to a more sympathetic and honourable level, one that is relevant to the contemporary challenges of personalisation, television, popular culture and the supposed lack of ideology?

The Soap as Saviour

Governments and politicians alike have embraced soaps and their actors as useful vehicles for their campaigns. The Dutch government, for instance, ponders how to convince soap producers to include health messages about the dangers of smoking (Deen, 2001). The Labour government has also considered how to get their messages across in TV-scripts, a move that journalists have condemned as a 'sinister scheme to woo the masses' (McSmith, 2000). The Tories would like the British soaps to include storylines that encourage marriage (Ward, 1999b). Both New Labour and the Tories have constructed their election broadcasts as small soap narratives

(The *Guardian*, 2000; Ward, 1999a). Soap celebrities have backed the Labour campaign in particular, just like Bill Clinton had a strong constituency in Hollywood. The paradox of the soap functioning simultaneously as a means of denunciation and as an instrument of support has been explained earlier; it is the gendered subtext that enables politicians and government to hail the soap as a means of support as long as it does not take over their core business. Journalists, however, by and large ridicule the incorporation of soap narratives and soap actors in policy and campaigning, in another expression of modernist discourse that considers entertainment separate from politics: '[Celebrity endorsements] provide the two crucial ingredients that spin doctors and journalists crave during election campaigns: a new storyline, and with a bit of luck, an attractive female twenty-something' (The *Guardian*, 2000). Of all the stories reviewed for this chapter, only a few judged that the soap provided an appropriate and stimulating narrative to cover politics and politicians. Mayor Giuliani's divorce and the Dutch tax-debate have already been mentioned. Timothy Garton Ash, a fellow at Oxford and Stanford universities also presents a diametrically opposed employment of the soap metaphor – elaborate, elegant and partisan – in a comment on the American elections, published in both *The Independent* and *The New York Times* (Garton Ash, 2000):

> Now, in living rooms from Caithness to Kosovo, Europeans are watching a new American soap opera. After 'Dallas' and 'Dynasty', we have ... 'Democracy'. The cast is familiar. Here again are the powerful women, with strong, partisan hearts and the shoulder pads of righteousness. ... Here are the silver-haired dynasts, advancing the interests of their houses with senatorial mien. ... For ordinary viewers to identify with, there is the walk-on ordinary person, here played by Theresa LePore, hapless inventor of the butterfly ballot. ... Does this mean the United States is making itself a laughing stock? Absolutely not. ... The basic message is a positive one: Every vote really does matter. And, like it or not, a soap opera is probably the best way to get this message across to the largest possible audience.

This seems to be written by a true believer in the genre, applying the soap metaphor not only in a well informed way (thus including female and sympathetic characters), but also recognising the potential of soap to involve people in personal and public issues and make them discuss them among themselves. In a later piece about the Milosevic trial, Garton Ash (2002) contends that the Serbian people are in a state of denial of the war crimes, a denial that is reinforced by the trial. He claims that the Serbian truth commission does not evoke the emotional response necessary for the nation to come to terms with its past. Serbian leader Kostunica says: 'we don't want a soap opera', but Garton Ash argues that soap opera might be one of the ways of breaking through 'the immensely strong psychological barriers of denial.'

> It was only the 1970s American soap opera *Holocaust* which finally brought home to ordinary Germans, through personalising and dramatising, the true horror of the Holocaust. Today, Serbs have one historical soap opera on their television screens: the Slobo and Carla show from The Hague. They urgently need another: a domestically produced reality show. Only when they get it will people like Dule [a Serbian acquaintance of Garton Ash] begin to face the facts and remember.

Garton Ash's use and promotion of the soap metaphor is highly exceptional in the plethora of cynical applications that characterise the work of ordinary journalists. His views reveal the bias in journalists' articulations of soap and politics more sharply. It is not simply a matter of different personal viewpoints on the relevance of soap. The difference has also to do with Garton Ash's position as an outside expert. Structural and ideological factors explain why journalists utilise the soap metaphor in their particular hostile manner. News values and organisational routines make the day-to-day news story primarily a negative one. The critical distance enabled by the soap metaphor fits easily into the professional routines that favour bad news and ignore good news. Time pressure and framing routines are as important for understanding journalists' views on politics as soap, as their personal dislikes (after having gone through all these stories, one wonders whether there *are* fans of soaps among journalists). In addition, professional ideology has developed in ways that make journalism one of the last bastions of 'high modernism' as Hallin (1996) has called it, believing in progress, rationality and universal truth or standards, and making it run parallel with classic conceptions of politics. Despite all the changes that journalism has gone through, including an increased attention to 'soapish' things such as human interest, private confessions and the like, the use of the soap metaphor in the prestigious newspapers examined for this chapter, shows that modernism still reigns supreme in the news rooms. It is therefore unlikely that the articulations of soaps and politics as journalists construct them, will enable the engaged investments that soaps are famous for, and that politics is in desperate need of. Only the occasional story, such as that described by Timothy Garton Ash, may provoke such audience reaction. That does not mean that the soap format is without potential for contemporary politics, it only means that it is unlikely to be accomplished in this kind of journalism. Soaps themselves may actually do a better job, as the huge critical and ratings success of the American series *The West Wing* suggests.

The West Wing is a weekly series that started on NBC in September 1999. It features the democrat president Josiah Bartlet (played by Martin Sheen) and his staff, showing how they operate in the face of major and minor political crises and events, and how their political work is continuously informed and transgressed by personal convictions and private matters. Like other series in this genre (*ER*, *The Practice*), it has a weekly plot and narratives that cover several episodes. The show has been exported to numerous countries and has received more awards than any other series before. Audience comments on the Internet suggest that the series invites an engagement and discussion with politics that is very often affirmative and admiring, but is also at times resolute and profound (http://us.imdb.com/comments). Martin Sheen's presidential character is often shown as setting an example for the real president: 'Can we have a President Bartlet instead of this Bush guy', or

'On countless occasions I've wished Josiah "Jed" Bartlet were real and sitting in the real Oval Office ... His character is not a saint, but one gets the feeling that there is a decent man with a passion for a job he loves but doesn't necessarily like doing'. Although West Wing stories are generally recognised as having been contrived for the purpose of good drama, they seem to give the audience 'the drift of how decisions are reached, the chain of command, the coddling up to Congress and the public at large, and of course the power play and influence peddling, the continual spin doctoring of public opinion.' Soap conventions enable this political drama to produce a hybrid understanding of politics, in which the different logics of rational policy development, ideological struggle, personal convictions and preferences, public relations requirements, incompetence and bureaucracy unite into a coherent and persuasive picture of 'best possible' political practice. The incorporation of private matters and personal weaknesses, in particular, simultaneously redefines prevailing notions of masculinity in politics, upholding it as a balanced mixture of public and private experience. That does not make for a practice that ensures equal access and participation for women, however, almost the contrary. Apart from press secretary C.J. Gregg (played by Alison Janney), the show features no women in power (her power is derived from being the president's mouthpiece), nor does it make room for any key black characters. The common defence line that the reality of politics is no different, does not hold here, for past and present American administrations employed more women and blacks in high positions than *The West Wing* does. Film and TV critic Lesley Smith has argued that *The West Wing* is actually about male bonding, with 'the ongoing delineation of male virtue the shows' main concern' (Smith, L. 1999). Masculine virtue in politics has clearly been redefined, no longer dependent on stoic, rational and unaffected behaviour. Virtues traditionally considered feminine, such as sensitivity, intuition and care have obviously passed into pop culture's notions of the ideal politician. Popular magazines too, have been seen to propagate such qualities in male politicians, but, as in *The West Wing*, this does not result in an equal place and appreciation of female politicians (cf. Van Zoonen, 2000b). The case of *The West Wing* even suggests that for politics to transform itself with the help of 'femininity', to be able to be the central theme of a soap, it needs to exclude women even more rigidly than before. One would not want to have one's masculinity questioned in the process, would one?

Summary

I have reviewed various articulations of soaps and politics for the reason that they seem to have become ever more frequent, and in the hope that some of the soaps' miraculous qualities of moving, engaging and mobilising people would transfer to politics. I have shown, however, that the dominant use of soap metaphors in politics, firmly anchored in modernist discourse, both brought down politics and depreciated the soap, by only exploiting its capacity to position the public as a detached and critical spectator. Within the confines of modernist discourse a more beneficial contribution for the soap was only made possible in a supportive role, as an endorser of parties or a narrative instrument for policy. This is very much in line with the traditional gender relations that are evoked by the subtexts of politics and soaps as respectively masculine and feminine genres. A metaphor for the role of soap in modernist politics would be the position of the First Lady, supportive but powerless. One needs to look outside of the public realm of politics and journalism in the area of popular culture to find an articulation of soap and politics that enables the public to engage and invest in. I have noted that the American series *The West Wing* does invite empathy with the public and private predicaments of politicians and suggests a hybrid understanding of politics. It does so, in one respect, by making virtues traditionally considered to be 'feminine' a central ingredient of political merit. Paradoxically, this happens at the expense of women featuring in the series, who are even less visible than in 'real' politics. While everything else that's solid melts in the air, traditional gender relations fly high and dry.

Notes

1 A search was conducted on the online archives of British (*Independent, Guardian, Times*), American (*New York Times*), German (*Frankfurter Rundschau, Die Welt*) and Dutch (*Volkskrant, Trouw, Algemeen Dagblad*) newspapers for the combination of the terms 'politics' and 'soap', in the last two years (January 1999–September 2001). The selection of newspapers was dependent on the existence of an easily accessible online archive. Only those articles were selected in which soap was used as a metaphor or symbol: articles about the soap preferences of politicians, for instance, were not used. The analysis was meant to provide a more detailed understanding of the range of interpretations of politics that the soap metaphor opens up and was not meant as a classic content analysis showing the number and distribution of metaphors among different countries and newspapers. The results therefore should be representative for the variety in discourse rather than for countries and newspapers (cf. Miles and Huberman, 1984).

2 Just as it is a joy to select them for the purpose of this chapter.

3 A particular Dutch policy enabling high school students to learn on their own, under supervision of a teacher.

4 Think, for instance, of the national excitement around the questions: Who shot JR? and Who shot Phil?

References

Aalberts, C. and van Zoonen, L. (2001) Politics in Popular Music. Paper presented at the Annual Conference of the Society for the Advancement of Social Economics, SASE. Amsterdam.

Ahmed, K. (2000) 'Seven Days that Spun Out of Blair's Control', *The Observer*, July 9.

Algemeen Dagblad (2001) 'Politici Delfzijl hebben ruggegraat van vanillevla', *Algemeen Dagblad*, September 11.

Ang, I. (1985) *Watching Dallas: Soap Opera and the Melodramatic Imagination*. London: Methuen.
Ayres, B.D. (1999) 'Political Briefing: Political Soap Opera Rivets Mississippi', *New York Times*, June 11.
Blackhurst, C. (2001) 'Hamilton: A Man Clinging to his Tattered Reputation', *The Independent*, August 11.
Boorstin, D. (1972) *The Image: A Guide to Pseudo-events in America*. New York: Athenaeum.
Broek, M. van den (2000) 'Sporen onder een vergeten viaduct', *Volkskrant*, December 23.
Brooks, J. (2001) 'Millbankers', *Guardian Unlimited*, June 5 At: http://politics.guardian.co.uk/news/story/0,502030,00.htm.
Brown, M.E. (1990) *Television and Women's Culture. The Politics of the Popular*. London: Sage.
Brown, M.E. and Gardetto, D.C. (2000) 'Representing Hillary Rodham Clinton: Gender, Meaning and News Media', in A. Sreberny and L. van Zoonen (eds), *Gender, Politics and Communication*. Creskill, NJ: Hampton Press, pp. 21–53.
Brownstein, R. (1992) *The Power and the Glory. The Hollywood–Washington Connection*. New York: Vintage Books.
Calhoun, G. (ed.) (1992) *Habermas and the Public Sphere*. Cambridge, MA: MIT Press.
Chen, D. (2000) 'In Dutchess: Politics, Sex, Suicide and a Big Man Behind the Curtain', *New York Times*, February 4.
Deen, F. (2001) 'Borst will vooral jeugd redden met 'kruistocht' tegen roken', *Volkskrant*, February 20.
Dillon, J. (2001) 'Labour Sets Out its (Tele)vision for Britain', *The Independent*, May 20. At: http://www.independent.co.uk/story.jsp?story=73491
Dowd, M. (2000) 'Liberties: Tin Cup Couple', *New York Times*, September 24.
Edelman, M. (1964) *The Symbolic Uses of Politics*. Urbana: University of Illinois Press.
Elshtain, J.B. (1981) *Public Man, Private Woman. Women in Social and Political Thought*. Oxford: Martin Robertson.
Faber, M.J. (2000) 'Srebrenica: de soap na het fiasco', *Trouw*, May 27.
Freedland, J. (2001) 'The Right is Left Bereft', *The Guardian*, August 22.
Garton Ash, T. (2000) 'A Reality Show that is Riveting the World', *The New York Times*, November 28.
Garton Ash, T.(2002) 'A Nation in Denial', *The Guardian*, March 7.
Geraghty, C. (1990) *Women and Soap Opera*. Cambridge: Polity Press.
Gidengill, E. and Everett, J. (1998) 'Metaphors and Misrepresentation. Gendered Mediation in News Coverage of the 1993 Canadian Leadership Debates',
Godschalk, B. (1999) 'Wat valt er nog te kiezen?', *Trouw*, 27 February.
Gordon, M.R. (1999) 'On Russia's Far East Fringe, Unrealpolitik', *New York Times*, February 14.
Grice, A. and D. Macintyre (1999) 'I Think This Government is Trying to Conduct Politics as a Soap Opera', *The Independent, December* 23. At: http://www.independent.co.uk/story.jsp?story=1451. Retrieved: September 6, 2001.
Gumbel, A. (2001) 'Dark Days for the Blue-eyed Boy of Condit County', *The Independent*, July 15.
Guardian (2000) 'Another Blow for Trust', *The Guardian*, October 17.
Haberman, C. (2000) 'NYC: Inviting an Invasion of Privacy', *New York Times*, July 8.
Habermas, J. (1989) *The Structural Transformation of the Public Sphere*. Cambridge: Polity Press.
Hagedorn, J. (2001) 'Another Chance for People Power', *New York Times*, March 16.
Hageman, E. (2000) 'Gewoon een uitglijer', *Trouw*, January 15.
Hague, W. (2000) 'Keynote Address to the Conservative Party Conference 2000', Edited version in *The Independent*, October 6. At: //www.independent.co.uk/story.jsp?story=10969. Retrieved: September 6, 2001.
Hall, S. (1991) 'Over postmodernisme en articulatie. Een interview met Stuart Hall' (On post-modernism and articulation. An interview with Stuart Hall), in S. Hall (1991), *Het minimale zelf en andere opstellen. (The minimal Self and Other Essays)*. Nijmegen. SUN.
Hallin, D. (1996) 'Commercialism and Professionalism in the American News Media', in J. Curran and M. Gurevitch (eds), *Mass Media and Society*, second edition. London: Arnold, pp. 243–65.

Hart, R. (1994) *Seducing America: How Television Charms the Modern Voter*. New York: Oxford University Press.

Hicks, J.P. (2000a) 'Bitter Primary Contest Hits Ethnic Nerve Among Blacks', *The New York Times*, August 31.

Hicks, J.P. (2000b) 'Vitriol Flows in Race for Congress', *The New York Times*, September 8.

Hobson, D. (1989) 'Soap Operas at Work', in E. Seiter, H. Borchers, G. Kreutzner and E. Warth (eds), *Remote Control: Television, Audiences and Cultural Power*. London: Routledge, pp. 150–67.

Hoedeman, J. and L. Nicolasen (2000) 'Van Hees vergat in PvdA gezag te verwerven', *De Volkskrant*, November 15.

Hoge, W. (2000) 'London Journal', *The New York Times*, December 23.

IMDb (2001) International Movie Database. User comments for *West Wing, The* (1999). At: http://us.imdb.com/commentsshow?0200276. Retrieved: November 22, 2001.

Independent (2000) 'Stop Acting Like a Soap Star', *The Independent*, July 18. At: //www.independent.co.uk/story.jsp?story=41040. Retrieved: September 6, 2001.

Iyengar, S. and D. Kinder (1987) *News that Matters. Television and American Opinion*. Chicago: University of Chicago Press.

Joseph, J. (2000) 'Yesterday's Viewing; The Prime Time Ministers', *The Times*, December 12.

Kalshoven, F. (1999) 'De herfstdip van Gerrit Zalm', *De Volkskrant*, October 2.

Kennedy, R. (2000) 'The Mayor's Separation: The Reaction', *New York Times*, May 12.

Kennedy, E. and S. Mendus (1987) *Women in Western Political Philosophy*. New York: St Martin's Press.

Kielinger, T. (2000) 'Indiskretionen aus dem Inneren Kreis der Downing Street', *Die Welt*, October 19.

Kington, M. (2000) 'That Old Game Show Called Politics', *The Independent*, August 31.

Kleinrensink J.J. (2001) 'Partijen zonder ideologie geven LN de ruimte', *Volkskrant*, June 12.

Krauss, C. (2000) 'Fujimori's Fall: A Nation's Lion to Broken Man', *New York Times*, December 3.

Krauss, C. (2001) 'An Upriver Battle for Votes in Peru', *New York Times*, June 2.

Landale, J. (2001) 'Soap Stars Help Blair Woo Young Vote', *The Times*, June 4. At: http://www.thetimes.co.uk/article/0,640–2001191070,00.htm.

Lanting, B. (2000) 'Van Amerikanen mag de soap nog wel even duren ('Americans would like this soap to last'), *Volkskrant*, November 17. At: http://www.volkskrant.nl/zoek. Retrieved: September 6, 2001.

Lichfield, J. (2001) 'Fugitive in Dumas Affair Confronts Accusers in Court', *The Independent*, February 8.

Liebes, T. and Katz, E. (1990) *The Export of Meaning*. New York: Oxford University, Press.

Macintyre, D. (2000a) 'Mr. Mandelson is More than a Star in a Soap Opera', *The Independent*, October 19.

Macintyre, D. (2000b) 'The Furore over Mr. Portillo Proves the Tories are in Crisis', *The Independent*, November 30. At: //www.independent.co.uk/story.jsp?story=42253. Retrieved: September 6, 2001.

Macintyre, D. (2001) 'The Iron Law of Politics Dictated that He Had To Go', *The Independent*, January 25.

Maguire, K. (2001) 'Masters of the Political Black Arts Go To War', *The Guardian*, March 10.

Mattelart, M. (1986) *Women, Media, Crisis: Femininity and Disorder*. London: Comedia.

McElvoy, A. (2001) 'How Will the New Labour Family Recover from its Tiff?', *The Independent*, April 4.

McLaren, M. (2000) 'Ignore these Nasty Politicians, London Needs an Independent Voice', *The Independent*, February 8.

McSmith, A. (2000) 'Is Big Brother Watching You Watching the Soaps?', *The Observer*, January 30.

Miles, M.B. and Huberman, M. (1984) *Qualitative Data Analysis. A Sourcebook of New Methods*. Beverly Hills, CA: Sage.

Modleski, T. (1984) *Loving with a Vengeance: Mass Produced Fantasies for Women*. London: Methuen.

Neve, B. (1992) *Film and Politics in America: A Social Tradition*. London: Routledge.
Norris, P. (1996) 'Women Politicians: Transforming Westminster?', *Parliamentary Affairs*, 49 (1): 89–102.
Postman, N. (1985) *Amusing Ourselves to Death*. New York: Viking.
Rawnsley, A. (2000) 'Tony's Still Winning the Ratings War', *The Observer*, July 9.
Rich, F. (2000) 'What's Love Got To Do With It?', *New York Times*, May 20.
Richards, S. (2000) 'We've Had Enough of the Soap Opera, Now What about Policy', *The Independent*, October 22.
Rother, L. (2000) 'Sao Paulo Journal: What Mayor's Wife Saw: A Tangled Tale of Graft', *New York Times*, May 5.
Schudson, M. (1998) *The Good Citizen. A History of American Civic Life*. New York: Free Press.
Sieter, E., Borchers, H., Kreutzner, G. and Warth, E-M (1989) *Remote Control: Television, Audiences and Cultural Power*. London: Routledge.
Smith, L. (1999) 'The West Wing: Reigning Men', *Pop Matters*. At: http://popmaters.com/tv/reviews/w/west-wing.htm. Retrieved: November 22, 2001.
Smith, A. (2000) 'Is Big Brother Watching You Watching the Soaps', *The Observer*, January 30. At: http://politics.guardian.co.uk.news/story/0,,456981,00.htm.
Smith, J. (2000) 'Hague Issues Poll Challenge at Blair', *The Independent*, October 5. At: http://www.independent.co.uk/story.jsp?story=10973. Retrieved: September 6, 2001.
Soetjipto, T. (2000) 'Suharto Land to be Searched for Son', *The Independent*, November 8. At: http://www.independent.co.uk/story.jsp?story=20491. Retrieved: September 10, 2001.
Sreberny, A. and van Zoonen, L. (eds) (2000) *Gender, Politics and Communication*. Creskill, NJ: Hampton Press.
Stephanopoulos, G. (2000) 'So How Will History Judge President Clinton?', *The Independent*, August 18. At: http://www.independent.co.uk/story.jsp?story=40641. Retrieved: September 10, 2001.
Street, J. (1997) *Politics and Popular Culture*. Cambridge: Polity Press.
Troost, N. (2001) 'Canada in de ban van politieke soap', (Canada under the spell of political soap), *Volkskrant*, July 21. At: http://www.volkskrant.nl/zoek. Retrieved: September 6, 2001.
Wahl-Jorgensen, K. (2000) 'Constructing Masculinities in the US Presidential Campaigns: The Case of 1992', in A. Sreberny and L. van Zoonen (eds), *Gender, Politics and Communication*. Cresskill, NJ: Hampton Press, pp. 53–78.
Ward, L. (1999a) 'In True Soap Style: Hague's Kitchen Table Couple Stick the Breadknife into Labour', *Guardian Unlimited*. At: http://politics.guardian.co.uk/news/story/0,,455432,00.htm. Retrieved: April 15, 1999.
Ward, L. (1999b) 'Hague Urged to Back Sex Advice Campaign', *The Guardian*, May 13.
Weimer, W. (2001) 'Politik als Soap', *Die Welt*, September 17.
White, M. (1999) 'Don't Edit Politicians, Campbell tells BBC', *Guardian Unlimited*, February 10. At: http://politics.guardian.co.uk/news/story/0,,455510,00.htm. Retrieved: September 6, 2001.
Wintour, P. (1999) 'Blair Scorns Fleet Street "Soap Opera"', *Guardian Unlimited*, January 31. At: http://politics.guardian.co.uk/news/story/0,,457215,00.htm. Retrieved: September 6, 2001.
Zippert zappt (2001) 'Die Leute vom Reichstag – Die politische Daily Soap', *Die Welt*, January 11.
Zoonen, L. van (1994) *Feminist Media Studies*. London: Sage.
Zoonen, L. van (1998a) 'A Day at the Zoo: Political Communication, Pigs and Popular Culture', *Media, Culture and Society*, 20 (2): 183–200.
Zoonen, L. van (1998b) 'Finally I Have My Mother Back. Politicians and their Families in Popular Culture', *Harvard International Journal of Press/Politics*, 3 (1): 48–64.
Zoonen, L. van (2000a) 'Popular Culture as Political Communication', *Javnost/The Public*, 7 (2): 5–19.
Zoonen, L. van (2000b) 'The Personalization of Politics: Opportunities for Women?', *International Journal of Political Psychology*. 9 (3 and 4): 19–35.

7

Citizen Consumers

Towards a New Marketing of Politics?

MARGARET SCAMMELL

It is an irony of our times that warnings about the 'capitalist threat' are now more likely to come from businessmen and women than politicians. Financier George Soros (1997) wrote famously of the threat of neo-liberalism, 'the belief in the magic of the marketplace', to democratic society. Body Shop founder Anita Roddick built an international reputation drawing attention to the 'ugly reality' of untrammelled global capitalism: gross inequality, forced labour, sweatshops, environmental poisoning and brutal repression of human rights. *Take it Personally* is the title and advice of her new book dedicated to the activists and grassroots organisations who challenge the 'myth of the global economy'.

In the midst of the backlash against globalisation, business leaders are increasingly discussing corporate citizenship, not just as prudent public relations, but as an imperative of the marketplace for multinational enterprises. At the 2002 World Economic Forum in New York the heads of 36 global corporate giants signed up to a 'framework for action', covering issues such as environmental quality, labour standards, human rights, equal opportunity and access, which was to make the case that social responsibility is profitable: business thrives best in democratic societies and corporate leaders have a direct interest in extending wealth and human rights to more people around the world.

This point of enlightened self-interest is given an imaginative Darwinist twist in Dickinson and Svensen's *Beautiful Corporations* (2000). They argue that in modern affluent society most people have what they need and much of what they want. People are not machines with an infinite capacity to consume, and because of this the old marketing standards of price and volume will not be enough for sustainable profits in the twenty-first century. Companies can no longer rely on increasing volumes and cutting prices. The more mature the markets, the more people's natural attraction to beauty will come into play. We are 'genetically programmed' to stop and stay with beauty, to that which delights the senses and pleases the mind, to intelligence and humanity. As choice increases so consumers will be drawn to the 'beautiful companies', those that seek an alliance of aesthetics with social responsibility, who realise that the pursuit of profit may destroy as much as it creates, and that integrity cannot be manufactured in any enduring way through cool advertising and public relations gimmicks.

Of course, this is a fantastically optimistic scenario, that markets will correct their own ugly reality such that beauty, inside and out, will become the essence of competitive advantage. It requires faith in consumers' taste and innate sense of citizenship, and a reversal of the historic truth that, as Robert Dahl (1998: 174–5) puts it, markets left to their own devices will inevitably inflict harm. However, 'beautiful corporations' *is* convincing as critique, rather than prediction, which in fairness is its intent. It is a powerful attack on the shallow cosmetic appeal of brand images set against the destruction of the environment, cultural diversity and human dignity. It suggests that the single-minded pursuit of profit, at any cost, may be increasingly unsustainable as business practice and goes against the grain of modern consumerism.

This chapter takes the spirit of this critique and applies it to politics. It will question, against the prevailing orthodoxy, whether politics might be improved by *more* not less marketing. This may seem curious since British parties are already 'highly professional market-oriented organisations ... geared to the needs of virtually permanent campaigning' (Webb, 2000). Moreover, political marketing is deeply implicated in the current concerns of democracy, considered a key contributor to 'the crisis of public communication' (Blumler and Gurevitch, 1995) and to public cynicism (Cappella and Jamieson, 1997). Marketing is more commonly seen as a problem rather than a solution for citizen disengagement.

However, this is not a plea for more of the same spin and manufactured imagery that is so characteristic of contemporary political communications. Rather the reverse. The spin, the usual propaganda of politics, is – let us use the word – ugly. It is not just that consumer critique, rather than party discourse, now discusses the big agenda of capitalist threat, poverty, environmental crisis and human rights – issues that were almost entirely absent from the major party campaigns and media agendas of the British 2001 general election, for instance. It is also that much mainstream political rhetoric seems locked in a time-warp fitting into the mass society scheme of propaganda outlined by Harold Lasswell's seminal examination of the First World War: polarise, simplify, repeat the message, personify and vilify the enemy. Under almost any pressure, from challenges at Prime Minister's Questions in the House of Commons to election campaigns, the ugliness principle holds sway: 'Vote/cheer for me because my opponent is more corrupt, less trustworthy, less competent, made a worse mess.' Negative campaigning, the predominant trend of political communications in the US over the last 15 years, is a scarcely more sophisticated version.

This is not to deny that politicians must operate in a world of ugly reality, and not of their own choosing. They must attend to the media ever-alert to splits, sleaze and the sensational story. They must deal with the electoral market as it is, seemingly lending itself to tight targeting of campaign resources and strict message discipline. However, it is to suggest that current campaigning styles may be increasingly unsustainable, the political equivalent of profit at any cost, and that clues to other, and maybe more appropriate ways, come precisely from the emerging critiques from within marketing. In short, parties and politicians, to the extent that they practice marketing, seem to rely on a model of product and promotion that is increasingly out of step with the modern market of citizen-consumers.

The Marketing Critique: corporate and consumer citizenry

The 'beautiful corporations' critique in large part depends on the premise of empowered consumers investing citizenship considerations into their everyday purchase decisions. The claim is that consumers are empowered in relation to producers, and their shopping habits are citizen-like to the extent that the goal of satisfaction of personal wants is tempered with wider social awareness, with a concern for impact on the public, increasingly global, realm. Both parts of this claim need to be demonstrated. Are consumers empowered? If so, how and in what ways? Is the new claim of powerful consumers any more believable than the old 'customer is king' mantra, offering the illusion of markets organised in the consumer interest while always serving the end of profit? Even if consumers are empowered, to what extent is citizenship an appropriate category?

Empowered consumers: the new marketing paradigm

People who spend constantly up to and beyond their means may not recognise themselves quite as empowered. However, a tilt in market power from producer to consumers is the basic idea underlying the predominant marketing paradigm of the last 30 or so years. At the heart of any definition of marketing is the 'marketing concept': an approach that 'puts the customer at the beginning rather than the end of the production–consumption cycle' (Baker, 1991). It is a philosophy of business that says that companies can best achieve their objectives by attending to customer wants and needs at the start, not just the end, of the production process. Marketing became the cornerstone of business philosophy because consumers empowered with greater choice were less susceptible to the allure of advertising and sales promotions alone.

New marketing theory now contends that the digital, global and de-regulated economy massively expands competition and choice, thereby substantially shifting further the power balance in favour of consumers. There is a mini-explosion of literature on marketing in the new economy. We focus here on the views of Philip Kotler, veteran US marketing theorist and a leading advocate of the application of marketing strategy and disciplines to politics. In his analysis, the main problem for business now is overcapacity (Kotler, Jain, Maesincee, 2002: ix): 'Customers are scarce, not products. Demand, not supply, is the problem. Overcapacity leads to hyper competition, with too many goods chasing too few customers. And most goods and services lack differentiation. The result: dog-eat-dog pricing and mounting business failures.'

Digital technology is re-writing the rules of the marketplace. It is democratising the information environment, transforming what Kotler calls the 'asymmetry' between sellers and customers. Sellers typically have had greater access to and control of market information and could effectively set the terms, while customers mostly relied on shortcuts such as brand recognition, reputation and consumer advice media. The Internet now allows buyers to compare prices and product attributes in minutes, facilitated by consumer information websites. Some sites encourage consumers to name their price – for airline tickets, hotels, holidays, mortgages – and see whether suppliers respond. Possibilities for exchange of information with other customers, about anything of mutual concern from holidays to health care, open up on the web. Beyond that, the Internet permits access to new worlds of user and expert information about virtually anything, and drastically lowers the costs of retrieval, in time, money and prior knowledge.

At the same time the consumer is offered considerably expanded choice. Digital deregulated markets lower the costs of entry for new producers and substantially reduce, or make irrelevant, barriers of time and space. The Internet consumer can shop any time and from any online country. Increasingly consumers can demand more precisely what they want. Customised and bespoke trade, formerly the province of wealthy elites is becoming more widely possible, as digital technology lowers the cost of manufacturing 'batches of one' in a kind of democracy of goods. Kotler et al. (2002: 36–7) suggest that this capability may transform the consumer into a 'prosumer', able to customise purchases from menus on sellers' websites.

These possibilities of information and choice are effectively transforming the market such that it is now the consumer, not the producer, who is the hunter. Increasingly producers will have to find products for customers, not customers for pre-designed products. They will have to turn their attention to the creation of 'customer portfolios', not product portfolios. They will have to focus increasingly on individual customer requirements, and develop strategies for keeping existing buyers ('customer lifetime value') because in the new environment the cost of attracting new consumers is much greater than the cost of building loyalty.

Kotler et al.'s new marketing paradigm, of 'customer relations management', comes close to an older, European tradition of marketing, from the Nordic School of Services. Its distinguishing feature is its emphasis on services.

It claims that marketing orthodoxy, associated with North American business schools and theorists such as Kotler, referred primarily to packaged goods and durables. In fact developed economies are service-dominated, with the service sector accounting for some two-thirds of GNP in the Western world (Gummesson, 1991). The sustainable success of services requires a form of marketing which differs from packaged goods in significant respects. First, services tend to be more reliant on promise and reputation. To some extent the sale of any good involves a promise to consumers, to perform certain functions or satisfy particular wants. However, in the case of services the promise and the reputation is normally the only thing that the seller can offer in advance of sale. The product cannot be physically sampled, tasted, touched or test-driven. Second, services are often long-lasting, banking, mortgages, insurance, for example. At the outset, customers buy into potentially years of provision from the service-provider. Such services often depend for profit on long-term custom. This is the basis of 'relationship marketing', in which the retention of existing customers determines sustainable profits. The more competitive and mature the market, the greater the imperative to retain customers and extract 'lifetime value'. Third, there is often no separation, as there is with packaged goods, between production, sales and delivery. 'For most service companies the majority of face-to-face contacts are not handled by salespersons; they are handled by those who produce and deliver the service or part of it – for example the contact between a waiter and a guest' (Gummesson, 1991: 67). All employees, therefore, who have contact with customers, are effectively 'part-time marketers'. They have a direct influence on customer perception of the product in markets almost entirely reliant on reputation. In these circumstances, the 'marketing function' cannot be satisfied by a specialised marketing department alone, it extends to all employees whose activities affect customer perception. Employees, therefore, form a vital audience – an 'internal market' in Gummesson's phrase – who must be persuaded by the company's mission and product quality, since their performance crucially influences external customer perception and continued loyalty.

Services marketing theory has provided some valuable insights for researchers of political marketing (Harrop, 1990; Scammell, 1999). Thinking of politics, and government, as a service theorises the importance of image – reputation – in politics, not just as an effect of television, but as an imperative of the marketplace. Reputation, based on record and leadership, is the only thing of substance parties can offer to voters in support of their 'promises' to govern (Scammell, 1999). Equally, the raising of reputation to a key variable helps explain why it is that voters may vote for one party while apparently preferring the policies of another; or indeed why it was that the Conservatives crashed to defeat in 1997 despite presiding over an improving economy. However, the significance of the idea of the *internal market* has been almost completely overlooked, both in the theory and practice of political marketing (Johansen, 2003).

In fact, in practice, parties may have been following the polar opposite strategy to that recommended by 'relationship marketing': by neglecting their memberships and core supporters. Members, activists, ordinary parliamentarians, and general constituency activities, have all become relatively peripheral to media-focused, leader-centred strategies intended to promote the party's reputation among the weakly-aligned target voters. A clear, centrally-controlled message may indeed be necessary for short-term electoral advantage. However, such benefits are not cost-free, according to marketing theory. Neglect of the internal market will most likely result in a less committed core and a diminution in the value, or even prospect, of face-to-face contact with the 'customers'. The result is greater distance between the organisation and its customers. It becomes more remote from the market and is discounting a vital resource of influence on customer perception. In the long-term, unless the organisation finds other ways to stay close to its market, competitive strength may decline. A similar point, from a more orthodox political standpoint, is emphasised in Seyd and Whiteley (1992) and Whiteley, Seyd and Richardson (1994), studies of Labour and Conservative memberships. They argue that there are clear political and electoral gains associated with robust memberships and local organisations. The de-energising of the parties' grassroots has diminished organisational capacity and capability to mobilise ordinary voters. The clearest case of this is the Conservatives, whose membership declined drastically during the Thatcher years and whose grassroots organisation was virtually wiped out in large swathes of the country. Paradoxically, the unprecedented electoral success of the Thatcher years sat alongside decay of the party (Whiteley et al., 1994: 1). The dire consequences of this neglect became abundantly evident following the Tories' historic defeat in 1997, and they were left to rebuild from a demoralised, shrunken and increasingly ageing base. Perversely perhaps, 'political parties in their struggle to get more market-oriented' have actually become less so, and have undermined their own long-term sustainability (Johansen, 2003).

Corporate citizens and consumer citizens

It is possible thus far to draw some lessons for the major parties, operating in not entirely dissimilar conditions of mature and highly competitive service markets. However, there is no real case as yet that sellers are beginning to view their customers as citizens, and only a few hints that market conditions may force them to. The case for this comes from two main sources: the marketing approach of radical entrepreneurs of whom Anita Roddick is the outstanding example; and the recent surge in interest in corporate citizenship.

Roddick's approach connects with a strain of sociological literature on consumption with 'its emphasis on liberation, the freedom to construct identities and the ability of consumers to empower themselves through the deliberate orchestration of commodity meanings ... ' (Hilton and Daunton, 2001: 8). Consumption in this view is not passive, nor necessarily an isolated, private action but an integral way in which people 'relate to themselves and the world through their relation to their own needs, through a relationship of reflexivity and choice' (Slater, 2001: 124). Consumption is a production process, according to Firat (1998), in a cultural theory echo of Kotler's more pragmatic 'prosumer': 'It often becomes an experience of finding self-expression, a recognition of purpose and identity.' Meijer (1998) argues further that consumer culture is 'an unmined source of civic capital': advertising with its power to amuse and annoy contributes to valuable public debate about civil attitudes and lifestyles. Consumption, and the reflexive, self-expressive consumer, is essential to the emergence of what Anthony Giddens (1991) calls lifestyle politics, characteristic of late modernity.

There are clear echoes of this type of thinking in the 'beautiful corporations' thesis. People seek happiness, as Dickinson and Svensen put it. Companies are mistaken if they imagine that mere accumulation is the route to consumer satisfaction because most of us do not seek happiness purely in the acquisition of more and more material possessions. For all the billions of dollars invested in cool brand images, corporations cannot 'lead youth culture, or inspire love or affection' (2000: 5). As public concern rises at the costs of globalisation, pollution, poverty and crass exploitation, so our instincts for happiness and beauty will drive consumers away from the guilty corporations. Aesthetic pleasure being roughly equal, consumers, if given the choice, will prefer the companies and products that do not pollute, disregard human rights, or subject people and animals to cynical cruelty. Roddick presents a view of a more directly political, 'vigilante', consumer (Roddick, 2001). People are increasingly willing to use their purchasing power as a kind of vote, she argues, and one that harnessed in collective action is capable of humbling corporate giants, such as Shell and Monsanto. 'Because the consumer movement deals with real issues that have an immediate impact on people's lives, it can build campaigns in a way that other movements cannot. It has the power to frighten corporations and governments because it asks questions that must be answered' (Roddick, 2001: 193).

More prosaic but roughly similar views of modern consumer behaviour underlie the emerging business case for corporate citizenship. It is tempting to react with scepticism to corporate citizenship, as yet another form of branding, dressed up with blue sky reports. Certainly, anti-corporate activists are unimpressed. Naomi Klein (2000: 433–4) notes with cynicism the rush by 'some of the most maligned multinationals on the planet – Dow Chemical, Nestle, Rio Tinto, Unocal' into partnership with human rights groups. Activist groups, such as Adbusters, specialise in exposing hypocrisy, and 'greenwash' in the claims of corporate advertising and public relations. Even promoters of corporate citizenship admit that the emergence of capitalist social conscience is primarily self-protection. As corporate responsibility consultant Bennett Freeman (2001) puts it: the anti-globalisation campaign 'has shifted the balance of power in global governance by putting company after company in sector after sector on the defensive as they are targeted, boycotted, sued or merely scrutinised and criticised on issue after issue'.

There is no doubt that the non-governmental organisation (NGO) phenomenon of recent years is driving business interest in corporate citizenship. The explosion in number of these groups is impressive. Keck and Sikkink's (1998) study of the transnational advocacy network traces the spectacular rise of international NGOs from the 1980s onwards, primarily in the areas of human rights, environment, women's rights and peace. After fairly slow growth from 1953–1973, the numbers nearly doubled from 1983–1993 and have multiplied many times since. The Union of International Associations estimates that there were some 23,000 international NGOs in operation in 1997, about four times the number of a decade ago. 'Scholars have been slow to recognise either the rationality or the significance of activist networks' (Keck and Sikkink, 1998: 2) but they are clearly now a major influence on global corporate behaviour. They have driven the issues that have forced the question of corporate responsibility from the 'campaigner's den into the boardroom' (Carr, 1999). They have threatened the expensively-built reputations and ultimately the bottom lines of company after company.

The success of the NGO-led campaigns has effectively made corporate responsibility an impossible issue to avoid, at least for large multinationals. Additionally, though, Freeman has found less 'cultural and intellectual resistance' in the boardroom to the idea that corporate responsibility might bring positive, rather than purely defensive, benefits. It has become clear, says Alice Tepper Marlin, President of the Council on Economic Priorities, that today's consumers are 'more sophisticated, and they are interested in more than just price' (Marlin, 1998). The idea of more socially-aware, citizen-like consumers is the essence of the business case for corporate responsibility. The boom in socially responsible investments (SRI) is only the most obvious example. From a tiny niche market SRI portfolios have grown rapidly, up by 36 per cent in 1999–2001 despite the stock market downturn. SRI is a minority but significant and increasing part of the investment business, accounting for about one in every eight dollars invested in the US stock market. Similar trends are evident in the sale of fair trade goods, organic and free range produce and non-animal tested cosmetics. They are significant because it takes only small changes in consumer behaviour to make substantial impact on company profits; if only 10 per cent of consumers switch products it is enough to make a huge difference in the marketplace (McIntosh et al., 1998). Roberts et al. (2002), in a paper prepared for the WEF cite MORI survey evidence of changing consumer attitudes, and the increased salience of corporate responsibility: 'The most comprehensive survey of consumer attitudes … involving 25,000 individuals in 26 countries, found that more consumers form their impression of a company on the basis of its corporate citizenship practices than do so on brand reputation … . With this level of public interest, it has tended to be the companies with the most direct relationships with consumers that have acted fastest.

Consumers and citizenship

Typically, 'citizen' and 'consumer' are considered opposite categories, the first outward-looking, embracing public interest, the second, self-interested, inward-looking and private. In fact, as Lizabeth Cohen (2001: 203) notes in respect of the US, no such simple distinction has held true historically. Citizen and consumer were 'ever-shifting categories that sometimes overlapped, other times were in tension, but always reflected the permeability of the political and economic …'.

Cohen traces a century-long tension in the US between two conceptions: 'citizen consumers' and 'customer consumers'. Citizen consumers emerged as a category of the citizenry with the rise of Progressivism, from the 1890s to the 1920s. They were identified as a broad-based constituency for political reform involving issues such as fair taxation, labour and consumer protections from exploitation, public ownership of utilities and ethical consumption. The notion revolved around the ideas of a 'fair shake at consumption' for working class consumers, and provided a 'powerful thrust in the drive for anti-trust legislation … as an attack on monopoly in order to preserve an America where consumers were best served by small, local, independent, self-governing businesses dedicated to a republican civic ideal' (Cohen, 2001: 205). The concept of 'customer consumers' emerged around the same time and was an idea of the consumer divorced from the more overtly political considerations. It centred on the philosophy of the free market: competition among relatively unfettered businesses would ensure quality goods at cheap prices to customer consumers.

Cohen argues that in the 1930s, President Roosevelt harnessed the idea of citizen consumers to the New Deal project for economic recovery. Consumers, as a voice of public interest, were included in New Deal agencies, establishing a new principle that the consumer had the right to representation in government policy. '… policymakers and the general public grew to consider consumers as a self-conscious, identifiable interest group on a par with labour and business whose well-being required attention for American capitalism and democracy to work' (Cohen, 2001: 205). This attention from the top, she suggests, encouraged opportunities at the bottom for otherwise unrepresented groups – women and African-Americans – to wield consumer power against political and corporate exclusion and exploitation. Women's groups orchestrated boycotts and protests against 'unfair pricing' and other forms of market exploitation. African-Americans mobilised consumer power for political rights: from the 'Don't Shop Where You Can't Work' campaigns to support for alternative black-owned co-operatives, 'blacks looked to the double-duty dollar to advance the race while they purchased' (Cohen, 2001: 208).

In the post-war economic boom the claims of the customer consumer emerged triumphant, against the citizen consumer arguments for retained rent and price controls. A new consensus between business, labour and government saw economic salvation in mass consumption; the duty of the good citizen in relation to consumption was merely to buy more and more, and the general benefits of increased prosperity would work themselves throughout society via the market. It was an elaborate ideal, says Cohen, of economic abundance and political freedom combined, and became almost the national religion. The 'consumer republic' was the blueprint for the US and for export to the democratic world. By the 1990s the 'customer consumer' had come to hold sway even in the realm of formal politics. Clinton–Gore's 1993 proposals to reinvent government, for example, listed 'putting customers first' as a top goal. However, this was not to reclaim the New Deal ideal of consumers representing public interest, rather it was to confirm a customer consumer orientation in the provision of public services. The watchdog citizen consumers of the 1930s and 1940s were replaced in the 1990s by citizens encouraged to bring 'a consumer mentality to their relations with government, judging state services much like any other purchased goods, by the personal benefit they derive from them' (Cohen, 2001: 220).

Matthew Hilton (2001: 241–60) charts a similar trajectory in Britain. The Labour government's 1999 White Paper, *Modern Markets: Confident Consumers*, is the culmination of decades during which the 'radical collectivist political critiques' of consumer society have been eliminated from the idea of the consumer. Labour, as Clinton–Gore before them, 'redefined citizenship to place "consumers at the heart of policy making"' (241), but this was consumers as self-interested shoppers, rather than the citizen consumer that historically was the heart of the cooperative movement and of Fabian socialist thinking. The kind of consumer power that inspired these movements was the idea that consumers through cooperative action could refashion economic life for the common good. Until and even beyond World War II, socialists, such as the Webbs and Harold Laski, sought ways to bring the 'cooperative commonwealth' into the institutions of the modern state. Gradually, amid the rising post-war affluence, the grand collective visions gave way to individual consumer advice; comparison between the goods on offer, warnings against manipulative advertising and high-pressure sales techniques. Consumer protection came to mean 'value for money', and protections against misleading claims and faulty goods. The consumer now meant the informed shopper, better able to negotiate her way through the range of offerings and to insist that product promises were fulfilled.

However, the citizen consumer, as both agent and concept, never quite disappeared on either side of the Atlantic. It was evident in the Civil Rights and later in the lesbian and gay rights movements, and in protests throughout the 1970s and 1980s concerning the environment and South Africa. In the US, Ralph Nader vociferously insisted on the central role of consumption in citizenship, against the arguments of business and labour that gave production political prominence over consumption (Nader, 2000). At the turn of the twenty-first century the citizen consumer is back with a vengeance and in the mainstream again. This time though s/he has emerged out of affluence, rather than poverty and necessity, and as a key figure of international, not merely national markets.

The New Age of Citizen Consumers

The term 'consumer activism' may and often does cover a huge spectrum from NGO monitoring of global corporations to 'anti-capitalist' demonstrations at meetings of the World Trade Organisation, to organised boycotts, to evidence of social concern in the habits of shoppers in supermarkets. Roddick puts all these activities together under the label 'the new consumerism'. Naomi Klein, whose *No Logo* is the closest to a manifesto for this activism, admits to some puzzlement of classification. Are we really talking about a movement? If so is it really anti-globalisation? Did the protests at the WTO meeting in Seattle signify a new 'global resistance' or merely a new kind of fashion statement: 'limitless frothy coffee, Asian-fusion cuisine, e-commerce billionaires and sappy Meg Ryan movies' (Klein, 2001: 81–2). Ultimately, she summarises it as a distaste and even rejection of 'the privatisation of every aspect of life, and the transformation of every activity and value into a commodity … It includes the way powerful ideas are turned into advertising slogans and public streets into shopping malls; new generations being target-marketed at birth; schools being invaded by ads; basic human necessities like water being sold as commodities; genes are patented and designer babies loom; seeds are genetically altered and bought; politicians are bought and altered.'

Klein does not put it this way, but what she describes is a revolt against the 'consumer republic'. The 'customer consumers' are converting the benefits of the consumer republic, shopping power and choice, into citizenship action. This idea more or less explicitly informs many of the proliferating websites falling into the broad consumer activist classification. There are clear echoes of the old 1920s cooperative union appeal for consumer power to change economic life

> We – the mass of common men and women in all countries – also compose the world's market. To sell to us is the ultimate aim of the world's business. Hence it is ourselves as consumers who stand in relation to all the economics of the world, like a king in his kingdom. As producers we each go unto a particular factory, farm or mine, but as consumers we are set by nature thus to give leadership, aim and purpose to the whole economic world (Peter Redfern, cited in Hilton, 2001: 246).

However, unlike the old cooperative movement there is no real indication as yet of any overarching theory of society, no ideological coherence, except as critique. Beyond a generalised concern at corporate power, the movement is characterised by diversity, fragmentation across specific issues and sometimes contradiction. Animal welfare and environmental activists' agendas may run counter to the claims of those promoting employment rights for multinational workers. Some ethical trade groups will work with multinationals while others continue to organise boycotts. Consumer groups campaigning at 'rip off' prices apparently share little in common with the more radical 'no logo' activists (Hilton and Daunton, 2001). For some, such as Naomi Klein, diversity is strength, a new politics appropriate for our postmodern globalised world. Most optimistically, Waterman (2001) sees potential in the consumer and NGO activism for labour internationalism, global solidarity between affluent consumers and workers in the developing world, leading to a revival of the humanist, emancipatory tradition that supposedly collapsed with the death of socialism.

The new consumerism is now itself subject to backlash. For critics, much of this activism is plain wrong-headed and perhaps even dangerously antipolitics. Contrary to the claims of protesters, economic globalisation is 'a powerful force for equality and poverty reduction'; there is a strong correlation between participation in international markets and domestic economic growth (Dollar and Kraay, 2002). For Charles Handy, the targeting of giant corporations, while understandable, misses the point that it is precisely those 'elephants' that can afford to maintain standards of acceptable capitalist practice (Handy, 2001). Standards would be no better, and certainly less easy to monitor without the giants. John Lloyd (2002) argues further that the anti-globalisation movement is a threat to social democratic politics. It offers critique without alternative, the prerogative of purely protest politics. It lumps together exploitative corporations with governing politicians in a too-simple but powerful emotional critique of greed and corruption. It is in short a kind of anti-politics whose consequences may undermine the entire social democratic project of sensible compromise between social justice and free markets.

These are all significant criticisms and it is worth being reminded that protest, however popular, is far from universally progressive. However, this is to overstate the significance of the highly-visible demonstrations and to underplay the major achievements of consumer activism. Lindblom's (1977) seminal critique of pluralist democracy in the 1970s warned of the threat to democracy of untrammelled corporate power, sufficient to skew the public agenda such that corporate power was a non-negotiable non-issue. The new consumerism has changed that. It has forced into the daylight a dangerously hidden issue. It has shattered the neo-liberal assumption that the massive multinationals had sufficient power to escape from politics. It has stopped in its tracks the slow creep of globalisation 'on velvet paws, under the guise of normality, rewriting societal rules of the game – with the legitimacy of a modernisation that will happen come what may' (Beck, 2000: 4). Above all, and this may be its most lasting achievement, it has restored to consumption the idea of citizenship. It is forcing markets to treat consumers as citizens.

Citizen consumers and the marketing of politics: lessons for parties

Clearly, there are parallels in the development of consumer and political markets. Just as the consumer is empowered through increased choice and vastly expanded resources of information, so too is the political consumer. Political interest options and resources await our convenience in astonishing abundance on the Internet. Just as the digital economy makes customisation increasingly possible for consumer goods, so it does too for politics, allowing us to tailor our political interest environment more closely to individual taste. The political consumer is increasingly the hunter rather than the hunted. In politics as in commerce there is a shift in the balance of market power from the producers to the consumers.

This new political market helps explain one of the more striking features of the much-discussed current 'crisis' of citizen engagement: that citizens are not turning off politics per se, they are turning away from the older established formal institutions of democracy. Thus we see public confidence in parties, politicians and governments is low and steadily declining throughout the established trilateral democracies, Japan, North America and Western Europe (Pharr and Putnam, 2001). Of the various institutions of democracy, 'no single institution is held in greater disrepute than the political party' (Diamond and Gunther, 2001: ix). Yet, while parties are struggling we see consistent evidence that levels of political interest are not declining and may be increasing in some countries (Bennett, 1998; Inglehart, 1999). Seyd et al. (2001) have found that in Britain 'repertoires of political engagement' may have broadened, even in the midst of media anxiety at voter apathy and the lowest electoral turn-out since 1918. The conventional wisdom about floating voters is being turned upside down. The undecideds of the past tended to be relatively uninterested in politics, compared to the partisan attached. Now we see correlations between better education, higher levels of political interest and *lower* levels of party loyalty.

This puzzle for politics is entirely predictable according to market analysis. Consumers are exercising their new choices in market conditions of oversupply compared to demand. At the same time insufficiently differentiated products are being reduced to dog-eat-dog competition. Kotler et al.'s description of a desperate market finds echoes in politics also, especially in the US trend over the last 10 years to negative campaigning, in which the short-term goal of victory outweighed longer term concern at potential damage to the overall market. The new commercial market of empowered consumers is provoking re-thinking of corporate strategy towards relationship marketing, towards investment in the idea of corporations and customers as citizens, and towards a 'beautiful' alliance of design and social responsibility. There may be appropriate lessons here for politics also. Three in particular suggest themselves:

1. Marketing theory indicates the increased importance of retention of existing customers, and especially in service industries, the crucial 'part-time marketing' role of employees;
2. It suggests that a 'customer consumer' orientation is no longer sufficient. Self-expressive citizen consumers are interested in more than price, results and delivery.
3. Aesthetics and style are substantial matters, and cannot be sustained by advertising and public relations alone.

Party sustainability and the internal market: core supporters and members

Of the three marketing recommendations for politics, this is the most surprising and the one most apparently at odds with current trends in political marketing. It is possible to discern similarities with the other two in the analyses of, for example, Labour's modernising architect, Philip Gould (1999), and policy adviser Geoff Mulgan. The latter's analysis of 'antipolitics' (1997) noted with concern the misfit between an increasingly democratic culture, through education, technology and consumer choice, and the formal institutions of politics. However, their remedies have tended to look outwards to stimulating new support and engagement, rather than inwards and to consolidation of the existing core. More recently a Demos analysis of 'de-politicisation' noted the importance of active memberships for general voter turn out, civic culture and the nurturing of new generations of political leaders (Bentley et al., 2001). Equally, however, the significance of membership is reduced by the parties' greater media resources and by increases in state, individual and corporate financial donations. Moreover, 'in a more complex and fast changing environment' it may be necessary to restrict policy development and campaign strategy to 'tighter professional teams'. These points are typical of standard political communication accounts: parties in their drive for target voters increase control at the centre to achieve organisational efficiency, clarity of policy, strategy and message. Active memberships may create as many problems as they solve. A too-intensive internal debate about goals and policy risks an external mediated image of division, generally regarded as a campaigning disaster. The more extreme members may be a liability. Both the Conservative and Labour Parties over the last 20 years have expelled or wound up extreme activist factions: the right-wing Monday Club and the Federation of Conservative Students in the case of the Tories, and in the 1980s the Trotskyite Militant tendency in the Labour Party.

The functional value of memberships for parties has long been debated in political science. Most importantly they supply and nominate candidates for office, mobilise electoral support and stimulate participation. It has become commonplace to suggest that the growth of communications technology marginalises members from one of the main tasks, mobilisation of voters. However, trends across democratic countries have not been uniform or unilinear. It is *not* axiomatic that mass-mediated 'marketed' campaigns marginalise memberships. Scarrow (1996) detailed German party efforts to encourage local activism and the high value placed by party leadership on members' activities as outreach workers, representatives of the party in broader society and even casual conversation. Effectively they were part-time marketers for the party. Perhaps not coincidentally Germany is one of the only European countries where membership increased from the 1960s to the 1990s. Labour too strove to build membership in its drive to election in 1997, increasing from a low of 261,000 in 1991 to 401,000 in 1997, although by mid-2001 they had slumped back to where they started.

Typically, however, parties have shifted from society to the state to safeguard their futures, preferring state money and protection to the increasingly difficult task of building and retaining membership, and to insulate themselves from the taint of corruption associated with private and corporate donations. This may work as 'survival strategy' (Bartolini and Mair, 2001) and it is clear from the example of the US that party labels can continue to dominate even while the organisations are effectively 'empty vessels' (Katz and Kolodny, 1994). However, a perception of the ever-more pronounced separation between state-protected parties and civil society is likely to contribute further to present party malaise. It may ultimately threaten long-term legitimacy. State protection reduces incentives for parties to stay close to their markets, may devalue the role of members and the importance of core supporters. Such neglect risks a vacuum that more aggressive political rivals may exploit. In Ireland, for example, Sinn Fein achieved breakthrough success in the 2002 general election in part by following a strategy of intensive canvassing of precisely those working class districts neglected by the mainstream parties. More generally Europe has witnessed the rise of the extremes in recent years, often 'anti-party' groupings led by charismatic figures capitalising on public disenchantment with the mainstream, notably Le Pen in France and Pym Fortuyn in Holland.

Citizen consumers rather than 'customer consumers'

Governments of both the centre left and right have moved towards a 'customer consumer' orientation, Cohen and Hilton argued (above), both in policy towards consumers in commercial markets and in the provision of public services. 'Value for money', the mantra of the Conservatives from Thatcher onwards, is evident also in Labour policy. Labour has continued

John Major's innovation of the Citizen's Charter to develop more responsive public services, with emphasis on delivery, performance and facilitation of customer complaints. Rhodes (2001: 106) argues that Labour policy towards the public sector confuses the distinction between responsiveness and accountability. The citizen's charter may induce improvements in responsiveness but in no way replaces political accountability because the consumer has no power to hold government agencies to account. 'Citizens have become consumers of services', he says. The charter is the government equivalent of 'the Consumers Association magazine', and probably less effective. The broader debate about 'empowering citizens to exercise democratic control' was muted throughout the 1997–2001 Labour government and none of the proposals in Labour's key policy document 'Modernising Government' offered a significant role to citizens.

Thus at a time when free markets are increasingly forced to consider customers as citizens, politics has discovered the customer consumer. It can easily be seen that such an approach is problematic and possibly self-defeating. Without considerable public investment, and attendant tax increases, public services will struggle to compete with the level of service and customisation offered in the private sector. By encouraging a customer mentality, government may simply be making a rod for its own back, fostering a culture of complaint rather than strengthening democratic control.

Both ideas, customer consumer and citizen consumer, informed Labour's analysis of the tasks of democratic government. Its assessment, as presented by Mulgan (1997), was of a public disenchanted with politicians who make big promises at election times and then fail to deliver, and who conduct debates among themselves, largely disconnected from the public. The remedies suggested included new ways for open dialogue with citizens; measures to represent public opinion in government through polls and citizens' juries; direct involvement through referenda and the Internet. Labour in government put many of these ideas into practice. The first few months in office saw a flurry of task forces, advisory groups and policy reviews, as wider civil society and private business were invited to help shape new public policy. It published a widely-welcomed freedom of information White Paper. It has experimented with deliberative democracy, in the form of citizens' juries, at local and regional levels. It is currently developing a citizenship curriculum for schools. It has sought, through the Internet, a more direct communication with the public. It claimed a world first with the establishment in July, 1999 of the People's Panel – 5,000 randomly selected voters who form a sort of permanent jury on the delivery of government services.

However, as suggested by Rhodes, the customer consumer orientation has come to predominate. Mechanisms of democratic inclusion have increased but tentatively and patchily. Some Downing Street insiders dismiss the People's Panel as a 'whingers' charter', the experiment with citizens' juries has made scarcely a dent on public consciousness, the task force initiative is tainted with the charge of 'cronyism' and pro-business bias (Scammell, 2001). The Freedom of Information Act greatly disappointed early hopes, ultimately implementing little more than the Conservatives' 1994 Code of Access. Fairclough's (2000) analysis, *New Labour, New Language?* concluded that for all the talk of initiating great debates, public inclusion amounted to little more than focus groups and promotional methods for engineering consent.

Style and substance

New Labour in 1997 had something of the 'beautiful corporation' about it. It fought on an agenda of social justice and inclusion and talked of an open, democratic style of political communication. Its advertising attempted to reward audiences with mainly positive and aesthetically pleasing messages. Its commitment to freedom of information was not an isolated policy, but as Tony Blair put it, a signal of 'cultural change', of a 'new relationship which sees the public as legitimate stakeholders in running the country and sees election to serve the public as being given on trust' (cited in Scammell, 2001: 526). This was to be a new, grown-up, open kind of politics.

Within a couple of years, spin and news manipulation came to be regarded as the hallmarks of Labour's communications. In contrast to the circumspection of its attempts to create open and democratic dialogue, Labour moved with gusto to exploit the machinery of government communications, significantly strengthening the control of Number 10, expanding the number of government press officers, multiplying the numbers of political special advisers with media briefs, increasing advertising until in 2001 the government was the country's largest single spender on commercials (Scammell, 2001). Over the past year, a succession of current and former Labour communicators has admitted the damage of spin. A famously leaked memo from Philip Gould in the summer of 2001 confirmed that 'spin no substance' was the first thought in voters' minds when questioned on Labour's image. The New Labour brand had been badly 'contaminated'. In an article in *The Times* (9 May, 2002), the Prime Minister's Press Secretary, Alastair Campbell, conceded that Labour's spin may have contributed to public antipathy towards politics. A week later, Peter Mandelson (2002), Labour's first spin doctor of the 'modernising' era, claimed that 'crude, clumsy', over-controlling spin had undermined public trust. He cited in particular the infamous email of Jo Moore, special adviser to the Transport Secretary, who within hours of the attacks on the World Trade Center on September 11, told colleagues that this was 'a good day to bury bad news.'

Labour's spin is just one of any number of examples of ugly political campaigning from Britain and the US in recent years. The British Conservatives in 1997, by admission of campaign insiders, waged an overwhelmingly negative campaign in a deliberate attempt to drive down the vote and minimise their inevitable losses (Cooper, in press). A viewing of US political advertisements and British party election broadcasts in recent years reveals not so much, as commonly thought, the influence of commercial advertising techniques, rather the continuing strength of a propaganda style and aesthetic. While commercials have become increasingly playful with narrative and image, much political advertising remains wedded to classic propaganda appeals of greed and fear and simple polarisation between good and bad, 'us' and 'the enemy'. Politicians operate under the permanent media spotlight, and often in warfare-like competition with opponents, where one's gain is the other's loss. These are not easy conditions to develop intelligent, attractive communications. However, this is the challenge for parties, or risk yet further distance from the market of citizen consumers.

Conclusion

Typically, in political communications research, marketing is seen as a problem in politics. At best it is an understandable response to the social fragmentation of modernity and the increasing autonomy of the media (Swanson and Mancini, 1996). At worst it has reduced political argument to the discourse of advertising (Jamieson, 1992), replacing substantive policy debate with focus-group tested soundbites, personality and show business pageantry designed to appeal to the least-committed voters. This is marketing as promotional politics, more attuned to the news values of the media and the mass consumer ratings of the polls than to the views of the engaged and debating public. It has elevated a consumer, rather than citizen, orientation in political campaigning and governance. In the process it has undermined the normative leadership expectations of representative democracy, undercut party structures, and bypassed what is left of the public sphere. Combined with a rise in cynical, news-value driven journalism, marketing is accused of contributing to a 'crisis of public communication' (Blumler and Gurevitch, 1995).

This is a brief summary of charges against political marketing. Impressionistically, if not in detail, it is an undeniably recognisable portrait. However, this is to depict marketing as purely self-interested and manipulative with no capacity for enlightened responsiveness to the rise of citizen consumers. It does an injustice to marketing's potential influence in politics. Consumer activism has forced a powerful political agenda on to the public stage to which business has been compelled to react, with a speed and innovation that makes politics seem sluggish. One does not need to believe in a utopia of beautiful corporations to see the force of its critique applied to the unappealing aesthetics of much political communication. One does not need to abandon scepticism to consider that marketing theory offers alternative ways to do political business, to deal with consumers as citizens, to value members and communicate with voters. Maybe politics needs more, not less, marketing.

References

Baker, M.J. (1991) 'One More Time – What is Marketing?' pp. 3–6 in M.J. Baker (ed.) *The Marketing Book*. Oxford: Butterworth-Heinemann.
Bartolini, S. and Mair, P. (2001) 'Challenges to Contemporary Political Parties', pp. 327–44 in L. Diamond and R. Gunther (eds) *Political Parties and Democracy*. Baltimore: Johns Hopkins University Press.
Beck, U. (2000) *What is Globalisation?* Cambridge: Polity.
Bennett, L. (1998) 'The uncivic culture: communication, identity and the rise of "lifestyle politics"', *Political Science and Politics*, 31(4): 740.
Bentley, T., Jupp, B. and Stedman Jones, D. (2001) 'Getting to Grips with De-politicisation' *Demos Briefing Paper*, London: Demos.
Blumler, J.G. and Gurevitch, M. (1995) *The Crisis of Public Communication*. London: Routledge.
Butler, D. and Kavanagh, D. (2002) *The British General Election of 2001*. Basingstoke: Palgrave.
Cappella, J. and Jamieson, K. (1997) *Spiral of Cynicism: the Press and the Public Good*. Oxford: Oxford University Press.
Carr, E. (1999) *'Earthly rewards': The World in 2000* London: Economist Publications.
Cohen, L. (2001) 'Citizen Consumers in the United States in the Century of Mass Consumption' pp. 203–22 in M. Daunton and M. Hilton (eds) *The Politics of Consumption*. Oxford: Berg.
Cooper, A. (in press) 'The Conservative Campaign' in J. Bartle, S. Atkinson and R. Mortimore (eds) *Political Communications: The General Election of 2001*. London: Frank Cass.
Dahl, R. (1998) *On Democracy*. New Haven, CT: Yale University Press.
Diamond, L. and Gunther, R. (eds) (2001) *Political Parties and Democracy*. Baltimore: Johns Hopkins University Press.
Dickinson, P. and Svensen N. (2000) *Beautiful Corporations*. London: FT/Prentice Hall.
Dollar, D. and Kraay, A. (2002) 'Spreading the Wealth', *Foreign Affairs*, 18 (1): 120–33.
Fairclough, N. (2000) *New Labour, New Language?* London: Routledge.
Firat, A. (1998) 'Rethinking Consumption', *Consumption Markets and Culture*, 3 (4): 284–96.
Freeman, B. (2001) 'Corporate Responsibility and Human Rights' paper delivered at Global Dimensions Seminar, New York, United Nations, 1 June.
Giddens, A. (1991) *Modernity and Self-Identity*. Cambridge: Polity Press.
Gould, P. (1999) *The Unfinished Revolution*. London: Little Brown.
Gummesson, E. (1991) 'Marketing Revisited: The Cruicial Role of the Part-time Marketers', *European Journal of Marketing*, 25 (2): 60–7.
Handy, C. (2001) *The Elephant and the Flea*. London: Hutchinson.
Harrop, M. (1990) 'Political Marketing', *Parliamentary Affairs* 43, pp. 277–91.
Hilton, M. (2001) 'Consumer Politics in Post-war Britain' pp. 241–60 in M. Daunton and M. Hilton (eds) *The Politics of Consumption: Material Culture and Citizenship in Europe and Asia*. Oxford: Berg.
Hilton, M. and Daunton, M. (2001) 'Material Politics: an Introduction' pp. 1–32 in M. Daunton and M. Hilton (eds) *The Politics of Consumption: Material Culture and Citizenship in Europe and Asia*. Oxford: Berg.
Inglehart, R. (1999) 'Postmodernisation Erodes Respect for Democracy, but Increases Support for Democracy', in P. Norris (ed.) *Critical Citizens*. Oxford: Oxford University Press.
Jamieson, K.H. (1992) *Dirty Politics*. Cambridge: Cambridge University Press.
Johansen, H. (2003) 'Political Marketing: More than Persuasive Techniques – An Organisational Perspective', *Journal of Marketing Special Issue: Comparative Political Marketing*, Vol. 2, Spring.
Katz, R. and Kolodny, R. (1994) 'Party Organization as an Empty Vessel' pp. 23–50 in R. Katz and P. Mair (eds) *How Parties Organize: Change and Adaptation in Party Organizations in Western Democracy*. London: Sage.
Keck, M. and Sikkink, K. (1998) *Activists Beyond Borders*. New York: Cornell University Press.
Klein, N. (2000) *No Logo*. New York: Picador.

Klein, N. (2001) 'Reclaiming the Commons', *New Left Review*, 9 (May/June): 81–9.
Kotler, P., Jain, D. and Maesincee, S. (2002) *Marketing Moves: A New Approach to Profits, Growth and Renewal*. Boston: Havard Business School Press.
Lindblom, C. (1977) *Politics and Markets*. New York: Basic Books.
Lloyd, J. (2002) *The Protest Ethic*. London: Demos.
McIntosh, M., Leipziger, D., Jones, K. and Coleman, G. (1998) *Corporate Citizenship: Successful Strategies for Responsible Companies*. London: Financial Times Management.
Mandelson, P. (2002) *The Blair Revolution Revisited*. London: Politico's.
Marlin, A. (1998) 'Foreword', pp. xi–xiii in M. McIntosh, D. Leipziger, K. Jones and G. Coleman, (1998) *Corporate Citizenship: Successful Strategies for Responsible Companies*. London: Financial Times Management.
Meijer, I. (1998) 'Advertising Citizenship: An Essay on the Performative Power of Consumer Culture' *Media, Culture and Society* 20: 179–81.
Mulgan, G. (1997) *Life After Politics: New Thinking For The Twenty-First Century*. London: Fontana Press.
Nader, R. (2000) *The Nader Reader*. New York: Seven Stories Press.
Pharr, S. and Putnam, R. (2001) *Disaffected Democracies: What's Troubling the Trilateral Countries?* Princeton, NJ: Princeton University Press.
Rhodes, R. (2001) 'The Civil Service' pp. 97–116 in A. Seldon (ed.) *The Blair Effect*. London: Little Brown.
Roberts, S., Keeble, J. and Brown, D. (2002) 'The Business Case for Corporate Citizenship' World Economic Forum at www.webforum.org.
Roddick, A. (2001) *Take it Personally: How Globalisation Affects You and Powerful Ways to Challenge it*. London: HarperCollins.
Scammell, M. (1999) 'Political Marketing: Lessons for Political Science' *Political Studies*, XLVII, pp. 718–39.
Scammell, M. (2001) 'Media and Media Management' pp. 509–34. in A.Seldon (ed.) *The Blair Effect*. London: Little Brown.
Scarrow, S.E. (1996) *Parties and their Members. Organizing for Victory in Britain and Germany*. Oxford: Oxford University Press.
Seyd, P. and Whiteley, P. (1992) *Labour's Grass Roots: The Politics of Party Membership*. Oxford: Clarendon Press.
Seyd, P., Whitley, P. and Pattie, C. (2001) 'Repertoires of Political Engagement', Paper prepared for the Elections, Public Opinion and Parties Conference, Political Studies Association, University of Sussex, 14–16 September.
Slater, D. (2001) 'Political Discourse and the Politics of Need' pp. 117–40 in W.L. Bennett, and R. Entman (eds) *Mediated Politics: Communication in the Future of Democracy*. Cambridge: Cambridge University Press.
Soros, G. (1997) 'The Capitalist Threat' *The Atlantic Monthly*. 279(2): pp. 45–58.
Swanson, D. and Mancini, P. (1996) *Politics, Media and Modern Democracy*. Westport, CT: Praeger.
Waterman, P. (2001) *Globalization, Social Movements and the New Internationalists*. London: Continuum.
Webb, P. (2000) 'Political Parties: Adapting to the Electoral Market' pp. 151– 68 in P. Dunleavy (ed.): *Developments in British Politics*, Vol. 6, 2000.
Whiteley, P., Seyd, P. and Richardson, J. (1994) *True Blues: The Politics of Conservative Party membership*. Oxford: Clarendon Press.

8

Lifestyle Politics and Citizen-Consumers

Identity, Communication and Political Action in Late Modern Society

W. LANCE BENNETT

Symbolic politics in democratic nations have transformed markedly in the past 50 years. Before the dawn of the global economy, the political arena in most democracies was drawn in broad ideological terms of labour, capital, religion and national mythology. Those symbolic constructions and the social and economic practices that embodied them enabled citizens within nations to imagine both common cause and meaningful conflict, and to channel political action – from voting for or against parties, to supporting or opposing taxation for social projects – into governmental institutions. .

At the height of mass nationalisms leading up to World War II, and continuing into the early decades of the Cold War, the central social science preoccupation with identity and politics was far removed from common concerns about identity politics today. In the 1940s and 1950s, many social scientists warned of the potential for widespread loss of self-autonomy and personal freedom due to over-identification with the grand symbols of nation, belief system and regime. Those worries stemmed from neo-Freudian theorising about the emotional insecurities of unprecedented individual freedom and the temptations of 'escaping' into emotionally programmed symbol systems. Not surprisingly, such concerns were directed initially at totalitarian regimes, beginning with the Fascism that triggered the Second World War, and continuing with the spread of Communism that fuelled Cold War fears (Lasswell, 1952, 1965; Fromm, 1941, 1960). Soon, however, the social analysis of the 1950s began to turn its lens toward domestic life in the democracies, discovering problems of conformity, mass psychology, socially stratified conspicuous consumption, and the substitution of party and group loyalties for independent thinking and opinion (Riesman, 1961; Wagner, 1996; Whyte, 1956).

The late modern period – defined roughly by the rise of global economic and communication systems since the early 1970s–presents a very different set of concerns about identity and the production of political meaning for individuals, society and politics. In the end game of modernity, national economic structures and the social institutions of nations have altered due to changes in global production, communication, and consumption. The cultural coherence of fundamental institutions (families, churches, civic associations, schools, careers and workplaces) is being challenged as individuals abandon old social roles: women leaving the home and entering career worlds, children spending more time with professional care-givers than with parents, and jobs and careers becoming less secure. Individuals today experience more frequent career changes, and greater senses of personal stress, risk and insecurity than in earlier periods of nationally and ideologically insulated economic and cultural life (Bennett, 1998; Beck, 1999, 2000).

This late modern era has spun 180 degrees in terms of challenges to individual identity. The old mass society dilemma of loss of self in the conforming crowd has been replaced by contemporary preoccupations with 'the identity project,' with its daily choices about managing one's persona, lifestyle, fashion statements, body displays, social and professional networks, and complex relationships with friends, family, and associates (Giddens, 1991; Turner, 1996). The concerns of social analysts in the recent period have been focused on the symptoms of mass de-identification with common institutions, symbols and authorities. As they disconnect from broad institutional constructions of identity and meaning, individuals become responsible for their own life choices, identities and destinies, while encountering less predictable social support and affirmation (Giddens, 1991). As a result, stress, depression, psychological disorder and generalised incivility become more familiar characteristics of life in advanced market societies (Lane, 1991, 1994, 2000).

Accompanying the drift from civil society and political institutions is a public celebration of lifestyle diversity and the attendant rise of a confessional and therapeutic media culture filled with talk shows and human relationship reality dramas. Those who still cling to the fragmenting modernist order fight the loss of binding institutions and public moral standards. Threatened by the personal freedoms of the age, once marginalised religious and ethnic orders have entered mainstream politics with a vengeance, ranging from Christian abortion clinic bombers in the US, to nationalist splinter parties across Europe, to Islamic militants attacking secular societies around the world. Much deserved attention has been paid to these fierce battles to establish religious, racial and other forms of imposed political identity (Hunter, 1991; Gitlin, 1995).

This chapter explores a more typical but less theorised citizen experience in the late modern period: the construction of highly personalised forms of identity politics anchored in lifestyles and consumer choices. What are the implications of these shifting citizen orientations both for conventional politics and for newly emerging political forms? Individuals whose meaning systems cohere narrowly around personal lifestyles, immediate social relationships and material values often find government and conventionally organised politics distant and hard to engage. From the standpoint of government and elected representatives, personalised and diverse citizen expectations are increasingly hard to satisfy. Yet when our political lens moves out beyond government, we find new forms of political expression taking shape that often channel individual identifications into surprisingly large-scale activities – such as community service, politically motivated consumer choices, and anti-globalisation protests – that Beck (1999, 2000) has called a sub-politics located at the margins of government. The discussion of these new political dynamics begins with a brief overview of the social conditions associated with the restructuring of late modern societies and the accompanying re-imaging of political cultures.

Social Change and The Rise of a New Politics

As individual identifications with common institutions and symbols weaken, the results may include citizen disaffection from nation states, governments, parties, church religion, and many election-centred patterns of political participation – trends that have been identified both in American (Putnam, 1995, 2000) and in various European democracies (Inglehart, 1997; Beck 1999). These trends have led some observers to sound alarms about the future of common national identifications (Rahn and Rudolph, 2001), and even about the health of democracy itself (Putnam, 2000). However, other observers have noted that society and democracy may simply be undergoing a period of historic change that is giving rise to new forms of political engagement and citizenship – rights-based (Schudson, 1998), lifestyle-oriented (Giddens, 1991; Bennett, 1998), social movement-centred (Tarrow, 1998), networked (Castells, 1997), sub-political (Beck, 1999), and even therapeutic (Giddens, 1991; Nolan, 1998). It is not surprising to find so many different views about the changing nature of politics. As Dahlgren points out in this volume, it is difficult to grasp the shape of change when it is in rapid progress and particularly when observers introduce different standpoints to make sense of it.

Despite disagreement about the future directions of politics and democracy, there seems to be broader agreement about the changing social conditions that confront citizens. The conditions noted below are associated with changes in: a) citizen roles and political identifications, b) the relations between citizens, representatives and government, and c) the ways in which political communication must adapt to get public attention and mobilise collective action. It should be noted that these conditions vary from nation to nation, and among different social, demographic and cultural groups within nations. However, due to the broad effects of economic globalisation across societies, some variations on these changes can be observed in most contemporary post-industrial democracies.

- Social fragmentation and the breakdown of civic institutions – parties, unions, churches and national service organisations (Putnam, 2000) – particularly as these institutions figure in the lives of younger and more cosmopolitan generations (Beck, 2000).
- Weakening social (for example, class) and political (for example, nation, party) identifications due to this greater freedom from groups and institutions (Inglehart, 1997).
- A resulting increase in freedom of choice over social identities, and preoccupation with identity management and lifestyle choices (Giddens, 1991).
- A growing sense of individual risk and of the complexity of these personal choices and political needs (Beck, 1999).
- The above conditions result in a weakening of central authority in public life. Individuals increasingly adopt their own authorities, and make more personal choices about competing information sources pertaining to health, science, moral values and public problems and their solutions (Bennett, 1998; Giddens, 1991).

All of these characteristics of late modern society promote the organisation of public life – its values, activities, and meanings – less in terms of familiar citizen roles based on duties and obligations, and more around lifestyle-oriented service and consumer activities. As the celebration of personal consumer choice fills the public spheres of advertising, entertainment content, and shopping displays, it also shapes conceptions of fundamental Western values such as freedom, rights and political representation. It is not surprising that politicians and interest organisations have adopted more personalised rhetorics of choice and lifestyle values to communicate their political messages to citizens. Indeed, political leaders in most countries have abandoned the old rhetorics of sacrifice and collective political projects in favour of promises of greater personal choices in basic policy areas such as health and education.

Even threats to national security – while still occasions for collective identification – are personalised with stories of heroes and villains. The 11 September 2001 attack on the United States even produced a national message to consumers. After Islamic militants flew airliners full of passengers into the World Trade Center and the Pentagon, President Bush urged Americans to show their attackers that they were not afraid of going on with their lives. He urged Americans to go shopping. In the year following those attacks, during a time of new warnings based on government intelligence reports, a national poll showed that national security against terrorism ranked fourth in importance below such personal issues as health care, education, and retirement security (National Public Radio, 2002).

Lifestyle politics, along with this new political consumerism through which lifestyles are expressed and addressed politically, offer useful frameworks for understanding changing conceptions of democracy and citizenship in late modern society. Some of these changes seem to undermine conventional electoral politics within nations, while others signal new directions of more cosmopolitan global activism. The next three sections of the chapter explore notable changes in electoral politics, popular ideologies and global activism.

The Transformation of Electoral and Interest Politics

The social fragmentation and de-identification associated with late modern society creates a dilemma for parties, political leaders and interest groups. The overarching problems involve how to achieve stable public opinion formation and coherent political mobilisation under conditions of increasingly fragmented identity formation and the decline of unifying symbols. The general result is an explicitly consumerist politics at the formal governmental level aimed at constructing and maintaining publics and their opinions. A core strategy in this new opinion process is to frame issues in terms of consumer considerations and bottom line policy outcomes. In the 2000 US election, the official website of the Bush campaign carried this to an extreme by providing a tax refund calculator in which potential voters could enter their income and family profiles and receive the amount of tax savings they would reap if an elected President Bush passed his proposed tax cut.

This political logic results in a vicious cycle in which citizens take more explicitly consumerist stances across a whole range of relations with the state, expecting more direct benefits and fewer collective goods, and demanding more choice in education, health care, and other areas of state services. This trend is now so pronounced that Christensen and Laegreid (2000) propose a new model of the state as 'the supermarket state,' which they see 'primarily as a provider of services responding to the demands of consumers or users'. Even national service obligations may be advertised in terms of personal lifestyle appeals. For example, US military recruiting advertisements at the turn of the millennium emphasised personal growth and career benefits, along with the fantasy, video game aspects of life in the army. One ad campaign even invited young people to join 'the army of one'.

Marketing Democracy

Professional communication consultants design issues and political positions for the demographic market segments most likely to advance their clients' goals. Given the challenges of finding broad social programmes and collective symbolic frames that advance strategic marketing goals, the political substance of consumerist politics is often reduced to an agenda of better jobs, tax cuts, and selected social service benefits. Broad social projects become difficult to sell unless they are packaged with fearful and negative appeals. Thus, expanding prisons became an easy sell in the US, while schools, libraries, parks, and other institutions withered.

The American populist style at the turn of this century expanded upon its Thatcherite ancestor in Britain, demonising government as a predatory force that limits the power of citizens as consumers and stifles the creativity of businesses through regulation. Promising more from government with less taxation became the winning formula. Yet, when governments, predictably, cannot deliver on such promises, both government and politicians end up falling out of favour, driving up the costs of winning votes back from demanding and self-centred citizen-consumers. Hence the spiralling costs of elections.

The political marketing strategies that have evolved in this era are like commercial campaigns in some ways and in other ways not. Staying on message and narrowing those messages to a few core themes are obvious parallels between the two worlds of marketing. Unlike adverts for soft drink and other products, however, the political product cannot be promoted as shamelessly by the latest sexy rock diva. The endless repetition of media events and messages centred around tightly scripted and managed candidates makes political campaigns a droning exercise for press, politicians and publics. Another distinction between mass-market commercials and political marketing campaigns is that the latter are often aimed at relatively small sections of the public. An ironic implication of this is that product campaigns for wide market brands such as Coke and Pepsi are likely to be far more democratic in their audience reach than campaigns between the Republican and Democratic brands.

The levels of social fragmentation and political de-alignment in American society also mean that few political appeals can be expected to generate more than 10 per cent of the vote. Thus, political messages may be sent to large numbers of voters, but they are often aimed at the relative few who may swing the outcome of the election or a public pressure campaign. As noted by Karl Rove, the chief political strategist for George W. Bush, education became the leading issue for his client because 'This year we picked up seven points in the suburbs over '96. Our education plan allows us to make further gains in the suburbs' (Lemann, 2001: 78). After the dismal failure of his national health care reform, Bill Clinton became a master of retailing small programmes and policies to multiple small constituencies.

Creating Political Brands

Consumer politics, like corporate advertising, is an expensive preoccupation. Even the seemingly simple act of branding a Republican proposal on social security insurance as a 'risky scheme' took the Clinton communication team more than a year of polling and marketing research. Moreover, since most such messages are not embedded in reinforcing social contexts (i.e., groups and institutions, which are now less central to people), they must be continuously reintroduced via the media to keep the attention of publics. To avoid these precious messages becoming lost in the noise of public communication, issue marketing is generally tied to larger strategies through which parties, candidates and interest organisations actively seek to brand themselves. Thus Bush became advertised as the education president, just as he was the education governor in his state of Texas before that. In an earlier era, Bill Clinton re-branded the Democratic Party by remarketing Republican initiatives such as family programmes for the middle class and welfare reform.

Political branding works, in part, because individuals identify less with old civil society groups that fed widely shared public values into politics. Contemporary publics have invested their identities in fluid social and professional networks (Castells, 1997), and in fashionable and socially exclusive *image tribes* that are constructed through consumer fantasies (Turow, 1997). Politicians, parties, public institutions and issue organisations have responded to the proliferation of these personalised social realities by employing the technologies of social marketing, and by adopting the discourse and methods of branding and positioning in their strategic political communication (Scammell, 1995; Blumler and Kavanagh, 1999). Thus, branded public experiences easily extend well beyond leisure, fashion and entertainment, to include the branding of parties, leaders and issue campaigns.

The Permanent Campaign

The communication dilemma inherent in this political branding process is that, similar to product branding, the communication campaigns required to keep a message or an image on the public mind must never stop. Politicians learn quickly that leadership success requires extending the election campaign throughout their time in office. The 'permanent campaign' is required not just for election, but for governing and policy success as well. This trend is more pronounced in the United States, but it is emerging in other nations too (Bennett and Entman, 2001; Scammell, 1995).

As explained earlier, the political marketing never stops because publics must be assembled and held together through continuous appeals that were not required in times of more stable social interests, broader political identifications and more central group memberships that enabled mobilisation through organisational ranks rather than through direct appeals to isolated individuals. A key question in all of this is: What happens to democracy? The short answer is that winning marketing strategies are often evaluated by professional communication consultants (whose advice is ignored at the peril of their clients) less in terms of whether the policies are sound, democratic participation is expanding, or people are happy with government and more in terms of how much political market share they generate for client parties and politicians. Following an address that I recently delivered to a prominent group of political consultants, the most prominent one of all stood up and asked what concern they should have about democracy, since they were being paid to win elections for their clients.

A natural by-product of calculating democracy only at the vote margin is the exclusion of large blocks of citizens from the discourse of elections and parties. As policies are marketed for their vote potential, those who are unlikely to shift the outcome of the election will hear few messages aimed at them. The excluded tend to draw the correct conclusions that they do not count politically. All of which suggests that while the market may be a reasonable principle on which to run an economy, it may be a very unreasonable one for a democracy. Yet, challenging the consumer rhetoric or the marketing calculus of the day is hard to do convincingly since the underlying ideological foundation for the late modern age has become neo-liberalism.

Ideology and The Transformation of Citizen Identity

The equation of free markets and democracy has long occupied the conservative sector of the marketplace of political ideas. However, Frank (2000) argues that what has changed in the recent period is the near monopoly of this position in many national and international idea markets today. With the expansion of globalisation and the death of rival socialist systems, neo-liberalism has been proclaimed the reigning idea system by leading political, economic and media elites in most nations. Compounding this triumph of market democracy, many labour-left parties have embraced globalisation and the neo-liberal trade economics that drive it. Witness, for example, Blair's reinvention of the Labour party in England, and the centrist-business shift of the Social Democrat-Green coalition forged by Schröder in Germany. Bill Clinton also pioneered this trend by re-branding the American Democratic Party in the service of middle class family values.

The resulting drift to the right in public discourse and party positioning reflects substantial public acceptance of personal choice and market deregulation as the leading ideologies for framing public issue discourse. Indeed, lifestyle politics implies an audience focus on consumption and private values. At the same time, many poor, minority, labour and left intellectual constituencies have been moved to the margins of contemporary public discourse. Indeed, the argument in the next section concerning the rise of new activism suggests that political progressives have lifestyles, too, and that human rights, environmental protection, and concern for the living standards of others enhance those lifestyles. Yet a popular ideological reformulation of such concerns in post-Marxian terms is inhibited. Those who suspect that another world (view) is possible are likely to be moved to the political margins with ever-present reminders from political leaders, business chiefs and media pundits that staying competitive in the global economy requires shrinking the public sector and privatising the responsibility for many of one's social needs.

This neo-liberal ideological backdrop of the time means that political consumerism is not just a metaphor for voter choices and policy preferences. Nor is the political consumer simply engaged with social choices – such as socially responsible buying and investing – that have political implications. Classic examples of the old consumer power in the modern period include the international Nestle infant formula campaign (Keck and Sikkink, 1998) and the grape boycott that helped unionise farm workers in California. Such actions have long been used to discipline corporations and economic interests alleged to be doing harm to workers or consumers. These conventional forms of political consumerism still exist, of course, and in some cases overlap with the new forms. The evolving political consumer is a new citizen, either conservative or progressive, whose choices define many relations with the state and whose sphere of political choice increasingly moves outside of government. As Rose explains it:

> Citizenship is no longer primarily realised in a relation with the state, or in a single public sphere, but in a variety of private, corporate and quasi-public practices from working to shopping. (Rose, 1999: 166)

Indeed, many observers have argued that for a combination of ideological and structural reasons, the real power of individuals in society is shifting from the core citizen roles of voters in the political/electoral realm, to the capacity of consumers to discipline the centres of corporate power in the economic realm. For example, Scammell argues that:

> The site of citizens' political involvement is moving from the production side of the economy to the consumption side. As workers, most of us have less power now for all the familiar reasons: technological revolution and economic globalisation, abetted by the deregulating governments of the 1980s and 1990s that systematically dismantled many of the legal rights of labour unions. As consumers, though, we at least in the developed North, have more power than ever. We have more money and more choice ... We are better informed shoppers ... Consumer rights and interest groups ... are now daily in our mass media. Environmental lobbyists and activists ... have a clear and central place in public debate and have demonstrated their ability to score direct hits against the multinationals: Shell and dumping of waste in the oceans, Monsanto and genetically modified foods, Nike and pay and working conditions in its Third World suppliers' factories. Just as globalisation squeezes orthodox avenues for politics through the state and organised labour, so new ones are being prised open, in consumer power. (Scammell, 2000: 351–2).

The extension of consumer action beyond governments and into the spheres of international political economy suggests the emergence of a global political order no longer occupied just by states, international organisations and NGOs, but by growing numbers of global citizens who are making their presence felt by corporations and trade regimes.

The Rise of Global Activism

At the same time that strains are introduced in conventional democratic politics by the transformation of societies and citizen identities, new areas of political action seem to thrive with the advent of lifestyle politics and consumer publics. For example, diminished national citizen identifications and cynicism about conventional politics seem not to have diminished individual concerns about justice, rights, environmental quality or other public problems. Membership of issue advocacy groups in the United States is growing (Putnam, 2000). Moreover, fluid political identities and greater freedom of political choice have liberated many individuals to become more cosmopolitan, learning about and engaging with cultural, economic, environmental and other human conditions on the planet (Tarrow, 2002).

These 'global citizens' now engage in a wide variety of 'politics by other means'. Some contribute to cause organisations that manage the political affairs of busy citizen-consumers. Others join, as media audiences and conscious consumers, the proliferating campaigns against corporations whose global economic strategies have created a sub-politics (Beck, 1999, 2000) that increasingly escapes the financial, environmental and labour regulations of nations. The many corporate (logo) campaigns waged in the current era indicate that activists are applying what marketing experts have long understood: that both consumers and companies are attentive and vulnerable to emotional attacks on unpleasant realities that may lurk behind the brand images of companies and their products (Klein, 1999). As one observer has noted, small organisations can have surprisingly large impacts: 'Increasingly, with multinational corporations gathering unparalleled power as the standard-bearers of freewheeling capitalism – in many countries, more powerful than the governments themselves – they are being held to account by shoestring advocacy groups like Global Witness that have filled the vacuum created by the end of the ideological contest between East and West, between capitalism and socialism' (Cowell, 2000).

The wave of demonstrations that swept the globe at the turn of the century (Seattle, Prague, Genoa, Sydney, Göteborg, Barcelona, and elsewhere) suggests that many different issue organisations are joining in common networks to try to reshape the global political economy at a more general level than is possible just through promoting specific issues or causes (Lichbach and Almeida, 2001). We may be witnessing the rise of a global political movement – one that is driven by the energy of younger cosmopolitan generations who are abandoning conventional national electoral politics. The magnitude and direction of this global citizen movement are reflected in the networked webs of organisations targeting the once veiled network of quasi-governmental economic policy organisations such as the World Bank, the International Monetary Fund and the World Trade Organisation. Following the protests at the WTO meetings in Seattle in the autumn of 1999, a coalition of 263 consumer advocacy groups created a world network under the name of Consumers International to press these global economic policy organisations on a variety of goals related to 'social justice and consumer protection in the global market' (Cowell, 2000).

The prospects for these new cosmopolitan politics are buoyed by the communication strategies employed by technologically savvy activists. Even as the costs of conventional political communication soar, Internet-based global issue networks have lowered the costs of activist communication. In addition, using familiar consumer brands and lifestyle icons as delivery vehicles for political messages boosts the effectiveness of activist communication. For example, using lifestyle logos such as Nike and GAP to brand the sweatshop labour issue has carried that issue into fashion columns, sports reporting and news programmes in a lifestyle language that passes through the media gates more readily than ideological discourse can. Attaching the icon of songbirds to the issue of fair trade coffee has brought networks of bird watchers and conservationists to the issue of sustainable local agriculture in ways that more conventional ideological discourse could not. In short, hooking political messages to brands and lifestyle symbols makes it easier to get media coverage and public attention for messages that would be hard to transmit otherwise to audiences that are not receptive to ideologies or radical political messages (see Klein, 1999; Bennett, forthcoming).

The uses of the Internet to transmit political information and coordinate actions in global activist networks, along with a steady stream of protests, brand attacks and culture jams, are challenging the legitimacy of the global economic order. As these cosmopolitan citizens formulate their own opposition sub-politics, they are demanding new political accountability systems aimed at holding the producers of all manner of products more accountable for the hidden human and environmental costs of corporate practices. Many organisations in this global movement are also exploring mechanisms for introducing greater transparency and public accountability into trade regimes, labour practices, environmental quality and other areas of corporate social responsibility. The development of a global social movement holds the potential to directly engage individuals as political agents in the globalisation process. The development of standards monitoring systems for forest products, food and fashion holds the potential to radically transform citizen roles, ideological frameworks, and the reach of democratic institutions in the future. *These developments signal new directions for global citizenship and democratic participation even as conventional politics within nations may be shuddering under the effects of globalisation.*

Conclusion

As political communication becomes more personalised, democratic systems groan under the rising costs of campaigning required to assemble publics and then to maintain their attention and support. In many cases, led by America, those rising political costs strengthen the influence of business interests on parties and elected officials due to the increasing private financing of polling, advertising, media time and other campaign costs. An irony of this vicious political cycle is that citizens often grow cynical about the corruption and insincerity of politics due to the staggering costs and formulaic results of polling, marketing and communication – even though those costs are driven in part by the challenges of reaching ever more isolated and sceptical individuals. Moreover, since it is easier to assemble publics through common threats and fears than through positive appeals, much of the resulting communication is negative and emotionally fearful. This elevates cynicism to the level of an informational defence strategy (Cappella and Jamieson, 1997).

As the social transformations associated with globalisation undermine the coherence and power of national institutions (for example, the power of nations to control their own internal labour markets and monetary systems), the power associated with traditional roles of citizens – as voters, party members, or organised workers – is often perceived to diminish as well. Yet new political forms are emerging even as old patterns erode. For example, many citizens recognise and resist the erosion of national political agendas and aim their actions, accordingly, at the emerging new centres of global politics: trade organisations, development agencies and global corporations and their products. Activist pressure on transnational economic organisations, along with the relentless targeting of companies in consumer campaigns hold the potential to transform citizenship, democratic institutions and ideologies in the coming era of politics.

The unanswered question at the dawn of this new era of democracy and citizenship is whether a new generation of global citizens will abandon the governmental institutions of the nation state on the grounds that those institutions have become captives of corporate sub-politics and global economic regimes. Can the fight to make corporations and economic systems more accountable to social values beyond profit calculations be waged effectively in the streets and in the symbolic arenas of media image and consumer behaviour? Perhaps the next question for the evolution of global democracy and citizenship is how citizen activists can use the power of a global consumer and lifestyle movement to turn the political agendas of national governments to the challenges of creating a more just international economic order.

References

Beck, U. (1999) *World Risk Society.* London: Blackwell.

Beck, U. (2000) *What Is Globalisation?* Cambridge, UK: Polity Press.

Bennett, W.L. (1998) 'The UnCivic Culture: Communication, Identity and the Rise of Lifestyle Politics.' *P.S.: Political Science and Politics*, 31 (December): pp. 741–61.

Bennett, W.L. (forthcoming). 'Consumerism and Global Citizenship: Lifestyle Politics and Logo Campaigns' in M. Micheletti, A. Follesdal and D. Stolle (eds). *The Politics Behind Products*. New Brunswick, N.J.: Transaction Books.

Bennett, W.L. and Entman, R.M. (eds) (2001) *Mediated Politics: Communication in the Future of Democracy*. New York: Cambridge University Press.

Blumler, J. and Kavanagh, D. (1999) 'The Third Age of Political Communication: Influences and Features,' *Political Communication*. 16: 209–30.

Cappella, J. and Jamieson, K.H. (1997) *Spiral of Cynicism: The Press and the Public Good*. New York: Oxford University Press.

Castells, M. (1997) *The Power of Identity. The Information Age*, Vol. II. Oxford: Blackwell.

Christensen, T. and Laegreid, P. (2000) 'New Public Management – Puzzles of Democracy and the Influence of Citizens.' Paper presented at the World Congress of the International Political Science Association, Quebec.

Cowell, A. (2000) Advocates Gain Ground in a Globalized Era. *The New York Times* International Business Section. Electronic Edition of December 18.

Edelman, M. (1964) *The Symbolic Uses of Politics*. Champagne: University of Illinois Press.

Edelman, M. (1988) *Constructing the Political Spectacle*. Chicago: University of Chicago Press.

Frank, T. (2000) *One Market Under God: Extreme Capitalism, Market Populism, and the End of Market Democracy*. New York: Doubleday.

Fromm, E. (1941) *Escape from Freedom*. New York: Avon Books.

Fromm, E. (1960) *The Fear of Freedom*. London: Routledge.

Giddens, A. (1991) *Modernity and Self-Identity: Self and Society in the Late Modern Age*. Stanford: Stanford University Press.

Gitlin, T. (1995) *The Twilight of Common Dreams: Why America Is Wracked By Culture Wars*. New York: Henry Holt.

Hunter, J.D. (1991) *Culture Wars: The Struggle to Define America*. New York: Basic Books.

Inglehart, R. (1997) *Modernization and Postmodernization. Cultural, Economic, and Political Change in 43 Societies*. Princeton, NJ: Princeton University Press.

Keck, M.E. and Sikkink, K. (1998) *Activists Beyond Borders: Advocacy Networks in International Politics*. Ithaca: Cornell University Press.

Klein, N. (1999) *No Logo*. New York: Picador/St. Martin's.

Lane, R.E. (1991) *The Market Experience*. New York: Cambridge University Press.

Lane, R.E. (1994) 'The Happy Mask of War and Violence: Lessons for Market Democracies.' Paper presented at the Seventeenth Annual Meeting of the International Society of Political Psychology, Santiago de Compostela, Spain, July 12–15.

Lane, R.E. (2000) *The Loss of Happiness in Market Societies*. New Haven: Yale University Press.

Lasswell, H.D. (1952) 'Democratic Character' in *The Political Writings of Harold D. Lasswell*. Glencoe, Ill.: Free Press.

Lasswell, H.D. (1965) *World Politics and Personal Insecurity*. New York: Free Press.

Lemann, N. (2001) 'Bush's Trillions: How to Buy the Republican Party of Tomorrow.' *The New Yorker*. February 19 & 26. pp. 72–ff.)

Lichbach, M.I. and Almeida, P. (2001) 'Global Order and Local Resistance: The Neoliberal Institutional Trilemma and the Battle of Seattle.' University of California Riverside Center for Global Order and Resistance.

National Public Radio. (2002) Opinion Poll of Most Important Issues for U.S. Public. Released May 20.

Nolan, J.L. (1998) *The Therapeutic State: Justifying Government at Century's End*. New York: New York University Press.

Putnam, R.D. (1995) 'Tuning In, Tuning Out: The Strange Disappearance of Social Capital in America,' *PS: Political Science and Politics*. 28: 664–83.

Putnam, R.D. (2000) *Bowling Alone*. New York: Simon & Schuster.

Rahn, W.M. and Rudolph, T.J. (2001) 'National Identities and the Future of Democracy,' pp. 453–67 in W. Lance Bennett and Robert M. Entman (eds) *Mediated Politics*. New York: Cambridge University Press.

Riesman, D. (with N. Glazer and R. Denney). (1961) *The Lonely Crowd*. New Haven: Yale University Press.

Rose, N. (1999) *Powers of Freedom*. New York: Cambridge University Press.

Scammell, M. (1995) *Designer Politics: How Elections Are Won*. New York: St. Martin's Press.

Scammell, M. (2000). 'The Internet and Civic Engagement: The Age of the Citizen Consumer.' *Political Communication*. 17: 351–55.

Schudson, M. (1998) *The Good Citizen: A History of American Civic Life*. New York: The Free Press.

Smith, P.J. and Smythe, E. (2000) 'Sleepless in Seattle: Challenging the WTO in a Globalizing World.' Paper presented at the meeting of the International Political Science Association, Quebec City, August 1.

Tarrow, S. (1998) 'Fishnets, Internets, and Catnets: Globalisation and Transnational Collective Action,' in M.P. Hanagan, L.P. Moch, and W. Brake, (eds), *Challenging Authority: The Historical Study of Contentious Politics*. Minneapolis: University of Minnesota Press.

Tarrow, S. (2002) 'Rooted Cosmopolitans: Toward a Sociology of Transnational Contention.' http://falcon.arts.cornell.edu/sgt2/contention.default.htm.

Turner, S.P. (1996) 'Introduction: Social Theory and Sociology,' pp. 1–20 in S. Turner (ed.), *Social Theory and Sociology*. Oxford: Blackwell Publishers.

Turow, J. (1997) *Breaking Up America: Advertisers and the New Media World*. Chicago: University of Chicago Press.

Veblen, T. (1961) *The Theory of the Leisure Class*. New York: Random House.

Wagner, P. (1996) 'Crises of Modernity: Political Sociology in Historical Context,' in S. Turner (ed.) *Social Theory and Sociology*. Oxford: Blackwell.

Whyte, W.H. Jr. (1956) *The Organization Man*. New York: Doubleday.

9

Reconfiguring Civic Culture in the New Media Milieu

PETER DAHLGREN

At any given historical juncture, the present often appears ambivalent. One finds contradictory processes at work, with any resolution or transition to a different set of circumstances seemingly quite unclear. Unquestionably the present state of democracy gives rise to such uncertainty. In the past decade or so, the catalogue of ills facing liberal democracies has become global common sense, with national variations that seemingly just confirm the general patterns. The formal systems seem stagnant and unresponsive, and citizens are 'dropping out', as manifested in declines in voting, party memberships, and in some places a marked growth in civic cynicism. Even civil society is not faring well, with patterns of disengagement continuing even on this front, as Putnam (2000) in particular has noted. At the same time, though, there have been other developments which give rise to some guarded optimism: there appears to be a growth in extra-parliamentarian political engagement, newer forms of involvement among social movements, activist groups, exponents of 'new', 'single issue', or 'lifestyle' politics, as well as a variety of citizen campaigns and global opinion-building efforts. To what extent these alternatives should be seen as 'balancing out' the negative trends is still a very open question.

For democracy there are thus good reasons to be worried, as well as to keep hold of hope. Seen from the standpoint of citizen engagement, the media's role readily occupies the spotlight: there have been many analyses arguing that media culture generally, with its emphasis on consumption and entertainment, has undercut the kind of public culture needed for a healthy democracy. More specifically, contemporary journalism is often charged with subverting democracy in its political coverage, via its growing commercialisation, sensationalism, trivialisation, personality fixation, horse-race mentality and so on. The charge is often two-fold: on the one hand journalism (and media culture more generally) contributes to an informational dumbing-down of the citizenry, on the other hand it promotes cynicism towards the political system and its representatives, as well as a congruent sense of powerlessness. (Contributions to this large literature have been coming both from academic corners, for example, Franklin (1997); Street (2001) and from media professionals (for example, Fallows (1997)). The more optimistic, upbeat interpretation of the media's role often arises when attention is shifted to the Internet and related new digital media. In these contexts the emphasis is on the newer forms of political engagement, rather than on traditional electoral politics (for example, Bennett, 1998; Bennett forthcoming; Castells 1996, 1997, 1998).

In this chapter I will not be arguing for optimism or pessimism in regard to democracy. What I wish to do instead is present an analytic framework that I have been trying to develop (cf. Dahlgren, 2000) relating citizens' political involvement and their uses of media – both the traditional mass media and the newer information and communication technology – to the concept of civic culture. It is my sense that the theme of political engagement/disengagement and the relevance of the media in this regard would benefit from a perspective that understands citizens' participation in terms of meaningful action and the cultural prerequisites for such action.

The idea of civic culture takes as its starting point the notion of citizens as social agents, and it asks what are the *cultural* factors that can impinge on the actions and communication of people in their roles as (multifarious) citizens. Civic culture, as I discuss below, is anchored in the practices and symbolic milieu of everyday life, or, if one prefers, of civil society. One of the assumptions here is that for a functioning democracy, there are certain conditions that reside at the level of lived experiences, resources and subjective dispositions that need to be met. The notion of civic culture grafts some fruitful elements from cultural theory onto some more familiar themes from political communication. The point of this modest 'cultural turn' is not just to highlight that such dimensions as meaning, identity and subjectivity are important elements of political communication, but also to specify empirical entry points into the study of citizens' media use that can help us to understand various modes and intensities of engagement. These dimensions, in dynamic interaction with each other, can be studied to examine how at any given point in time they might serve to promote or to hinder engagement.

In what follows, I first present a short overview of the civic culture framework, and then model it as a circuit comprised of six dimensions – each of these being a door to empirical inquiry. The actual interplay between these dimensions configures the character of civic culture at any point in time and in any specific social location. With each dimension I try to suggest some possible media articulations. From there I summarise some of the major changes in the media landscape and their relation to democracy. I end with some snapshots from the realm of the Internet, which point to reconfigurations of civic culture within the dynamics of (as yet) marginalised progressive political engagement.

Civic Culture: Towards an Analytic Frame

The search for explanations as to why many people, especially among the young, are withdrawing from the democratic political process, or simply not entering it, and thereby indirectly renouncing their roles as citizens, can go in a variety of directions. Likewise, the challenge to clarifying why in fact people may become engaged in politics – and may even develop new forms of engagement – can be met in various ways. It is my sense that we might be able to understand some of the dynamics of engagement/disengagement by going via the concept of culture. The frame of civic culture is not an ambitious 'theory'; it does not anticipate being able to offer full explanations about citizens' democratic participation or lack of it. Hopefully, however, it can enhance our understanding of human action and meaning-making in concrete settings.

Cultures consist of patterns of communication, practices and meaning; they provide taken for granted orientations – factual and normative – as well as other resources for collective life. They are internalised, intersubjectively: they exist 'in our heads', as it were, guiding and informing action, speech and understanding. If we were to say that culture only exists at the moment of speech or action, we would lapse into a behaviourist view. Similarly, if we argued that culture rigidly steers all speech and action, we stumble into determinism. Culture thus must be treated as providing road markers for likely patterns of doing and thinking, but never directing automatically. There is thus always a dimension of potentiality in cultural analysis – possibilities that we analytically assert exist, but that we can never assume always to be actualised.

The notion of civic culture links up with notions of 'strong' or 'radical' democracy, participatory and 'deliberative' democracy, as well as a view of citizenship that is associated with neo-republicanism (cf. Barber, 1984; Beiner, 1995; Benhabib, 1996; Bohman and Regh, 1997; Elster, 1998; Eschele, 2001; van Gunsteren, 1998; Mouffe, 1992). I will touch more upon these themes below. It thus has a normative base: civic culture is not just a 'good thing', but a necessary one for democracy. Given that the foundation of the civic culture frame is the citizen – agent, this frame is thus interested in the processes of becoming – how people develop into citizens, how they come to see themselves as members and potential participants in societal development. Liberal theory, for example, tends too often to postulate a mature citizen who enters into the public realm, fully formed, as it were. The question of how s/he gets there is largely ignored, or at best is seen as something to be understood in terms of individual psychology.

Civic culture as a concept is not new and my reformulation carries over some traditional elements from political science/political communication. American political scientists in the Cold War era tried to map democracy's cultural variables using large-scale survey techniques together with functionalist views on social integration (Almond and Verba, 1963; 1980). My point of departure is somewhat different; in using the concept, I wish to update it and avoid what I take to be elements of psychological reductionism and ethnocentrism. Also, my view of culture is constructionist and materialist, rather than systemic; it is the connection with contemporary cultural theory that enhances the utility of the civic culture concept. If the more familiar concept of the public sphere points to the politically relevant communicative spaces in daily life and in the media, civic culture points to those features of the socio-cultural world – dispositions, practices, processes – that constitute pre-conditions for people's actual participation in the public sphere, in civil and political society. In short, these preconditions involve cultural attributes prevalent among citizens that can in various ways facilitate democratic life. This view of civic culture has obvious parallels with the work of Robert Putnam (2000), though he does not make explicit use of the term. In his political sociology, 'social capital' is the core concept (see below).

The notion of civic culture that I employ is anchored in everyday life and its horizons, and can thus be seen as an important region of the Habermasian lifeworld, with its negotiation of norms and values (see Habermas' more recent formulations of civil society and the public sphere: Habermas, 1996, esp. Chapter 8). Extending this line of thinking, civic culture, as a part of the lifeworld, is vulnerable to colonisation from the system of politics and economics. Civic culture, in other words, is shaped by an array of factors. Even the legal system is of utmost importance here: constitutionalism is essential, with functioning institutions that can guarantee among other things the rule of law, democratic decision-making, the separation of powers, individual rights of expression, assembly, association, religion, etc., fair and recurring elections and accessible and alternative sources of information. Also, factors of social structure, economics, education, organisational possibilities, infrastructure, spatiality, can all have their impact. For our purposes here, however, we turn our attention to the media factors in shaping civic culture, whose true significance is still only emerging.

Civic culture can, nevertheless, prevail even in the absence of many of these important social, political and legal factors, as we saw in several countries when the Communist system began to collapse. A civic culture is thus potentially both strong and vulnerable: it helps to promote the functioning democracy, yet it sits precariously in the face of political and economic power. It can shape citizens, via various 'technologies of citizenship', as Cruikshank (1999) calls them, such as education – and I would emphatically add the media – that can serve to empower or disempower.

There is a conceptual and empirical tension between the notions of 'civic' and 'political'. Without going into an etymological digression, we can note that 'civic' pertains to citizen, as does the related word 'civil' when used for example in 'civil society'. Citizenship points to formal membership and the right as well as the capacity to participate in the development of society. It also has subjective dimensions, discussed below. 'Civic' should thus be understood as a prerequisite for the (democratically) political, a reservoir of the pre- or non-political potentiality that becomes actualised at particular moments when politics arises.

This tension is replayed in the couplet 'civil and political society'; the boundary is difficult to specify with certainty and may indeed be as much temporal as social or spatial. Usually we think of civil society as the broad arena of social interaction, associations and organisations bounded by 'the state' on the one side and 'the market' on the other. The major empirical problems of these boundaries aside, contemporary thinking about civil society often underscores the socialisation and acculturation to democracy that civil society promotes, a key argument in Putnam (2000). But just where and how does the 'civil' or the civic' become 'political', and what is the relationship between 'the political' and 'politics'?

Here I would refer to what was said above about culture as a potential: civic culture is an analytic construct that seeks to identify the possibilities of people acting in the role of citizens. This is a role which can have non- or pre-political aspects (as often is the case in civil society), but which may open up toward 'the political', and indeed evolve into formalised politics. The key here is to underscore the processual and contextual dimension: the political and politics are not simply given, but are constructed via word and deed. Mouffe (1999: 754) highlights the distinction between politics and the political:

> By 'the political' I refer to the dimension of antagonism that is inherent in all human society, antagonism that can take many forms and can emerge in diverse social relations. 'Politics', on the other hand, refers to the ensemble of practices, discourses and institutions that seek to establish a certain order and to organise human coexistence in conditions that are always potentially conflictual because they are affected by the dimension of 'the political'.

Thinking of civic culture as a resource, a storehouse of assets that individuals and groups draw upon and make use of in their activities as citizens, calls to mind the notion of 'social capital'. Edwards and Foley indicate in their introduction to a collection analysing Robert Putnam's ideas about civil society and social capital (Edwards et al., 2001), that the latter term has a number of origins and uses. The work of Bourdieu and the American sociologist James Coleman are among the most prominent in this regard, yet it is in Putnam's work where the term becomes most directly relevant to the theme of democracy. Here social capital is viewed as residing in social connections within networks of reciprocal relations (Putnam, 2000: 21–4). These social ties involve shared values, trust, reciprocity; they are both an individual and a social good. Putnam's notion of social capital encompasses bonding (exclusive, intra-group ties) and bridging (inclusive, linking up with other groups). He points out that social capital can obviously have a dark side: bomb-planting terrorist groups, racist organisations and so on also have manifest social capital, but in profoundly anti-democratic ways.

These conceptualisations of social capital underscore its character as a *resource*, but the term as such does not lend itself to analysis of the processes of meaning-making. We need to go beyond the social variables and dynamics and make a cultural turn. The following section attempts do this by presenting civic culture as a circuit with six dimensions.

A dynamic circuit

The civic culture concept does not presuppose homogeneity among its citizens, but in the spirit of neo-republicanism it does suggest the need for minimal shared commitments to the vision and procedures of democracy, which in turn entails a capacity to see beyond the immediate interests of one's own group. Needless to say, this is a challenging balance to maintain. However, different social and cultural groups can express civic culture in different ways, theoretically enhancing democracy's possibilities. Groups and their political positions are always to some extent in flux, and individuals can embody multiple group loyalties.

Conceptually, civic culture can be modelled as an integrated circuit, the six dimensions of which have a mutual reciprocity. Briefly, the six dimensions, discussed below, are: values, affinity, knowledge, practices, identities and discussion. Together, my aim in deploying them is to underscore a constructionist perspective and highlight the processes of meaning that characterise civic culture at any given point in time.

Values

It should be underscored that values must have their anchorings in everyday life; a political system will never achieve a democratic character if the world of the everyday reflects anti-democratic normative dispositions. We can distinguish between substantive values such as equality, liberty, justice, solidarity and procedural ones, like openness, reciprocity, discussion, responsibility/accountability, tolerance. Even support for the legal system (assuming it is legitimate) is an expression of such virtue: democracy will not survive a situation of widespread lawlessness. However, just how such values are to be applied in practice, can of course be the grounds for serious dispute – and at times should be. This is precisely why the procedural norms and mechanisms take on extra importance. Resolution of conflict, striving for compromise in situations where consensus is impossible, is a key task for a democratic society and requires a commitment to the rules of the game.

The mass media largely tend to reinforce the commitment to democratic values (even by invoking them in sensationalist scandals), and it can be argued that support for the democratic rights of individuals is something that is spreading globally via media representations. Schudson (1998) in his historical survey of citizenship in the US argues that the cementing of the values of individual rights particularly offers grounds for a qualified optimism regarding democracy's future. In regard to the new interactive media, it can be argued that the virtues of democratic communication – the circulation of information, horizontal and vertical contact, deliberation, etc. – have greater potential, even if that is not always achieved in practice.

Affinity

I have in mind here something less ambitious than 'community' – rather, a minimal sense of commonality among citizens in heterogeneous late modern societies, a sense that they belong to the same social and political entities, despite all other differences. They have to deal with each other to make their common entities work, whether at the level of neighbourhood, nation state or the global arena. If there exists a nominal degree of affinity, for example, conflicts can then become enacted between 'adversaries' rather than 'enemies', as Mouffe (1999) puts it, since an awareness of a shared civic commonality is operative. This commonality is grounded in a realisation among all groups of the mutual need to maintain democracy and adhere to its rules. Community of the more compelling kind, with pronounced affect, may (at best) also exist, but I am here deliberately avoiding a strong communitarian argument as a foundation for democratic society, as I think this simply puts the threshold at unnecessarily high a level.

Civic affinity blurs into civic trust. Here too I aim for a modest level. Certainly a degree of trust in government and other major institutions is important, but in the civic context we must also add trust between citizens. Putnam (2000: 136) distinguishes between 'thick' trust based on established personal relationships, and 'thin trust', the generalised honesty and expectations of reciprocity that we accord people we don't know personally but whom we feel we can have satisfactory exchange with. That individuals can experience some degrees of thick trust is obviously necessary for psychological and social well-being, but thin trust becomes especially relevant in civic contexts.

Knowledge

Knowledge, in the form of reliable, referential cognizance of the social world is indispensable for the vitality of democracy. A subset of knowledge is competencies, and in particular, the skills to deal communicatively in the sociopolitical world are pivotal. Some degree of literacy is essential; people must be able to make sense of that which circulates in the public sphere and to understand the world they live in. Education, in its many forms, will thus always retain its relevance for democracy, even if its contents and goals often need to be critically examined.

While it seems rather obvious that people must have access to reliable reports, portrayals, analyses, discussions, debates and so forth about current affairs, it is also becoming more challenging to specify access to knowledge, as socio-cultural heterogeneity increases and as the media landscape evolves. Access also includes issues of linguistic capacity and cultural proximity. This of course reiterates the need for multiple public spheres, characterised by sufficient autonomy and diversity to address and incorporate different groups. Thus, precisely what kinds of knowledge and competencies are required by whom for the vitality of a civic culture can never be established once and for all.

There is a further nuance needed too. Modes of knowledge are evolving, especially among the young, in keeping with cultural changes. New media technologies can promote new modalities of thought and expression, new ways of knowing and forms of communicative competencies. With regard to both knowledge and competencies, we must take into account the array of different forms and inflections that can exist between individuals and groups. This on the one hand speaks to and for democratic pluralism, yet on the other hand we must be alert to the question of the efficacies of different modalities of knowledge in the face of dominant power. For example, intuitive forms of knowing and expressive modes of communication among some groups may not always be politically effective in a political culture where the elites operate within the terms of technocratic rationality.

Practices

Democracy must be embodied in concrete, recurring practices – individual, group and collective – relevant for diverse situations. Such practices help generate personal and social meaning to the ideals of democracy. They must have some element of the routine, of the taken for granted about them, if they are to be a part of a civic culture, yet the potential for spontaneous interventions, one-off, novel forms of practice, needs to be kept viable. In a sense, civic culture needs meta-rules for breaking the normal rules. Elections can be seen as a routine form of practice in this regard, but a civic culture requires many other practices, pertinent to many other circumstances in everyday life, to civil and political society. For example, organising campaigns, holding meetings, and managing discussions, can be seen as important practices of the lifeworld that have bearing on civic culture; these in turn obviously link up with knowledge and competencies.

Across time, practices become traditions and experience becomes collective memory. Today's democracy needs to be able to refer to a past, without being locked in it. New practices and traditions can and must evolve to ensure that democracy does not stagnate. The mass media obviously contribute here by their selective representations (and exclusions) of ongoing political life, including its rituals and symbols. Yet the newer ICT (information and communication technology) increasingly takes on relevance as more people make use of the newer possibilities and incorporate these as part of their political practices (for example, activist mobilisation via the Internet).

Identities

In the recent expansive literature on citizenship an important theme has been its subjective side (cf. Mouffe, 1992; Clarke, 1996; Ellison, 2000; Isin and Wood, 1999; Preston, 1997). While the formal and legal attributes of citizenship are no less central today, many observers emphasise the importance of understanding citizenship also as a form of identity, often analytically linking this to elements in lived everyday culture. Today, identity is understood as plural: in our daily lives we operate in a multitude of different 'worlds' or realities; we carry within us different sets of knowledge, assumptions, rules and roles for different circumstances. All of us are to varying degrees composite people. For democracy to work, people need to see themselves at least in some way as citizens, though it should be clear that few people find that the actual word 'citizen' gets their adrenaline flowing – what is at stake is not a label, but the subjectivity of membership and efficacy. Citizenship is central to the issues of social belonging and social participation.

To see citizenship as one dimension of our identity may also help us to avoid letting our democratic ideals generate a predefined, one-size-fits-all portrait of citizenship that is sociologically and psychologically unrealistic. There are many ways of being a citizen and of *doing* democracy. Identities of membership are not just subjectively produced by individuals, but evolve in relation to social milieus and institutional mechanisms. We should see the citizen component of late modern individuals as increasingly multidimensional and protean.

Discussion

Discussion among citizens is a cornerstone of the public sphere and a key to most formulations of neo-republicanism, radical or 'strong' democracy and certainly deliberative democracy. This dimension has a 'meta'-quality about it, however: it is through discussion – or, more simply, talk – that much of the substance of the other dimensions becomes actualised, circulated and reinforced. At the same time, the specific attributes of citizens' talk, and not least the factors that can impinge on it, can be seen as an integral element of civic culture. We can empirically investigate civic talk by examining, for instance, its various discursive modes, its spatial and contextual sites and settings, its social circumstances. We might look at what tacit rules are operative in these contexts, and how mechanisms of social etiquette about talk can either promote or hinder the practices of public discussion. Eliasoph (1998), reveals in a detailed ethnographic study the troubling socio-cultural patterns that inhibit discursive practices in American civic culture, contributing to what she calls the 'evaporation' of the public sphere. A good deal of civic discussion today takes place on the Internet, not only in explicit public fora, but also within varieties of online journalism and within the networking of activist organisations and mobilisation.

Clearly, not all the communicative interaction of everyday life should be treated as civic discussion; in fact, I am sure that only a small portion of it is. Yet, we cannot always know in advance just what talk of a pre-political nature will, within the context of ongoing interaction, turn, perhaps indirectly, towards the political. There has recently been some argument as to whether political talk among citizens is best understood as grounded in the informal flowing character of everyday speech, or should rather be seen as a separate and distinct mode of discursive activity. Schudson (1997) has made the controversial case that 'conversation is not the soul of democracy'. His point is that 'conversation' is basically about sociability. Political discussion, on the other hand, is about solving problems, finding solutions to conflicts; it is purposive, goal-oriented. Democratic deliberation is not 'spontaneous'; rather it is civil, public and not even necessarily egalitarian. It opens up the door for social discomfort, seemingly the opposite of what is usually intended with conversation.

However, it appears that Schudson and others are operating with an understanding of political discussion that is rather bounded, indeed, one might call it 'formal'. Political discussion thus is associated with a specific kind of context; it becomes situationally distinct from other modes of talk. One can certainly work with this kind of definition, but the neo-republican perspective would claim that while these formal contexts do exist, we need to look beyond these settings. It emphasises instead the permeability of contexts, the messiness and unpredictability of everyday talk in order to put forward the view that 'the political', and thus the individual's role as citizen, is never *a priori* given, but can emerge in various ways, to which political analysis has to attend.

Democracy and civic culture in the evolving media milieu

The media as institutions that shape so much of our symbolic environment, that provide resources for information, and for interactive communication, become salient – in different ways – at each of the six dimensions. I begin this section by specifying in a summary way the prevalent vectors of change in the media and their potential significance for democracy.

Here we can make use of an extensive contemporary literature (cf. Herman and McChesney, 1997; Lacroix and Tremblay, 1997; Sussman, 1997; McChesney, 1999; Baker, 2002; Bagdikian, 2000; Preston, 2001; Axford and Huggins, 2001; Bennett and Entman, 2001; Croteau and Hoynes, 2001). This literature indicates mutually reinforcing structural and technological trends that are dramatically changing the media landscape, among them proliferation (i.e., ever increasing media output), commercialisation, concentration, convergence, globalisation, and digitalisation.

The general analytic consensus here is that at least in terms of the mass media in the industrialised nations, these developments are not at present contributing to a more robust democracy with engaged citizens. Of course there are exceptions, as one moves to more detailed levels of analysis. The current negative role of the mass media can be exemplified in a variety of ways.

Thus, from familiar angles, we can strongly hypothesise that overarching mass-mediated ideological climates will have a bearing on the dimensions of civic culture. One might suggest, for example, that the observed rise in cynicism toward the political system is in part a response to portrayals that in various ways undercut traditional democratic values and identities, making them appear naive and outdated. The case that is made for the mass media contributing to political disengagement by their very modes of representation thus certainly needs further research.

From a related perspective, in a period when market neo-liberalism has such a prominent position in media discourses, it is not surprising to witness that economism permeates much political discourse. Politics, not least as manifested in election campaigns, accentuates the 'bottom line' of budgets, rising social costs, measures for cut-backs, etc. Normative visions, emphasising democratic values, become increasingly in short supply as financial calculations marginalise other concerns. We find also that the sections for 'economic news', both in the press and on television, have been expanding. This is partly a result of more coverage being devoted to economic and financial matters. However, we also see that many topics of social and political character increasingly end up in the economic sections of newspapers and programmes, here framed as economic rather than social or political issues.

In tandem with economism we find consumerism as an ideological vector in political discourses too. While the role of the citizen has become increasingly entwined with that of the consumer in late modern society and the two can no longer be seen as directly antithetical, the discursive modes of consumerism accentuate market relations and individual satisfaction, rather than democratic principles and such values as justice, equality and solidarity.

As another example, we can note that the democratic values of openness and tolerance, which we can readily link to the dimensions of identity and affinity, certainly took a drop after the traumatic events of 11 September, 2001. Not just the USA, but even many countries of Western Europe, witnessed a contraction of the public sphere in the wake of the launching of the 'War Against Terrorism'. The media by and large contributed to a drastic polarisation in the public climate by reproducing and legitimating the power elite's message 'You are either totally with us or you are supporting terrorism'. This left little room for political nuance or for analysis of the social origins of terrorism. The experiences of 11 September – not least in their mediated form – gave rise to a strong manifestation of civic support among Americans.

This positive turn, however, was embedded in a troubling atmosphere of 'Us *vs*. Them' that emerged in the US as well as in other Western countries, underscored by the harassment of people with Arab or Muslim features. (In Sweden, for instance, a number of Iranian immigrants were also – albeit 'erroneously' – victimised.)

Identities and affinities have also been at stake in the recent successes of right-wing populist parties in Western Europe who have been strongly pushing anti-immigration policies. The road to harmonious and democratic multicultural societies is rough, to say the least, and the origins of racist and anti-immigrant sentiment are complex. While the 11 September events no doubt fuelled these fires, we must also look at the routine mechanisms of journalism. The edict 'bad news is good news' is particularly problematic here. In many Western European countries, large segments of the citizenry have little or no personal contact with immigrants. Their perceptions are shaped to a great extent by media images. In the logic of daily journalism, immigrants figure most often in 'negative' news: social problems, crime, costs for welfare and social services. Obviously there is no quick fix to be had here, but from the long term horizon of civic culture, serious self-reflection is in order. Even the *non*-journalistic positive visibility in the media of people with appearance, speech or names that signal 'immigrant' is crucial.

Among the perennial dilemmas of democracy has been the generally low level of political knowledge among citizens, a problem that pollsters and other social scientists have been wrestling with since the 1930s (cf. Lewis, 2001). As I mentioned earlier, we must be prepared for the dimension of knowledge and competency to take new forms as media culture evolves. Yet, for most of the citizenry most of the time, basic referential knowledge in the form of factual information is still highly relevant, and the traditional role of journalism has not yet been eclipsed, even if its circumstances are changing. The public, however, also bears a responsibility and established patterns of media use are a key – and clearly problematic – element in the practices of civic culture.

It is all too easy to stockpile a litany of negative features about the mass media's role in shaping civic culture. Obviously many claims, assumptions and hypotheses need to be nuanced by empirical investigation. Moreover, it becomes all the more difficult to simply isolate 'the mass media' as unified actors; their power is relative to other institutions and actors and they are by no means thoroughly homogeneous. We should continue to register the positive import they can have for civic culture, even if the gap between ideals and reality is at times painfully large for many citizens.

Net reconfigurations

One of the claims often made with regard to journalism is that the world is so vast and complicated that it is impossible for any one journalistic organisation to cover it adequately. In this light, the emergence of the Internet with its capacities for personalising and targeting information retrieval, coupled with the fragmentation of the public, becomes highly relevant. The media trends noted above – commercialisation, concentration, etc. – can be seen in the newer interactive media as well, even as this distinction between mass and interactive media becomes increasingly difficult to maintain. The older media move into the Internet, and it in turn manifests more attributes of 'mass communication'. The Internet's political economy suggests that its development is quickly veering toward the commercialisation that characterises the traditional media model (Patekis, 2000). It has by now also become an integrated element in the dynamics of global capitalism (Schiller, 1999). Market logic together with emerging legal frameworks may well serve to diminish this as a properly 'communicative space' (Lessig, 1999; 2001).

However, despite the threat to its civic potential, for the time being it is in particular the capacity for 'horizontal communication' that has focused attention on the Internet's special role and status in the development of new or alternative extra-parliamentarian politics.

At the outset of this chapter I made reference to contemporary discussions of democracy and how they often consist of two different narratives, one a lament of sorts, about stagnation, disengagement, cynicism, the other an acclamation heralding a growing vitality of engagement in the newer, alternative extra-parliamentarian politics. While this is a schematisation in the extreme, it still may serve a heuristic purpose here, as I give closer attention to the Internet.

During the 1990s, as the discussions about the poor health of democracy intensified, the Internet was rapidly leading a media revolution. It did not take long for many observers to connect the two phenomena in an optimistic way. That new information and communication technologies are revolutionising just about all spheres of life in late modern society is of course no news (cf. van Dijk, 1999; Slevin, 2000), but there remains ambiguity as to the extent to which they are enhancing democracy (cf. Hague & Loader, 1999; Dahlgren, 2001). Two varying perspectives seem to be emerging. One view posits that while there have been some interesting changes for democracy, on the whole, the import is modest; the Internet is not deemed yet to be a factor of transformation. Among some of the evidence for this perspective (cf. Hill and Hughes, 1998; Margolis and Resnick, 2000; Kohut, 2000) we can find:

- The use of the Internet for civic and political purposes is definitely a minor activity compared to its uses, for example, in entertainment and shopping. Even other, non-news information-seeking on the Internet (for example, health, finance, consumer matters) surpasses that of current affairs and journalism.

- There has not emerged a vast increase in the number of politically engaged citizens. Most people are not politically active, nor have they become so because of the Internet. While the ideological spectrum of discussion on the Internet is broader than in the mass media, this has not had much impact on voting patterns or party loyalties.
- One vision has been that the Internet would empower the powerless. This has not been substantiated, and marginalised groups have not as yet had major impacts on power relations in society.

Margolis and Resnick (2000: 14) conclude that 'There is an extensive political life on the Net, but it is mostly an extension of political life off the Net'. So while the major political actors may engage in online campaigning, lobbying, policy advocacy, organising and so forth, this perspective posits that there does not seem to be a massive political change in sight. The argument is that the Internet has not made much of a difference in the ideological political landscape, it has not helped mobilise more citizens to participate, nor has it altered the ways that politics gets done.

This evidence cannot be lightly dismissed, but what should be emphasised is that this perspective is anchored in sets of assumptions that largely do not see beyond the formal political system, and the traditional role of the media in respect of the system. Indeed, much of the evidence is based on electoral politics, in the US. While the problems of democracy are acknowledged, the view is that the solutions lie in revitalising the traditional models of political participation and patterns of communication. Other scholars alternatively take as their point of departure the understanding that we are being ushered into a new, transitional era in which the certitudes of the past in regard to how democracy works are now problematic. Democracy is seen to be, precariously, at a new historical juncture.

However, any serious consideration of the current and future health of democracy cannot simply dismiss the central importance of electoral politics, as if a more robust democracy will emerge by blithely side-stepping the traditional, formal structures and procedures. New politics can challenge, inspire and help renew traditional politics, but cannot fully replace this fundamental core of a democratic system. We must retain a view that encompasses both and underscores the articulations between them. From such an horizon the various dimensions of civic culture must be seen as ever-relevant for electoral politics, even if it means confronting severe problems. Yet at present, it is clearly in the fissures generated by the turbulence of the traditional media, and changing socio-cultural patterns, that we can begin to glimpse the best hopes for a civic culture and democracy that are resourced by the Internet.

In their recent survey of the available research from political science, Graber et al. (2002) note '… the literature on interest networks and global activism seems particularly rich in examples of how various uses of the

Internet and the Web have transformed activism, political pressure, and public communication strategies .... Research on civic organizations and political mobilization is characterized by findings showing potentially large effects of new media and for the breadth of directly applicable theory' (Graber et al. 2002: 3–4). We should proceed with caution here, keeping in mind that it is indeed as yet a very small minority of the population that is civically and politically engaged online, and that the political uses of the Internet are modest compared to other uses. Yet there, in the margins, may be something profound that is beginning to take shape in how democracy gets done. If we switch lenses and look from this alternative view, there is evidence that speaks for a much more robust contribution. Even a cursory examination of the *kinds* of civic communication present on the Internet – and the engagements and activities beyond the Internet to which such communications often point – will tell us that there is a vast array of serious and highly competent manifestations that reflect and promote robust reconfigurations of the prevailing civic culture. Looked at from the standpoint of any and all of our six dimensions, there *are* clear alternatives emerging on the Internet. I cannot here attempt any comprehensive overview, but will point to a few suggestive examples that seek to foster civic engagement in democratic and politically progressive ways. I use as a convenient starting point for this excursion the website of the Center for Communication and Civic Engagement (CCCE) at the University of Washington (www.engaged citizen.org/). The Center has not only many links and other resources, it also carries out research on new forms of democratic participation, with an emphasis on Internet use.

Among the topics being studied here are the campaigns against the WTO, IMF and the World Bank, as well as the Microsoft anti-trust campaign, various campaigns for human rights and about political consumerism. The anti-sweatshop movement also figures prominently (see the European branch at www.cleanclothes.org). The actors behind the websites have widely different profiles; they range from NGOs and foundation-sponsored non-profit organisations to social movements, political activist groups, labour unions, church groups, professional collectivities from various fields, and even in some cases, commercial entrepreneurs who believe that business can be combined with progressive social values (for example, www.working forchange.com). Some of the activist groups/networks are well-established and have been in existence a long time, while others, such as Attac (www. attac.org/) are newer.

Under the rubric 'Citizen Search Engines' on the CCCE site are a number of what could be called 'civic portals': websites that usher into vast alternative public spheres. Global Exchange, for example (http://globalexchange. org/) is an umbrella site dedicated to 'building people-to-people ties'; it not only has links to such broad themes as the global economy and to many ongoing campaigns, but also to sites offering 'Education for Action', and

'Reality Tours'. Action Without Borders (www.idealist.org/), another civic clearing-house, has links to 27,000 organisations, 186 ongoing campaigns, and circa 6800 volunteer opportunities. That these websites and those they link to support democratic values is obvious, but they clearly also encourage values that are congruent with participatory versions of democracy. The emphasis on activism, engagement, networking, community and so on, points to values that differ markedly from those found in the mainstream media, where collective civic and political action outside the formal political arena is usually treated with restraint if not scepticism. Indeed, there are a number of websites that explicitly address such issues as civic values and community with an educational perspective (for example, The Civic Network: http://civic.net).

The emphasis on networking, information sharing and alliance building also underscores the sense of civic *affinity*. There is a strong neo-republican tone that promotes a climate of solidarity and trust among activists, a feeling of commonality between all those who in various ways are struggling for progressive social change. One is continuously invited to join this quasi 'community of activists'. These are groups that are critical of 'the system', especially as it manifests itself in neo-liberal globalisation, but in a left-liberal reformist way; there is little in the way of revolutionary rhetoric. Looking at an established (since the late 1980s) website like the Institute for Global Communication (IGC) (www.igc.org/), which also functions as a sort of meta-organisation, we find in turn extensive links to PeaceNet, EcoNet, WomensNet, and Anti-racismNet, suggesting some more areas in which new modes of civic culture are emerging. IGC together with other organisations launched the Association for Progressive Communication (APC) in 1990 (www.apc.org/), comprised of 25 active member organisations and 40 affiliates working in 130 countries. The APC provides effective communication and information-sharing to NGOs and citizen activist groups; the IGC and APC also cooperate with the UN in a number of ways. Affinity is thus becoming increasingly cosmopolitan, even if notions about 'global citizenship' are contested in the academic literature. An optimistic perspective on this pertinent theme is found in Castells' trilogy (1996, 1997, 1998), as well as in Delanty (2000) and Barber (2000); more sceptical accounts that underscore the tenacity of nation-state identity are offered by Miller (2000) and Schlesinger (2000).

Within this sprawling political terrain one can notice some social distinctions between the presumed target audience/users. Thus, Democracy 2000 (www.democracy2000.org/) is aimed at community leaders, law makers, educators and the like, while Reclaim the Streets (http://rts.gn.apc.org/) seemingly addresses groups that are younger and less established – and more militant. Such social distinctions remind us of the importance of diversity even *within* the realm of alternative public spheres, yet, despite the different rhetoric and target groups, such sites each in their own way both manifest and argue for strong civic affinities, for the commonality and trust necessary for a viable civic culture.

Knowledge is a strongly highlighted dimension in this terrain. Most of these websites have updates, news, analyses, links to resources, etc.; information-sharing tools are common (including Internet skills), and there is a climate of self-help, that suggests learning by both doing and studying. On many of these websites there is not only a sharing of information and experience, but also coverage of current events – often of course specific to the focus of the website. For example www.corpwatch.org/ monitors the actions of major corporations and financial institutions, while www.oneworld.org/ emphasises news about environmental issues and democracy. In fact, what is emerging is a vigorous and serious alternative journalism. Some websites are even explicitly and exclusively geared to presenting alternative journalism, e.g. www.alternet.org/, www.zmag.org/, www.fair.org, www.indymedia.org/. There are even sites dedicated to critically monitoring the mainstream media (cf. www.mediachannel.org/). While there have been recent studies of what happens when journalism goes online (for example, Pavlik, 2001), even from critical perspectives (cf. Hall, 2001), the perspective is largely on actors from the dominant mass media moving into the Internet. Even a recent ambitious and useful study of alternative media (Atton, 2002) just begins to scratch the surface of this important development.

One would have to make a detailed study of the knowledge and competencies promoted on these websites to speak in any authoritative manner about them. But impressionistically it seems that there is both a strong emphasis on practically useful as well as analytic knowledge, which implicitly and not infrequently explicitly challenges the dominant frames of reference and lines of interpretation that are found in the mass media. In many cases, though not all, the knowledge and competence derive 'horizontally', that is, they are shared among engaged citizens, and have less of a hierarchical, professional register.

In terms of practices, there are of course many that are advocated. It could be argued that knowledge and competency development are indeed among the foremost practices here. A list of the kinds of practices fostered would be both long and unsurprising; we could simply summarise by saying that the kind of citizenship envisioned on these websites is one that is constituted *in and through* practices: democracy is something that is *done*, enacted by citizens in various contexts. This sense of doing democracy is obviously integral to the kinds of identity found. It is through the many forms of civic activity in cooperation with others that one constructs and maintains citizen identities. One can sense a classic dialectic hovering between the lines on many of these websites: they intend to provide the knowledge and competencies needed to participate; the thus empowered citizen engages in practice, leading to new knowledge and competencies – as well as a strengthened civic identity. The mode of address often suggests this. Under www.idealist.org/, for example, is a section for 'Kids and teens'. There we can read things such as, 'Think you're too young to start your own organisation? Maybe you'll reconsider after seeing what these kids have done'. Also: 'Take the lead: have an idea for changing your neighborhood, your school or the world? Find resources, project ideas and organizations that can help get you started'.

Discussion appears on many of the sites, but of course it can be argued that the parameters are narrow, given the relatively homogeneous political character of most of the participants. I mentioned above that the dimension of discussion is a sort of meta-category, where values, affinity, knowledge, etc. are circulated and at times generated. It is this kind of discussion that has to do with reinforcing the general worldview, exchanging experiences, cementing collective identity, and weighing strategic options for activities that is most prevalent, rather than debate between opposing views. On the journalistic sites one finds more examples of discussion with varying viewpoints, though the spectrum of positions tends to be narrow, as might be expected.

As the public sphere extends out to the Internet, and the terrain of new politics continues to grow, mainstream journalism on the Internet will need to keep the communicative spaces open between the pre-political and the political, between traditional and new politics. We should remind ourselves that we are still only in the first stages of a new media era, and clarity about the significance of these media may well have to wait a while, as citizens develop new ways of being 'seeker, consultant, browser, respondent, interlocutor, and conversationalist' (McQuail, 1997: 129).

The trends in modern democracy articulate in complex ways with the evolution of the media. Mediation is entwined with the declining engagement in traditional electoral politics, as well as with the emergence of a newer, informal politics. A functioning democracy requires a creative interplay between new and traditional politics. At present, this development has not appeared on the horizon but a more expansive civic culture framework will allow us to recognise it when it does.

Note

I would like to express my thanks to John Corner for helpful suggestions on an earlier draft of this chapter.

References

Almond, G. and Verba, S. (1963) *The Civic Culture*. Princeton: Princeton University Press.
Almond, G. and Verba, S. (eds) (1980) *The Civic Culture Revisited*. Princeton: Princeton University Press.
Atton, C. (2002) *Alternative Media*. London: Sage.
Axford, B. and Huggins, R. (eds) (2001) *New Media and Politics*. London: Sage.

Bagdikian, B. (2000) *The Media Monolopoly* 6th ed. Boston: Beacon Press.
Baker, E.C. (2002) *Media, Markets, and Democracy*. Cambridge/New York: Cambridge University Press.
Barber, B. (1984) *Strong Democracy: Participatory Politics for a New Age*. Berkeley: University of California Press.
Barber, B. (2000) 'Globalizing democracy'. *The American Prospect* 11(20), Sept. Online: www.prospect.org/archives/V11-20/barber-b.html.
Beiner, R. (ed.) (1995) *Theorizing Citizenship*. Albany: SUNY Press.
Benhabib, S. (ed.) (1996) *Democracy and Difference*. Princeton: Princeton University Press.
Bennett, L. (1998) 'The Uncivic Culture: Communication, Identity, and the Rise of Lifestyle Politics'. *Political Science and Politics*, 31(4), pp. 741–61. Also available at: www.apsanet.org/PS/dec98/.
Bennett, L. (2000) 'Coming into Europe?'. Paper presented at the Unesco conference on *Global Public Space, Media and the Information Society*, Santiago de Compostela, Nov. 16–19.
Bennett, L. (forthcoming) 'Consumerism and Global Citizenship: Lifestyle Politics, Permanent Campaigns, and International Regimes of Democratic Accountability'. In M. Micheletti et al., (eds) *The Politics Behind Products: Using the Market as a Site for Ethics and Action*. New Brunswick, NJ: Transaction Press.
Bennett, L. and Entman, R. (eds) (2001) *Mediated Politics: Communication in the Future of Democracy*. New York: Cambridge University Press.
Bohman, J. and Regh, W. (eds) (1997) *Deliberative Democracy*. Cambridge, MA/London: MIT Press.
Castells, M. (1996) *The Rise of the Network Society*. London: Blackwell.
Castells, M. (1997) *The Power of identity* London: Blackwell.
Castells, M. (1998) *End of the Millennium*. London: Blackwell.
Clarke, P.B. (1996) *Deep Citizenship*. London: Pluto.
Croteau, D. and Hoynes, W.H. (2001) *The Business of Media: Corporate Media and the Public Interest*. Thousand Oaks, CA: Pine Forge Press.
Cruikshank, B. (1999) *The Will to Empower: Democratic Citizens and Other Subjects*. Ithaca, NY: Cornell University Press.
Dahlgren, P. (2000) 'Media, Citizens and Civic Culture' pp. 310–28 in M. Gurevitch and J. Curran (eds) *Mass Media and Society*, 3rd (ed.) London: Edward Arnold.
Dahlgren, P. (2001) 'The Public Sphere and the Net: Structure, Space and Communication' in L. Bennett and R. Entman, (eds) *Mediated politics: Communication in the future of Democracy*. New York: Cambridge University Press.
Delanty, G. (2000) *Citizenship in a Global Age*. Buckingham, UK: Open University Press.
van Dijk, J. (1999) *The Network Society*. London: Sage.
Edwards, B., Foley, M.W. and Diani, M. (eds) (2001) *Beyond Tocqueville: Civil Society and the Social Capital Debate in Comparative Perspective*. Hanover, NH: University Press of New England.
Eliasoph, N. (1998) *Avoiding Politics: How Americans Produce Apathy in Everyday Life*. Cambridge: Cambridge University Press.
Ellison, N. (2000) 'Civic-Subjects or Civic-Agents? The Structure-Agency Debate in Late Modern Perspective.' *Theory, Culture & Society* 17, 148–56.
Elster, J. (ed.) (1998) *Deliberative Democracy*. Cambridge: Cambridge University Press.
Eschele, C. (2001) *Global Democracy, Social Movements, and Feminism*. Boulder: Westview Press.
Fallows, J. (1997) *Breaking the News*. New York: Vintage Books.
Franklin, B. (1997) *Newzak and News Media*. London: Edward Arnold.
Gamson, W.A. (2001) 'Promoting Political Engagement' pp. 33–55 in L. Bennett and R. Entman (eds) *Mediated politics: communication in the future of Democracy*. New York: Cambridge University Press.
Graber, D.A., Bimber, B., Bennett, L., Davis, R. and Norris, P. (2002), 'The Internet and Politics: Emerging Perspectives' in M. Price and H. Nissenbaum, (eds). *The Internet and the Academy*. London: Peter Lang Publishing.

van Gunsteren, H.R. (1998) *A Theory of Citizenship*. Boulder: Westview Press.
Habermas, J. (1996) *Between Facts and Norms*. Cambridge, MA/London: MIT Press.
Hague, B.N. and Loader, B.D. (eds) (1999) *Digital Democracy*. London: Routledge.
Hall, J. (2001) *Online Journalism: A Critical Primer.* London: Pluto Press.
Herman, E. and McChesney, R. (1997) *The Global Media*. London: Cassell.
Hill, K.A. and Hughes, J.E. (1998) *Cyberpolitics: Citizen Activism in the Age of the Internet*. Lanham, MD: Rowman and Littlefield.
Isin, E.F. and Wood, P.K. (1999) *Citizenship and Identity*. London: Sage.
Kohut, A. (2000) 'Internet Users are on the Rise, But Public Affairs Interest Isn't'. *Columbia Journalism Review*, Jan/Feb. Online: www.cjr.org/year/00/1/kohut.as.
Lacroix, J-G. and Tremblay, Gaëtan. (1997) 'The "Information Society" and Cultural Industries Theory', Special Issue of *Current Sociology* 45(4): 1–162.
Lessig, L. (1999) *Code and Other Laws of Cyberspace*. New York: Basic Books.
Lessig, L. (2001) *The Future of Ideas: the Fate of the Commons in a Connected World*. New York: Random House.
Lewis, J. (2001) *Constructing Public Opinion*. New York: Columbia University Press.
Lundquist, L. (2001) *Medborgardemokratin och eliterna*. Lund: Studentlitteratur.
Margolis, M. and Resnick, D. (2000) *Politics as Usual: the Cyberspace 'Revolution'*. London: Sage.
McChesney, R. (1999) *Rich Media, Poor Democracy: Communication Politics in Dubious Times*. Champaign: University of Illinois Press.
McQuail, D. (1997) *Audience Analysis*. London: Sage.
Miller, D. (2000) *Citizenship and National Identity*. Cambridge: Polity Press.
Mouffe, C. (ed.) (1992) *Dimensions of Radical Democracy*. London: Verso.
Mouffe, C. (1999) 'Deliberative Democracy or Agonistic Pluralism?' *Social Research* 66, 745–58.
Pavlik, J.V. (2001) *Journalism and New Media*. New York: Columbia University Press.
Patekis, K. (2000) 'The Political Economy of the Internet' in J. Curran, (ed.), *Media Organizations in Society*. London: Arnold.
Preston, P.W. (1997) *Political/Cultural Identity*. London: Sage.
Preston, P.W. (2001) *Reshaping Communications*. London: Sage.
Putnam, R. (2000) *Bowling Alone: The Collapse and Revival of American Community*. New York: Simon & Schuster.
Schiller, D. (1999) *Digital Capitalism*. Cambridge, MA: MIT Press.
Schlesinger, P. (2000) 'The Nation and Communicative Space', pp. 99–115 in H. Tumber, (ed.) *Media Power, Professionals and Policies*. London: Routledge.
Schudson, M. (1997) 'Why Conversation is not the Soul of Democracy'. *Critical Studies in Mass Communication*, 14(4): 297–309.
Schudson, M. (1998) *The Good Citizen*. New York: The Free Press.
Slevin, J. (2000) *The Internet Society*. Cambridge: Polity Press.
Street, J. (2001) *Mass Media, Politics and Democracy*. London: Palgrave.
Sussman, G. (1997) *Communication, Technology and Politics in the Information Age*. London: Sage.
Tambini, D. (1999) 'New Media and Democracy: The Civic Networking Movement'. *New Media and Society* 1(3): 305–29.
Wilhelm, A.G. (2000) *Democracy in the Digital Age*. London: Routledge.

10

Popular Culture and Mediated Politics: Intellectuals, Elites and Democracy[1]

JON SIMONS

The popular public

The predominance of the mass media in contemporary democratic processes provokes considerable anxiety on the part of many political and cultural critics about the potential pernicious effects of the media on democratic politics. Such critics deploy a variety of arguments to express their concerns about democracy in a mediated age, but perhaps a common feature of their concerns is that the cultural context in which democracy operates is inhospitable. The cultural context is one of popular culture that is produced, disseminated and consumed in and through media technologies. The most influential thesis about the inappropriateness of popular or mass culture for 'genuinely' democratic politics was established by the Frankfurt School theorists Horkheimer and Adorno (1993) in their paradigmatic essay written in Los Angeles during World War II. Their analysis of the commodification of culture, organised along the lines of a capitalist industry, led them to conclude that the very mode of mass culture functions to promote the ideological deception that real human needs are fulfilled by the consumption of culture reduced to entertainment. By organising conformism and promoting a substitute gratification, the culture industry 'impedes the development of autonomous, independent individuals who ... would be the precondition for a democratic society' (Adorno, 1991: 92).

This view rests on a Marxist logic according to which if people were able to make a genuinely enlightened, substantively rational democratic choice, they would not accept capitalist domination. This view has been absorbed by significant tendencies in cultural studies that remain pessimistic about the democratic potential of popular culture. For the pessimists, the commercial and corporate organisation of media technologies entails that mass cultural activity is commodified in a capitalist media industry that maintains the hegemony of the ruling class. If so many people voluntarily consume and enjoy the products of the mass culture industry then they are dupes who are manipulated and deceived by the cultural opiate they consume. Consequently, culture as well as politics may have been democratised, but only under conditions that make a complete sham of democracy. The capitalist economy and the dominant classes are not only unchallenged by popular contest, but actually enjoy popular acclaim.

The pessimists about popular culture are thus also pessimists about democracy, for reasons which are to a large extent grounded in Marxist and neo-Marxist analyses of the social, political and cultural conditions identified with capitalism. Just as Marx argued that political emancipation would not itself bring human emancipation, so do pessimistic cultural theorists argue that what is described as popular or mass culture is nothing like 'a culture that arises spontaneously from the masses themselves, the contemporary form of popular art' (Adorno, 1991: 85). In the case of both mass culture and democratic politics under capitalist conditions, the enlightened, emancipatory potential of popular action is frustrated. I will not take issue with that view in this chapter, as pessimists rightly argue that it is surely problematic that today's popular culture and media industries are structured along capitalist lines of production and consumption. I do, however, suspect that at least some of the anxiety about the mediated politics and some of the pessimism about popular culture relate not only to the constraints of capitalist conditions but also to the actual popular nature of much mediated culture and democracy itself. In other words, I have my own anxieties about elitist, anti-democratic tendencies masquerading as concern for 'genuinely' popular culture and politics. Moreover, I argue that intellectual distrust of popular culture leads some cultural elites to overlook the possibility that popular culture is actually a hospitable terrain for democratic politics, in that it is a risky arena in which the political elites of contemporary liberal capitalist societies are forced to conduct politics.

At the heart of my argument is an understanding that the notion of the political 'public' has expanded since the days of Jürgen Habermas' reading public (1989) and Neil Postman's typographic America (1985), which are discussed below. Since the beginning of liberalism, the meaning of the term 'public' has shifted from a narrower, more elitist sense of an educated and bourgeois public, to a broader, more populist one that refers to all citizens. The incremental equivalisation of 'public' and 'popular' has occurred on two fronts that have huge significance for democratic politics. First, the inclusion of the property-less, the working classes, women and younger people in the electorate with the expansion of universal suffrage means that the political public is now mostly the same as the adult population of liberal democracies.[2] Popular sovereignty became really popular. Earlier on in the process of democratisation thinkers such as J.S. Mill had hoped that the new public would become more 'cultured', but along a second front culture was itself becoming more 'popular'. The public sphere was no longer the privileged terrain for the production, dissemination and appreciation of elite culture, but one constituted by media technologies which generated audiences for entertainment more so than for politics (Dahlgren, 1991: 16–17). The popular culture of print media, cinema, radio, TV, recorded music, video and the Internet are almost synonymous with the growth of media technologies that could reach the whole people.

The consequence of these roughly simultaneous developments is that democratic electoral competition, by which democratic government is legitimised, is fought out not only on the terrain of ruling and perhaps alternating political elites and their intellectual legitimisers, but also on the terrain of popular culture. Media technologies are thus crucial for democratic government because they mediate between the general sphere of popular culture and the narrower domain of formal government (Hartley, 1996: 81). However, one should not think of the communications media as halfway between elite, official, highly educated culture and popular, low-brow culture. Media traverse the whole social array, constituting even publics as erudite as the readership of this book. The point is, rather, that political publics such as those who constitute the 'chattering Westminster classes' or the Washington insider circles must rely on and engage in much broader media relays to secure popular consent. Political elites must be able to mediate with the popular cultural publics constituted by media technologies, which are largely orientated to entertainment and generally commercial and corporate in their organisation. The principles of democratic government require competing political publics, however narrowly defined they are in social terms, to immerse themselves in 'popular reality' which is 'a democratised mediasphere' (Hartley, 1996: 29). My suspicion is that academic intellectuals who lack the cultural capital to operate successfully in the democratised mediasphere instead blame mediated culture and politics for the shortcomings of democracy.

Popular Mediated Culture Under Suspicion

One reason for my suspicions and anxieties is that it is not only Marxist-inspired criticism that has such a low regard for the democratic potential of popular, mediated culture. The breadth of suspicion, if not hostility, towards popular culture from critics claiming to uphold democratic values is a strong indication that such suspicion is not based only in a Marxist critique of the commodification of culture, but also in a certain disdain for the very forms of popular culture. Significantly, a good deal of contemporary mediated, popular culture is televisual in form, combining visual and aural media along with some textual elements. The mediasphere at the heart of our culture is what Régis Debray (1996) calls the 'videosphere', which has succeeded the 'graphosphere' in which print-based media predominate. The switch from one mode of mediation to another has posed specific problems for the particular class of intellectuals (who are now often professional academics) whose mode of reasoning is written and verbal, and whose form of cultural capital has been invested almost entirely in the typographic media. Indeed, there are good grounds for holding that the loss of typographic cultural capital suffered by such intellectuals is the main symptom of the current crisis of intellectuals that Zygmunt Bauman (1992) and Mike Featherstone (1988), among others, have recognised.

Postmodernism and postmodernity appear, according to this analysis, to be the projection of the sense of crisis experienced by intellectuals in contemporary culture and society. Bauman characterises the crisis as the loss of a legitimating authority for intellectuals that they gained in alliance with the knowledge-hungry and knowledge-generating modern state. Intellectuals earned the 'right to tell others ... what to do, how to behave, what ends to pursue and by what means' by establishing 'universal standards of truth, morality, taste' (Bauman, 1992: 14). Bauman exaggerates the authority of intellectuals, but is closer to the mark when he discusses the extent to which the domain of the intellectuals, namely culture, has been absorbed by the market. In this case, Bauman's position is closer to the Frankfurt School thesis about the commodification of culture, a thesis that has been extended by Jameson (1984) to understand postmodernism as the cultural logic of late capitalism, under which culture has ceased to be superstructural in relation to the economy. According to Jameson, the loss of relative autonomy in relation to the mode of production diminished the critical distance discernible in modern art and culture, which was in effect the space in which intellectuals could exercise their critical role. Jameson thus offers another perspective from which to understand postmodernism as the loss of intellectual authority, in this case in respect of intellectuals as critics rather than as allies of the state.

While analyses such as Jameson's are useful insofar as they focus on the problematic relation between intellectuals and culture under postmodern conditions, they concentrate mostly on an analysis of the capitalist relations of production and consumption of culture. Yet, as stated above, there are good grounds to suspect that the crisis of intellectuals pertains not only to such matters, but also to an aesthetic, but not disinterested, distaste for the mediated forms of popular culture. Intellectual authority, understood either as a legislative or a critical function, is not abstract but must be practised in cultural forms and by means of cultural techniques. The authority of intellectuals in modernity was invested in typographic cultural forms and techniques. Following Bourdieu (1984), an intellectual preference for print culture rather than televisual culture, for the graphosphere rather than the videosphere, appears as a difference in class taste through which the ruling classes attempt to deploy cultural capital to assert their distinction. Under contemporary circumstances, however, there is a disjunction between the corporate power of the media and entertainment industries that produce and disseminate most popular culture, and the intellectual cultural capital of the middle classes, which is for the most part still typographic in form, derived from investment in academic education. This disjunction can probably be explained by the transitional character of postmodernism, one consequence of which is that, contrary to Jameson's view, cultural critical distance is sustained between dominant cultural forms and cultural capital invested in residual cultural forms.

It might thus appear that, from the perspective of Marxist-oriented criticism, there is a critical advantage to the investment of cultural capital in print culture rather than televisual culture. I would, however, wish to argue precisely the opposite. The intellectual attachment to typographic culture obscures the critical potential within the contradictory nature of popular culture. While bearing in mind the problematic, commodified character of mediated culture, we should distinguish between the capitalist conditions under which most popular culture is produced and consumed and its aesthetic and technical forms. As Stuart Hall (1998) has argued repeatedly, precisely from a neo-Marxist perspective, the effects of cultural domination should not be read off simply from the capitalist modes of cultural organisation. Equally, the televisual cultural forms of popular culture should not be criticised on the grounds that they are the forms chosen by the media corporations.

The distaste of some intellectual and cultural critics for the very forms of popular culture indicates that what is at stake is not the sort of critical perspective sought by Jameson but the loss of intellectual authority characterised, albeit in an exaggerated way, by Bauman.[3] It is this distaste, which can be explained by the loss of cultural capital invested in typographic culture, which underlies a range of non-Marxist critiques of the pernicious effects of popular, mediated culture on democratic politics. As often as not this distaste for popular culture is posed in what W.J.T. Mitchell (1986: 3) calls the 'rhetoric of iconoclasm' that expresses an antipathy to images. Iconoclastic critique entails the 'twofold accusation of folly and vice, epistemological error and moral depravity' (1986: 197). An example of such iconoclasm is popular cultural critic, Daniel Boorstin's, classic of 1961 *The Image*, which presaged Baudrillard's theme of hyperreality: 'We have become so accustomed to illusions that we mistake them for reality', he wrote of the illusions of advertising, public relations and political rhetoric (Boorstin, 1992: 6). Since the 'Graphic Revolution' (not to be confused with the graphosphere), which has increased the manufacture, storage, transmission and dissemination of images dramatically by means of communications technologies, 'Vivid image came to overshadow pale reality' (1992: 13). Boorstin characterises images as 'pseudo-ideals' which are planned to be believable, appealing to the senses, and simplified.

The pernicious effects of political, commercial and corporate images are to obscure reality, to the extent that people try to fit in with images, subverting their faculties of judgement. 'The Graphic Revolution has made the hypnotic appeal of the image take the place of the persuasive appeal of the argument' (1992: 192), a point that brings Habermas to mind. Just as consumers know what they want from advertising images, so 'the citizen can see himself in the mirror of the opinion polls', so that 'Public opinion ... becomes more and more an image into which the public fits its expression' (1992: 238). The multiplication of images has degraded our epistemological standards, leading to a shift 'from an emphasis on "truth" to an emphasis on "credibility"' (212). The only way we can break the powerful hold of images on ourselves is through an act of epistemological will that allows us to see our mediated, imagistic, commercialised culture as an illusion. Boorstin calls on us to 'try to reach outside our images' to reality, recommending that 'each of us must disenchant himself' (1992: 260). His book, a product of typographic culture, is the means to disenchantment.

Habermas has, or at least used to have, a similar view. In his early book *The Structural Transformation of the Public Sphere*, Habermas (1989) traces the rise of the public use of verbal, critical reason by the European bourgeoisie. The idea of critical judgement in coffee house and *salon* society was characterised by the parity of the participants and the authority of the better argument. The exercise of power was subjected to a public tribunal of reasoned critique, in which the habit of critique was developed by a reading public. Albeit in a restricted, bourgeois and male-dominated milieu in which face-to-face rather than distant communication is privileged, the technology of printing and the practice of reading constituted a public that could claim to criticise government in the name of the people. However, the public sphere has been transformed in contemporary welfare capitalist society so that its embodiment of critical reason has been lost. The mass media generate a pseudo-public sphere in which cultural consumption entails no discussion of what is consumed, claims Habermas. 'The replacement of a reading public that debated critically about matters of culture by the mass public of culture consumers' has been accompanied by 'psychological facilitation' of the digestion of culture in which the optical and acoustic dilute or replace the verbal (1989: 168). Consent is engineered by 'sophisticated opinion-molding services under the aegis of a sham public interest' (1989: 195), while the public's acclamation (often of personalities) is required rather than the rational legitimation of authority. Propaganda and advertising merge as the public authority addresses citizens as consumers. Parties try to woo floating voters using the techniques of the mass media and by appealing images, such that 'old style propagandists give way to advertising experts' (1989: 216). Political messages are reduced to slogans, and appeals are made to 'unconscious inclinations'. In contrast, Habermas argues that it is through verbal communication, through reasoned deliberation, through communicative reason that must be presupposed by the intersubjective linguistic bond, that the enlightened notion of publicity may not only be an organisational and normative principle of contemporary society but can also be institutionalised in democratic practice.[4]

The argument about the depraved nature of televisual culture in relation to the esteemed nature of typographic culture is made explicit by Neil Postman in his *Amusing Ourselves to Death* (1985), a book that he describes as 'an inquiry into and lamentation about ... the decline of the Age of Typography and the Ascendancy of the Age of Television' (1985: 8). The crux of Postman's argument is that 'the media of communication available to a culture are a dominant influence on the formation of the culture's social and intellectual preoccupations' (9) to such an extent that 'media are implicated in our epistemologies' (17), thereby shaping and constraining the concepts of truth and forms of truth-telling available to a culture. Drawing in part on Boorstin's analysis, Postman's argument is directed against forms of mediated communication that debase public discourse, not against the commodified form of mediation as in Marxist-oriented critique.

The contrast between print culture and televisual culture could not be drawn more sharply than it is by Postman. Typographic culture was 'generally coherent, serious and rational; and then ... under the governance of television, it has become shrivelled and absurd' (1985: 16). In print culture, intelligence 'implies that one can dwell comfortably without pictures, in a field of concepts and generalisations' (26). In the typographic culture that typified colonial America and the United States until the invention of the telegraph, literate audiences had long attention spans and could follow complex political arguments. Advertising as well as political discourse 'assumed that potential buyers were literate, rational, analytical' (59), presenting their products in propositions that could be assessed as being either true or false. Postman goes as far as to say that 'the words "true" and "false" come from the universe of language, and no other' (74), even though this undermines his argument that televisual culture has its own concepts of truth and reality, albeit an inferior, 'dangerous and absurdist' (27) epistemology in comparison to a print-based epistemology. In contrast to the latter, televisual culture, which is entirely geared to entertainment, 'requires minimal skills to comprehend it, and it is aimed largely at emotional gratification' (88–9). In one of his most telling assertions, Postman states that 'by substituting images for claims, the pictorial commercial made emotional appeal, not tests of truth, the basis of consumer decisions' (131). He thereby draws the line between typographic culture and televisual culture very clearly. The former is one in which communication is linguistic, requiring developed skills of literacy and attention, in the form of propositions that can be assessed rationally in terms of their truth or falsity. The latter is a culture in which communication is visual, pictorial and imagistic, requiring short attention, and which appeals to the emotions to support a sense of reality 'without much coherence or sense' (79). Drawing on the resources of a residual print culture, Postman calls for national salvation through the exercise of 'media consciousness' (28) and a process of 'demystification' (166).

Does Televisual Culture Destroy The Intellect?

There are many arguments that can be deployed against Postman's thesis, arguments that are also effective against other critiques that implicitly rely on a value-preference for typographic rather than televisual culture, as is the case with both Boorstin and Habermas. An easy point to latch on to is Postman's preference for a residual rather than an emergent cultural form, which suggests that he is clinging to an outmoded form of cultural capital, rather like an early modern scholar berating the decline of Latin and the knowledge of the ancients.[5] Postman also assumes that early print culture was always high-minded and serious, but the early modern press was as given to scurrilous excess as today's tabloids (Hartley, 1996: 24). Postman also misses the point that the 'media consciousness' he desires would require a new form of 'literacy', a set of new skills required for competence in assessing televisual rather than typographic truth claims. Perhaps such 'visual literacy' can be modelled on the semiotic notion of 'reading' images proposed by Roland Barthes (1977) and extended by Gunther Kress and Theo van Leeuwen (1996) into a distinct notion of 'visual literacy'. Or perhaps the very metaphor of 'reading' images is misplaced in that it is locked into a linguistic model of cognition, which, as Barbara Maria Stafford (1996) has argued, is itself symptomatic of a broader logocentrism that still pervades intellectual culture. Such logocentrism can be explained in material terms as investment in typographical cultural capital.

In contrast, Stafford regards 'serious training in visual proficiency' (1996: 22) as an indispensable part of humanistic education, but insists that such proficiency should be based on the acceptance of the 'intelligence of sight' and an understanding that 'imaging ... remains the richest, most fascinating modality for configuring and conveying ideas' (4). She argues for an alternative, analogical, model of understanding by means of images that draws on cognitive science and advocates the 'knowingness of visual communication' (5). She has no sympathy for the prejudice, expressed by Postman, that images 'pose a special epistemological problem, in ways that written words do not' (43). Stafford considers the evidence from a branch of neuroscience to support her case that 'understanding, imagined as a combinatorial and synthetic physical function, has the potential for taking into account a broad range of multisensory endeavors' (8). In relation to this, the linguistic model of cognition underlying print culture appears truncated, desensitised and disembodied.

Although one might do well to be wary of some of Stafford's (1999) speculations about the notion of analogy solving the 'binding problem' in neuroscience[6], she surely has a strong point against Postman's thesis that typographic culture engenders a superior epistemology to televisual culture. One of the main sources she draws on from neuroscience is Antonio Damasio, who argues that 'images are the currency of our minds' (1999: 319) in that thought is a flow of mental images, some conscious, others not, some visual, others not. Significantly, this tendency in neuroscience undermines the belief attacked by Stafford, upheld by Postman, implicit in Habermas and consistent with an entire linguistic turn in philosophy.[7] Moreover, Damasio (1994) would also reject Postman's dualist and masculinist assumption that reason and emotion are not only distinct but opposed, on the grounds that emotional investment is a fundamental part of human cognition and reasoning. Similarly, Daniel Goleman (1996) has popularised the view that a full account of human intelligence must incorporate its emotional aspects, which is obviously as significant for intersubjective relations as linguistic communication. If televisual culture does indeed engage emotions by engaging a broader range of senses than print culture, it may well be that it provides a means of communication and truth-telling that is more in tune with human brains and cognitive capacities, as currently understood, than typographic culture. If that is the case, then it would appear that the logocentrism identified by Stafford in intellectual culture, as well as the antipathy to emotional and pictorial modes of intelligence expressed by Postman, are good grounds for my suspicion that there are some elitist tendencies at work in criticisms of popular, mediated culture.

It may also be surmised that if televisual culture is more in tune with human cognitive capacities it is more 'democratic', in the sense that it does not require the same degree of specialised training as print culture or perhaps even a new kind of visual literacy. Earlier on in the process of democratisation thinkers such as J.S. Mill had argued for a principled connection between democracy and education, hoping that the demand for the former by the working class would promote the expansion of public education, while experience of the former would have an educative effect on the new electorate. Perhaps televisual culture is child's play compared to print culture, requiring skills of attention, retrieval, searching, collating and sense-making that can be picked up through interactive use of digital television controls and the computer screen. Perhaps some of those skills or cultural habits evade the older, linear-minded, literate generation, who thus fail to see the wealth of information alluded to in political images.

Perhaps, also, televisual culture does not require the same sort of attention that print culture does. Walter Benjamin rejects the 'commonplace' argument that new media of reproducible art that depend on changes in the organisation of human sense perception, most notably film, are simply 'a diversion for uneducated, wretched, worn-out creatures [and] a spectacle that requires no concentration and presupposes no intelligence' (1968: 240–1). The mistake of critical and political commentators such as Postman, Habermas and Boorstin is to take the 'disreputable form' in which the new mode of participation appeared as its essential character, thereby repeating the 'ancient lament that the masses seek distraction whereas art demands concentration from the spectator' (239). Benjamin does not accept the dichotomisation of distraction and concentration, instead writing of 'reception in a state of distraction', as a result of which '[t]he public is an examiner, but an absent minded one' (240–1). The new media of art such as film are matched by a new mode of participation that does not require attention for it to tackle difficult and important tasks. While Benjamin's remarks remain suggestive, we should be open to the possibility that the political public does not need to sit through a three hour speech to understand and possibly criticise the ideas and policies, as well as personalities, of democratic contestants.

Or perhaps it may be that the normative concept of attention referred to by Postman has been transformed since the late nineteenth century by new social organisations of perception and vision. Jonathan Crary (1999: 1) argues explicitly that Benjamin's notion of 'modern distraction can only be understood through its reciprocal relation to the rise of attentive norms and practices'. Although new technologies of vision trained observers how to connect attentively to the disciplinary organisation of labour, education and mass consumption, Crary is adamant that even this new form of attention should not be associated with visuality alone but with mixed modalities of perception, which relates back to earlier points raised by Stafford about 'multisensory endeavors' and Damasio about non-visual images. Seen in this light, it would seem that Postman has again missed the point of his own argument that historical changes in the media of communication are linked to changes in a culture's intellectual and social preoccupations, which would include its normative notions of attention. No doubt, then, that the form of democracy and its discourse has changed since the early days of American politics and the largely typographic culture in which its public sphere was constituted. Not only politicians, but even some academic intellectuals have adapted to the videosphere, and perhaps the disdain with which 'media intellectuals' are regarded by many academic intellectuals is further evidence of the latter's desperate appeal to typographic cultural capital. This brings us back precisely to the main argument of this chapter, about whether or not the popular, mediated, televisual culture of today is as inhospitable to democracy as its critics contend; and about whether or not this kind of culture is inhospitable to intellectuals whose cultural capital is invested in typographic culture.

Popularity and Democratic Government

These considerations lead directly into the debate between cultural populists and pessimists raised at the beginning of the chapter. According to the 'populist' perspective, the apparent one-way technological flow of the mediation of culture is resisted by the active interpretation of messages by 'the people' who retain their ideological or cultural autonomy. In broad terms, I agree with the view of Stuart Hall, who has been claimed by both sides in the debate (Storey, 1998: 429), that the better perspective is one between 'the two alternative poles of that dialectic – containment/resistance' or 'pure "autonomy" or total encapsulation' (Hall, 1998: 443, 447). Ordinary people are not cultural dupes, yet the effects of cultural domination should neither be denied nor simply read off from the capitalist modes of cultural organisation. Although there is little dispute that most media, and hence much popular culture, is organised as commercial enterprise, it is also through its commercialisation that so much culture develops popular styles and is made accessible to so many (Thompson, 1995: 10, 27, 76). As one of the populists, Hartley (1996: 47), points out, the cultural publics of modernity have always also been consumers, while the capitalist mode of production and distribution of popular culture does not determine its interpreted meanings. Culture and political consent have been genuinely democratised in terms of their scope.

The extent of that democratisation can be grasped by further consideration of the 'popular'. Hall's preferred yet uneasy definition of 'popular' 'refers to that alliance of classes and forces which constitute the "popular classes". The culture of the oppressed, the excluded classes ... The people versus the power bloc: this is the central line of contradiction around which the terrain of culture is polarised' (Hall, 1998: 452). It is this antagonistic relation that makes sense of a descriptive definition of 'popular' as what 'the people' do, because it is contrasted with what elites or dominant classes do. It is the power relation that matters, not the shifting boundaries between and the content of 'popular' and 'elite'. Moreover, whereas the pessimist perspective regards popular culture as a site of class domination, Hall's approach figures it as a site of a struggle, though 'necessarily uneven and unequal, by the dominant culture, constantly to disorganise and reorganise popular culture' (447). As a result, popular cultural forms are contradictory rather than coherent: 'alongside the false appeals, the foreshortenings, the trivialization and short circuits, there are also elements of recognition and identification' (447–8). In the late nineteenth and early twentieth centuries 'a developed and mature working-class audience' was inserted 'into a new kind of *popular*, commercial press' which was 'organised by capital "for" the working classes' at a time both when the media were being reorganised along technological and commercial lines and popular democracy was being contained (445). Yet, even the present day heir of that press 'wouldn't get very far unless it were capable of reshaping popular elements into a species of canned and neutralised demotic populism' (448). Or perhaps identification with those elements allows for more contradiction than the terms 'neutralised' and 'demotic' allow, terms that indicate the depth of Hall's ambivalence about popular culture and its potential. If popular culture is both 'where hegemony arises and ... one of the places where socialism might be constituted' (453) then the contradictions must resist neutralisation.

Despite Hall's awareness of the contradictory nature of culture, including popular culture, he tends too much toward a dichotomy of either containment or resistance, either hegemony or socialism, because he is still focused on a central contradiction between people and power bloc. If popular culture correlates with the oppressed and excluded, does that not afford it a normative value of 'progressiveness' which would be the inverse of the aesthetic-political value of high or elite culture, something like an inverse class distinction and alternative form of cultural capital? (Bourdieu, 1984). If cultural forms are contradictory, does that not suggest that any such valuation of political culture could adhere only to an ideal type, an idealisation equivalent to the 'authentic, autonomous "popular culture" which lies outside the field of force of the relations of cultural power', which Hall (1998: 447) argues does not exist? In other words, some of Hall's formulations suggest that genuine popular democracy exists in ideal form in popular culture, though the overall thrust of his argument would be that popular culture is one of the places – and I would say the most likely place – in which it might be constituted.

Some of the problems of over-emphasis on Hall's dichotomy between the people and the power bloc in his analysis of popular culture can be read off from an essay on news and popular journalism by John Fiske (1992), who is one of the populists. Following the dichotomy, he looks for distinct characteristics of popular rather than elite culture in the tabloid culture that flourishes in the marketplace. However, his account of journalism is not attentive enough to the contradictory nature of popular culture, and rather too focused on one of its genres, the tabloid . Even in his focus on that genre, Fiske says both that tabloid culture 'flourishes in the market-place' and that 'popular culture is made by the people out of the products of the mass-media – it is not imposed upon them', producing 'information that contradicts that of the power-bloc' (46–7). Fiske implicitly ascribes to the people an autonomy and agency that exists outside the relations of power that produce subordination.

By contrast, I would argue that the popular public readerships of the tabloid news are constituted with their agency as subjects of the power relations that traverse state, market and culture. It is not only culture that is necessarily contradictory, but also agency, because the very power relations that constitute subjects with agency also locate them in positions of domination and subordination. My approach differs from both Fiske and Hall in its focus on the constitution of 'the popular' as cultural forms and the 'public' as both a form of agency and an object of government. The popular public has no agency or autonomy that is not constituted by political technologies including the media.[8] But at the same time that there is no guarantee, as some populists might like to believe, that the popular public will be constituted as an agent of resistance to dominant culture, it is also unlikely that it will be governed as a passive consumer of commodified culture.

As mentioned above, the conduct of democratic politics through popular, mediated culture involves risks for political elites, which is an effect of the gap between official democratic politics and popular culture. This gap is understood by Bourdieu (1984) as a difference in class taste through which the ruling classes deploy cultural capital to assert their distinction. Political elites also conduct their politics distinctly, in language and styles that render it relatively inaccessible to those less well-educated. However, in democratic polities the gap presents elites with a challenge that threatens the legitimacy of democratic government and denies them the level of popular acclaim that they seek. Even as political elites blame the people for their political apathy (Fiske, 1992: 60), they also endeavour as far as possible to connect to popular cultural forms for electoral competition in order to reduce voter apathy, at least among those from whom they expect support. Politicians seek endorsements from and coverage by tabloid newspapers. Like celebrities, they develop recognisable images with which people can and wish to identify, sometimes drawing on their skills as popular cultural performers in their efforts to become celebrities and sustain their public visibility (see Street, in this volume). Recognising that they operate in the same sphere of popularity as the market, political elites turn to the expertise of advertisers to 'sell' themselves. In brief, the competition for popular consent occurs to a great extent on the terrain and in the forms of popular, commercialised culture.

Of course, this 'dumbing down' of politics such that personalities prevail over policies and style over substance is repeatedly condemned by political and cultural elites (very often the same elites that conduct politics in this way), as being the basis for the argument that popular culture is inhospitable to democracy. Yet, this very lament should be heard as a complaint about the terms on which democratic government is legitimated. On the one hand, elites and ruling classes rely on their cultural capital to maintain their positions of cultural and political domination. On the other hand, democratic competition requires them to divest themselves of much of that capital to engage in popular reality, especially their typographic, academic capital. In doing so, they are also forced to engage in popular forms, such as the tabloid genre, and hence to acknowledge, even if only instrumentally, popular claims that contradict their own perspective on reality. The elites who operate successfully in the videosphere must thus generate and invest in quite different forms of cultural capital than the typographic forms recommended by critical academic intellectuals. Democratic legitimation of political elites paradoxically requires them to perform the cultural forms of those who are structurally subordinated in the political, economic and cultural system. Intellectual elites who have no authority other than their typographical cultural capital (which may mean only academic intellectuals) may thus prefer not to engage on the risky terrain of the popular, but instead to expend their residual cultural capital in critique of popular, mediated culture that is the domain of democratic politics. As a result, some intellectuals arrive at the paradoxical position of condemning democratic politics in the name of democracy.

The contradictions that elites must deal with do not arise only in the context of political democratic competition, but rather those contradictions reflect and are paralleled in popular culture. The contradictory nature of popular culture means that the very same TV programmes or cultural events can be both containment and resistance, both regressive and progressive, and thus truly dialectical. In the same way, one might add, political parties and movements can be simultaneously progressive and regressive. Focusing on TV rather than journalism, Fiske (1987) describes the necessary features of popularity in television; features that apply to other mass media and to democratic politics too. From the side of the audiences, he notes their activity in producing a range of meanings and pleasures in relation to a variety of social positions that extend beyond Hall's dualistic model of 'dominant' and 'oppositional' readings. He also notes that television can only be popular, appealing to many different audiences, if it is polysemic and prone to semiotic excess. Ironically, then, although corporate media producers may seek to control polysemy and ensure that their message is decoded the way they encoded it, their products are only popular if they allow for meanings that show some of the contradictions of capitalism or the antagonisms that fissure any hegemonic articulation. Fiske says that television 'promotes and provokes a network of resistances to its own power whose attempt to homogenize and hegemonize breaks down on the instability and multiplicity of its meanings and pleasures' (324).

The resistances that are part of the risk for elites are also in part a consequence of the possibilities for action at a distance that media technologies enable. Thompson (1995: 29) notes that mass communication involves a structured break between producers and receivers, such that the cultural elites have no direct feedback about how their messages are being received and interpreted by audiences. As Hall (1981) explains, the audience is not a passive mass, because signification also requires active interpretation. Audiences 'decode' messages 'encoded' by broadcasters. Encoding and decoding are both moments in the process of mediation that consist of the articulation of connected but separate practices. As media research has noted, the message as encoded by the broadcasters may not have its intended effect if members of the audience interpret it according to negotiated or oppositional codes, or a variety of codes, instead of the dominant one.

One is reminded of Foucault's dictum that 'where there is power, there is resistance' (1978: 95). Resistance to hegemonic or elite representations exists in the inconsistencies between different media producers, different genres within media, different types of media, between media producers and media consumers, as well as between different audiences. Popular culture is a risky terrain for elites because it is a terrain in which versions of reality and practices that produce cultural capital are challenged. Fiske (1987: 326) says of television that 'far from being the agent of the dominant classes, it is the prime site where the dominant have to recognise the insecurity of their power'. The source of their insecurity is not that they are confronted with 'the people' in opposition to their 'power-bloc', but that in acknowledging the interests and styles of those among whom TV is popular, they are forced to produce contradictory rather than hegemonic programmes to achieve higher ratings. The cultural elites that produce TV programmes and other genres of popular culture for commercial consumption can (and do) succeed only in so far as they fail to assert their own cultural class privilege.

Fiske is careful to distinguish between politics and entertainment and there is certainly good sense in his point that resistive readings of TV programmes do not translate directly into political opposition (1987: 326). However, it is precisely the overlap between democratic politics and popular entertainment that makes politics as risky to elites as TV. Perhaps it is because of that risk, and the necessary divestment of at least some of their cultural capital, that so many elites are disdainful of the decline of politics into popular culture. Even the official, mainstream news that Fiske claims does not connect with popular culture is considered to have fallen into an 'infotainment' genre. Yet it is only through the allegedly fallen nature of public affairs and politics that they can become popular.

In part this is another feature of the class distinction between media and political elites and most of their audiences. However, class is not the only relevant distinction. The youngest potential voters are generally keen consumers of popular culture but reluctant to 'buy' the products of the political market. The gap is even more acute when the popular culture of ethnic minorities is not articulated with any political elite. Condoleeza Rice does not rap. More generally, the commercialisation of popular culture means that access to it varies according to economic resources. Access to terrestrial TV is very wide, although the advent of cable has put some areas, notably many key sports features, beyond the reach of many. There are some who are economically excluded from the sphere of popular culture and thus cannot be constituted through media technologies as a political public.

Moreover, commercial culture no more has a secret formula for reaching all its potential markets than political culture does. According to Anne Cronin (2000) the consumer-citizen imagined, addressed and generated by advertising industries more often than not has a masculinist identity based on creativity and innovation. When political elites address themselves primarily to consumer-citizens their message is unlikely to be decoded as they desire by those who do not identify themselves in that way, be it on the grounds of class, race, age or gender. The risk elites face is also one of physical as well as social distance, both of which mean that elites cannot be sure that the risk they take in divesting cultural capital and acknowledging contradictions has actually paid off. Surveys, public opinion polls and focus groups are all techniques employed to try to minimise the risk, but they too involve distance and hence the risk of uncertainty.

The main source of uncertainty, however, does not lie in the distance between producers and receivers, or elites and audiences. In other words, the 'risk' of democratic government is not primarily one of communication, which would imply that the elites and audiences are pre-existing entities possessing their particular capacities, interests and tastes. My approach to democratic politics attends to the constitution of political publics by media technologies of popular culture. Individuals, categories of person and social groups are constituted as publics and audiences in popular culture. Publics and audiences, both elite and popular, act on each other in efforts to conduct the actions of others. In democratic politics the actions of elites are governed and thus constrained not only by each other and the resistance of popular publics, but also by the democratic nature of government.

The democratic 'public' (which is actually a series of sometimes overlapping, sometimes distinct publics) must not only be amenable to being governed, but must also be governed in a way that enables it to govern the government. In a minimal sense the public must have enough of its own agency to replace one set of representatives with another, which relates to the public as a negative limit on democratically organised states. Yet, in a more general and significant sense, the negative operation of public power is possible only if government and the governed are constituted differentially. While democratic governments claim to rule the people in the name of the people, they are not themselves 'the people' but representatives of them. In order to succeed in democratic competitions, elites must engage in and perform popular cultural forms, and so would prefer to be as close to the popular as possible, yet cannot entirely participate in the contradictory character of 'the popular'. Governments engage in risk and face constraint when they follow the contradictions of popular culture, dividing themselves in semiotic excess, sensationalism, parody and scepticism. Governments do this all the time – in effect resisting their own actions – but while this impairs the effectiveness of government it sustains the representativeness of government by performing characteristics of popular culture. 'Joined-up government' would not actually be very popular, in so far as the characteristics of popular culture demand 'mixed' government. Even under capitalist conditions of commodified culture, in which the public is governed by media technologies and through popular culture, the mediated public governs the government through the latter's contradictory participation in popular culture.

Conclusion

The main thrust of this chapter has to been to argue that there is a structural and necessary relation between the popularisation of culture and the democratisation of politics. The popularisation of politics provokes concern that popular consent is not real but mediated, becoming a mere simulacrum of democratic consent. As has been argued, such anxieties are expressed by pessimists in the debate about popular culture. Moreover, they are also similar to pessimistic assessments of the radical, popular potential of liberal democracy. According to this view, popular democracy is a sham because it does not enable genuinely popular consent to government in an unequal society in which the majority are subordinated to the few, or in which everyone is subordinated to the bureaucratic state and capitalist economy. As the anarchist adage goes – it doesn't matter who you vote for, the government gets in every time. Or as Marx understood, political emancipation does not itself bring human emancipation. I would not disagree with the view that democratic societies are still structured by inequality and subordination. However, I would not ascribe the failure to date of representative democracy to bring its peoples closer to human emancipation to the pernicious influence of the media and the inhospitable terrain of popular culture. It is surely problematic that today's popular culture and media industries are structured along capitalist lines of production and consumption, as the pessimists rightly argue. Yet the popular character of culture is not wholly determined by those capitalist relations, just as democratic states are not merely the executive committees of the bourgeoisie. Moreover, I suspect that much of the intellectual pessimism about popular democracy and culture should be understood as a lament about the loss of effective cultural capital, capital that has been invested in typographic rather than televisual culture.

Indeed, could it be otherwise that appeals for consent are couched in popular cultural forms, or that the public of mass democracies is constituted by means of media technologies that depend on and disseminate popular culture? My approach to these issues understands political media technologies not as aberrations in the light of democratic theory but as the practices of 'actually existing' representative democracy. The popular cultural forms of political technologies do not deserve to be condemned in themselves, as no mass democracy could function outside of popular culture. Genuine popular democracy does not exist, fully formed, in the publics constituted by the media technologies that also constitute popular culture. But if genuine democracy is to flourish, it will most likely be in popular culture and through mediated politics.

Notes

1 This chapter draws on earlier published work and conference papers, as well as developing themes from earlier essays. I have borrowed some passages from Simons (2000a) and Simons (2000b). My main debt is to both Simons (2002a) and especially to Simons (2002b), in which I develop the argument that media are political technologies for constituting and governing political publics. Both those articles were developed from a paper presented at the Second

Annual South Carolina Comparative Literature Conference, *History, Technology and Identity: After Foucault*, University of South Carolina, March 16–18, 2000, as well as the *Finding the Political* conference, London, 27 January 2001. I am grateful to those who made comments on the paper on those occasions and in the review process of the published papers, as well as to the British Academy who funded my travel to the conference in South Carolina. I would also like to thank John Corner and Dick Pels for their helpful comments on an earlier draft of this chapter.

2 The exceptions who do not have the right to vote are various categories of refugee, immigrant, migrant, and in some cases, prisoners and the mentally ill. The requirement to register for voting in effect also reduces the extent to which the adult population is included in suffrage.

3 For this reason, I also understand Adorno's (1991: 88) rebuttal of the charge of 'cultured snobbism' as another instance of the assertion of intellectual authority dressed up as critical analysis.

4 I have argued against Habermas' later presentation of deliberative democracy as the antidote to the pathologies of mediatised politics in Simons (2000a).

5 The terms 'residual' and 'emergent' are borrowed from Williams (1994).

6 I am grateful to Arthur Piper for his critical insight into Stafford's overly ambitious argument.

7 Damasio's view is consistent with Wittgenstein's position that thinking is the activity of working with signs, be they verbal or pictorial. See Mitchell (1986: 42).

8 I have made a case elsewhere for understanding media technologies as technologies of government that constitute political publics. See Simons (2002a) and Simons (2002b).

References

Adorno, T. (1991) 'Culture Industry Reconsidered', pp. 85–92 in J.M. Bernstein (ed.), *The Culture Industry: Selected Essays on Mass Culture*. London: Routledge.

Bauman, Z. (1992) *Intimations of Postmodernity*. London: Routledge.

Barthes, R. (1977) *Image, Music, Text*. London: Fontana.

Benjamin, W. (1968) *Illuminations*. New York: Schocken.

Boorstin, D. (1992) *The Image*. New York: Vintage.

Bourdieu, P. (1984) *Distinction*. Cambridge, MA: Harvard University Press.

Crary, J. (1999) *Suspensions of Perception: Attention, Spectacle, and Modern Culture*. Cambridge, MA: MIT Press.

Cronin, A. (2000) *Advertising and Consumer Citizenship: Gender, Images and Rights*. London: Routledge.

Dahlgren, P. (1991) 'Introduction' pp. 1–24 in P. Dahlgren and C. Sparks (eds) *Communication and Citizenship*. London: Routledge.

Damasio, A. (1994) *Descartes' Error: Emotion, Reason and the Human Brain*. New York: Avon.

Damasio, A. (1999) *The Feeling of What Happens*. London: Heinemann.

Debray, R. (1996) *Media Manifestos*. London: Verso.

Featherstone, M. (1988) 'In Pursuit of the Postmodern', *Theory, Culture and Society* 5: 195–215.

Fiske, J. (1987) *Television Culture*. London: Methuen.

Fiske, J. (1992) 'Popularity and the Politics of Information' pp. 45–63 in P. Dahlgren and C. Sparks (eds) *Journalism and Popular Culture*. London: Sage.

Foucault, M. (1978) *The History of Sexuality, Vol. 1*. Harmondsworth: Penguin.

Goleman, D. (1996) *Emotional Intelligence*. London: Bloomsbury.

Habermas, J. (1989) *The Structural Transformation of the Public Sphere*. Cambridge: Polity Press.

Habermas, J. (1996) *Between Facts and Norms: Contributions to a Discourse Theory of Law and Democracy*. Cambridge, MA: MIT Press.

Hall, S. (1981) 'The Structured Communication of Events', pp. 269–89. in David Potter et al. (eds) *Society and the Social Sciences*. London: Routledge and Kegan Paul.
Hall, S. (1998) 'Notes on Deconstructing "the Popular"', pp. 442–53 in John Storey (ed.) *Cultural Theory and Popular Culture*, 2nd edn. London: Prentice Hall.
Hartley, J. (1996) *Popular Reality*. London: Arnold.
Horkheimer M. and Adorno, T. (1993) 'The Culture Industry: Enlightenment as Mass Deception', pp. 120–67 in M. Horkheimer and T. Adorno, *Dialectic of Enlightenment*. New York: Continuum.
Jameson, F. (1984) *Postmodernism, or the Cultural Logic of Late Capitalism*. Durham, NC: Duke University Press.
Kress, G. and van Leeuwen, T. (1996) *Reading Images: The Grammar of Visual Design*. London: Routledge.
Mitchell, W.J.T. (1986) *Iconology: Image, Text, Ideology*. Chicago: University of Chicago Press.
Postman, N. (1985) *Amusing Ourselves to Death: Public Discourse in the Age of Show Business*. London: Methuen.
Simons, J. (2000a) 'Ideology, Imagology and Critical Thought: The Impoverishment of Politics', *Journal of Political Ideology*, 5(1): 81–103.
Simons, J. (2000b) 'Critical Images as Critical Theory', paper presented to the *Social Theory 2000 conference*, May 11–14, 2000, Lexington, Kentucky.
Simons, J. (2002a) 'Aesthetic Political Technologies', *Intertexts*, 6(1): 74–97.
Simons, J. (2002b) 'Governing The Public: Technologies Of Mediation And Popular Culture', *Cultural Values*, 6(1&2): 167–81.
Stafford, B. (1996) *Good Looking: Essays on the Virtue of Images*. Cambridge, MA: MIT Press.
Stafford, B. (1999) *Visual Analogy*. Cambridge, MA: MIT Press.
Storey, J. (1998) *Cultural Theory and Popular Culture*, 2nd edn. London: Prentice Hall.
Thompson, J. (1995) *The Media and Modernity*. Cambridge: Polity.
Williams, R. (1994) 'Selections from *Marxism and Literature*' pp. 604–8. in N. Dirks, G. Eley and S. Ortner (eds) *Culture/Power/History: A Reader in Contemporary Social Theory*. Princeton: Princeton University Press.

11

Marked Bodies

Environmental Activism and Political Semiotics[1]

BRONISLAW SZERSZYNSKI

I want to start this chapter by considering two political gestures from 1990s Britain, gestures captured in emblematic photographs taken during that decade's many direct-action protests against the British road-building programme. The wave of these protests started at Twyford Down in 1992, but over the next few years similar protests took place at dozens of rural and also some urban sites across the country. Protesters at these events were typically drawn from two distinct social groupings – local residents, often quite 'establishment' in background and outlook, and young, unemployed and geographically mobile 'eco-warriors', living in on-site protest camps (Doherty, 1996; McKay, 1996; Seel, 1996). These camps were established at a chosen site on the route of a planned bypass or motorway – generally rural and wooded – and consisted largely of home-made shelters called 'benders'. During eviction by the construction company's security guards and police, the protestors would move to tunnels, tree houses or rope walkways, locking themselves on using handcuffs or bicycle 'D-locks'. After eviction, during the construction process, protesters would turn their attention to the harrying of construction workers and the occupation or 'monkey-wrenching' of construction plants (Doherty, 1997; Doherty, 2000).

In the first of my two images (Figure 1), one taken near Newbury, a distant figure in a yellow jacket clutches near to the top of a lone surviving tree in an otherwise denuded area carved out of woodland. The tree, which fills the full height of the image, has been stripped of its lower branches, and sags slightly to the left over a woodpile. In the foreground two police officers stand as if waiting, with their backs to the camera, clad in bright yellow day-glo costume; in the distance a crowd of figures, similarly dressed, stand around seemingly indifferent to the tree-top vigil. In the second image (Figure 2), taken a few years earlier on Twyford Down, two protesters blow giant horns over the enormous cutting already made into the chalky hillside. Again, day-glo clad figures stand around in the middle distance at the bottom of the cutting.

Figure 11.1 *Environmental road protest, UK. Newbury bypass. The remaining tree in the chase camp has a temporary reprieve thanks to a protestor. Copyright and credit: Nick Cobbing/still pictures*

Figure 11.2 *Environmental protest, UK. Twyford down. Members of the donga tribe lament over the devastation of the countryside. Copyright and credit: Nigel Dickinson/still pictures*

How do we *believe* in these radical gestures? What do the gestures mean? These are emotionally charged images from emotionally charged protest events. But what role does emotion actually have in their authentication as political gestures? How does the meaning of the gestures relate to what the protesters or we might be feeling? How *can* we know what these anonymous figures might have been feeling anyway? This welter of questions raise with them some fundamental issues in the social sciences, particularly those concerning the relation between meaning, intention and interpretation.[2] Where does the meaning of *any* act lie – in the intentions of the actor, in the interpretation of the analyst, in the interpretation of a particular community, or somewhere else entirely? However, I will suggest that the relationship between these perennial questions and this particular research object are more intimate than is usually the case with research objects. Because of the way that the protest gestures under consideration are both intensely personal and intensely public, the tensions and instabilities surrounding their interpretation are an inherent feature of the acts *themselves*, and inherent in a specific way that is not always the case with political acts. The tensions over interpretation are thus turned from a methodological problem to be *solved* to a characteristic to be *understood*. The labyrinth of conflicting construals of these acts should not be seen as something to be navigated to its final, stable terminus, but as something to be mapped and plotted – including its confusions and reversals.

Let us first enter this labyrinth by attempting an initial theoretical reading of these images, reconstructing their visual grammar (Kress and van Leeuwen, 1996). The first photograph is a long shot, which conventionally is used to frame an impersonal relationship between the viewer and the 'represented participants', the figures in the image. Either through angle or distance the latter all appear as ciphers, types; the main individualising feature of the small figure on the tree is the *negative* mark of their lack of day-glo yellow. The second composition is a medium shot of the foreground figures, a shot that tends to signal a social encounter; but the shot is at a sideways angle to the two protesters, suggesting a certain detachment. We observe what is occurring as an onlooker, not as someone directly addressed by the gesture. The protesters are also marked out as different to the norm, and probably to us, by their hair and clothes; the man on the right seems to be wearing khaki trousers and an open tunic over his bare chest; the woman on the left a sarong and heavy boots.

All three people are strangers. We do not know them. They are unlikely even to be local to the protest locations. Neither are they celebrity politicians, like most politicians today, media 'personalities' about whose private lives we often know more than we do those of our neighbours, and of whom we have to make sense as a person before we can understand or judge their work in office (Sennett, 1986: 265).

But at the same time, as political communications these actions are *not* of the kind that we can read in abstraction from the individuals performing them, or from the moment of their performance. There is no simple code for the reading of these strangers' acts. They are not members of parties or organisations whose policies and principles might be read in order for us to understand their actions. Unlike the dramaturgy of earlier models of protest – the CND march, for example – this is a protest that cannot simply be reduced to a simple textual message or demand (Kershaw, 1997: 274). Despite the media accusations of their being a hired 'rent-a-mob', the protesters do *not* appear to us as mannequins wearing a conventional costume, or as actors playing a role. We are invited to understand their signs, their gestures, as in some way extensions of their personal being. Rather like the nineteenth century romantic actor or musician, in their actions there is an emphasis on immediate meanings immanent in the act of performance itself, rather than on re-presented meanings buried in a pre-existing text (Benjamin, 1973; Sennett, 1986: 199). These actions appear as the auratic externalisation of a profound inner passion by emotional-political virtuosi.

However, despite the hypersingularisation of these actors and their actions, they also appear to us as a type, rather as do those who are pictured in the images of distant suffering that Luc Boltanski (1999) considers. Around each of Boltanski's moral patients 'crowds a host of replacements' (Boltanski, 1999: 12). In a similar visual-aesthetic logic, the moral agents in our two images are at once singularised *and* generalised. In terms of the semiotics of Peirce (1991), the protesters' actions appear to us as *indices*, as natural signs that reveal their inner cause and referent of individual commitment and passion as authentically and directly as heat signals a fever. But at the same time the actions also signify *beyond* themselves, connoting through an exemplary logic the wider movement, its cosmology and values (Eyerman and Jamison, 1998: 172). It just *happens* to be this protester, and not that one, who is performing the given action. And as I will argue, just as the individual protest actor is generalised in this visual logic, synechdocally invoking the wider movement in the reader's mind, this generalisation is accompanied, if haltingly, by a second generalisation, that of the *action*. The aesthetic typing of the protest actors in the images plays an important role in allowing the actions to be more than momentary expressions of authentic emotion, and thus to politically signify. And central to the operation of this typological visual logic is aesthetic style.

The aesthetic style of the eco-warriors – including dreadlocks or mohican, boots, khaki fatigues and natural fabrics – is a complex bricolage drawing on a number of different sources. It takes components from established subcultural styles such as punk and hippy, adapts tribal imagery borrowed from pre-modern, small-scale societies, and ironises elements of mainstream Western culture (McKay, 1996).[3] Some protesters adopt a deliberately 'crusty' style, combining dirt – a necessary result of life on the road and in camps – with body-piercing into a 'grotesque' style, a mark of opposition to conventional life (Hetherington, 2000: 96). This can be seen as a specific and highly fertile example of the more general use of emblems or 'badges' – formal or informal, mobile or fixed, conventional or representational, ascribed or elective visual symbols that are used to signify membership of a civic or political community (Szerszynski and Urry, 2001).

The adoption of style plays a role in constituting the movement as a neo-tribe or Bund, a form of sociation that facilitates elective, affectual and value-rational identities and forms of action (Hetherington, 1998; 2000; Maffesoli, 1996). In neo-tribal sociations style is 'a means through which identity markers and indications of belonging are expressed' (Hetherington, 1998: 56). However, it also plays a part in stabilising the political semiotic, but in a way that does not always succeed. The legitimacy of the often-illegal actions depends on marking out the group as one obeying a higher moral law, in a way that lifts them out of the surface of the social. But at the same time the eco-protesters' marked-out nature also makes them vulnerable to being seen as Other in a way that exactly *denies* them the right to speak beyond their own boundaries, to make the powerful prophetic moral claims that they do. Particularly in a style-dominated age the adoption of a style can hamper the generalisation of actors and actions that is necessary to this ethico-political praxis. By entering this labyrinth of unstable and conflicting interpretations I want to explore the dilemmas raised by a very particular kind of style politics.

Social Movements, Style and Semiotic Creativity

Students of youth culture such as Paul Willis argue that symbolic activity is not some expendable luxury, but 'necessary work', necessary to human life – 'not extra but essential to ensure the daily production and reproduction of human existence' (Willis, 1990: 9). However, Willis argues that such activity does not just reproduce but can transform – the interest is not just in the symbolic activity but crucially in symbolic *creativity*. They are interested in the shifts in the meaning of words, things and practices – however small – that people are able to effect (1990: 11).

In order better to understand this symbolic creativity it is useful to draw on Saussure's (1966) distinction between *langue* and *parole*. Language (*langue*) is a system, an autonomous, abstract set of rules and conventions of meaning (semantics) and combination (syntax); speech (*parole*) is an individual act of communication, which draws on and selects from language in the abstract. This is related to another distinction made by Saussure, that between paradigmatic and syntagmatic relationships between signs. A paradigm is a set of signs within a given language system from which we can make a selection. A syntagm is a combination of chosen signs made in a particular performance of language (*parole*), whether spoken or written. So in acts of communication or semiosis, *parole*, we draw on *langue*, consciously or unconsciously selecting elements from paradigms, and combining them into syntagms.

But in the notion of symbolic creativity in youth cultures, Willis is saying *more* than that people have freedom of choice to select from paradigms as they construct their syntagms – that the act of *parole* is a free operation within the fixed system of a *langue*. He seems to be suggesting that people also have the ability to alter systems of meanings, to shift signs from one paradigm to another, to detach signifiers from a given signified and attach them to another, and so on. Conditions of contemporary consumer capitalism, where signs are commodified and further destabilised by their circulation outside natural, 'organic' communities of communication and reception, can give ordinary people more agency in symbolic practices. Received signs can be turned into 'made messages', given new, personal or group-based meanings, and sent out again through different communities. Making messages in this way, adapting and reusing in everyday life the circulating signs of modern culture, is for Willis a key part of symbolic work and creativity (Willis, 1990: 133–7).

Just as cultural theorists have focused on youth culture as a particularly intense site of cultural and semiotic creativity, something similar might be said for social movements. For the Italian sociologist Alberto Melucci, new social movements such as environmentalism are *also* cultural laboratories for the generation of new – and in their case overtly oppositional – codes. He suggests that in a highly mediatised information age, power resides largely at the level of control over symbolic codes and schemes of meaning, so it is here that social movements increasingly concentrate their work – at the level of symbol and meaning. At the public, political level, movements thus engage primarily in acts of symbolic challenge to dominant understandings. At the level of everyday life, such movements act as enclaves of experimentation, within which individuals do not so much satisfy personal needs, but enact different forms of life, forms that rely on the contestation and altering of society's dominant codes (Melucci, 1989; 1996).

In a similar way, Eyerman and Jamison in their discussion of the role of music in the life of social movements argue that social movements are deeply cultural, providing a context for cultural expression and innovation, and drawing on cultural activities as resources for political praxis (Eyerman and Jamison, 1998). Social movements invent new aesthetic principles and collective rituals to sustain themselves and communicate with wider society, and at the same time can also act as a source for new ideas, aesthetics and practices that diffuse into wider society.

But symbolic creativity in subcultures is not simply a continuous fluid process of change. Youth subcultures have been analysed in terms of the internal coherence of the ensemble of objects and the kinds of behaviour that their creativity produces – their *style* (Hebdige, 1979). Drawing on the work of the anthropologist Lévi-Strauss, Hebdige describes style in terms of *bricolage* and homology (Lévi-Strauss, 1962). Style is assembled out of its constituent elements – dress, appearance, language, music genres, bodily comportment etc. – through a process of selection, combination and recontextualisation. Within this style each element can be seen as homologous, as symbolically fitting, with each of the other elements.

Social movements can exhibit high degrees of homology in their material style, in that elements of style are used to symbolise values and commitments.

In his analysis of the performance of identity in social movements, Kevin Hetherington distinguishes between identity and identification. Identity is play, bricolage, the combination of discrete elements from diverse contexts in a topologically complex ensemble. Identification, in contrast, encourages homology, the ordering of elements into some coherent package (Hetherington, 1998: 28). Hetherington points out that, unlike the genuine pre-modern *bricoleur*, contemporary subcultures 'begin with the homology rather than the bricolage', in that they 'begin with a set of values and beliefs that helps order the outlook on the world', and on the basis of these values select elements to build into their style that are already consistent with these values (2000: 98–9). We can go on to observe that within *oppositional* subcultures such as those under consideration here, the homology is often even greater than in other subcultures. The value-rational character of oppositional sociations, and their outward-facing dimension to their group habitus, their desire to speak to the rest of society, means that their *bricolage* is at least partly governed by and expressive of their cosmology and values (Eyerman and Jamison, 1991; 1998).

Publicity, Actors and Artists

But how do these sociations signify to the rest of society, and what role does their subcultural style play in this signification? In order better to understand both the distinctive nature of this kind of political semiotic, and the specific problems it faces, it is useful to return to Richard Sennett's seminal account of the rise and fall of 'public man'. Sennett makes a case for a parallelism between theatre and urban public life, suggesting that eighteenth century theatre provided a cultural resource that helped make possible the urban public sphere (Sennett, 1986: 38–42). First, both face the shared problem of arousing among an audience forms of belief in the persons and actions of those unknown to us. In the urban world of strangers, as in a theatre, the meaning and sincerity of utterances and gestures cannot be stabilised by reference to any knowledge of the person's private life, since as a rule we have no access to it. Second, both realms offer a shared solution, in the form of rules of audience response, rules that restrict interpretation to the immediate context but provide ways nevertheless of meaningfully interpreting and responding to actions. Third, modern urban life was made possible by the rise of a public geography beyond the local and intimate, ordered by this common code of how to read and move through it, involving a concomitant imaginary which facilitated the belief in people personally unknown to us. Fourth, this public geography and its common code enabled a genuinely public mode of expression, where utterances and gestures are read in a way that necessarily detaches them from the enunciator, itself a precondition for modern politics. In a public geography social expression is seen 'as presentation to other people of feelings which signify in and of themselves, rather than as representation to other people of feelings present and real to each self' (1986: 39).

In the eighteenth century this social expression relied heavily on a dress code. Although in homes at that time all classes wore simple, loose-fitting natural garments that were expressive of the body and its needs, on the street dress was increasingly used conventionally, to mark out social positions. Whether or not the social position implied by the costume corresponded to that of the wearer was less important than that it was recognisable. Similarly, there was little interest in adapting or customising costumes to better express the identity of the wearer. The point was not so that people would know with whom they were dealing, but that, on the public street, through dress codes people were able to behave *as if* they knew with whom they were dealing. Public life was constituted through what might be called an 'actorly' metaphor. The real person, the mannequin on whom the costume was draped, was a mystery – one engaged with the character not the actor behind it. Interpreting people's actions did not require one to penetrate through to their private persona and intentions; interpretations were grounded not in a metaphysic of interiority but in an agreed conventional code.

It was only in the nineteenth century that this artificiality was replaced by a more expressive use of clothes and public performance. In the emergent notion of the modern 'personality', appearances were seen as revealing and expressing the real self – masks were faces (Sennett, 1986: 152). In this new situation dealing with strangers became the more complex task of reading the individual behind and expressed in the costume. In public life expression turned from the presentation of a mask to the authentic revelation of one's unique personality, and the problems of discerning what is authentically felt – by others, but by oneself too. A complementary source for understanding this shift is provided by Lionel Trilling in his account of the displacement in nineteenth century public life of an ethos of sincerity by one of authenticity (Trilling, 1972). Whereas *sincerity* relies on the private–public distinction, in that it consists in the public expression of private feelings, *authenticity* requires its erasure, in that authentic expression is understood as the continuous revelation of inner feeling. In sincerity, expression to others may include disguise and self-censorship, as the focus is still on the content of what is expressed; in authenticity, the focus shifts to genuineness – whatever is felt has to be revealed. The realisation and expression of one's true, inner self becomes a moral duty in its own right (Taylor, 1991). With the shift from sincerity to authenticity, Sennett suggests, comes the breakdown of publicity, its replacement by a semiotic regime of subjectivised expression, and the loss of the objectivity of signs.

In contemporary protest actions, I want to suggest, we can see a further step in this move away from 'actorly' notions of public performances towards more 'artistic' ones, but this time it is a step *back* into the public realm, claiming a different and more passionate kind of objectivity. In order to explore this, let us return to the gestures of the strangers in my opening images, and the philosophical questions they raise. How do we ground our interpretation of them? By reference to a shared impersonal code of political expression? In the form of our own moral response as audience (Boltanski, 1999)? Or in their own authenticity, flowing as they appear to do from the authentic moral feeling of the protesters?[4] The protesters are strangers, but strangers who use an expressive, subjectivised semiotic code, rather than an objective, public one. However, they are also marked-out strangers – strangers who expend some of their cultural work in distinguishing themselves from wider society. In the next section I will explore the role this plays in constituting the movement as a cultural laboratory – a sociation that can experiment with new semiotic codes. In the following section I will discuss the role this marking-out also plays in the 'political generalisation' of their protest actions – the task of making them signify beyond the act itself, invoking the wider values and cosmology of the movement.

Citizenship and Difference

If environmentalists want themselves and their actions to signify more widely – to speak *to* the world, and to speak *for* the planet – why would they want to mark themselves out as different? To survive and to function as a cultural laboratory, a certain degree of marking-out is essential. But I am suggesting that something else is also going on here – that the marking-out is integral to their functioning as a sign to society as a whole (Melucci, 1989: 60; 1996: 357–60). The link between the visual marking-out of social groups and their appearance as citizens has been made by others. Hannah Arendt pointed out that, as the labouring classes started to take a public role as participants in society, they felt compelled to adopt their own costume, the *sans-culotte*, which gave them their name in the French Revolution. For Arendt this visual marking-out of themselves as a distinct group was necessary if their group interests were not to be simply absorbed into the rest of the social sphere as private interests.[5] Ironically, it thereby allowed them for a time to represent not just themselves and their own group interests but the people *as a whole* (Arendt, 1998: 217–9).

It could perhaps be said that radical environmentalists in a similar way mark themselves out as a group in order to try to speak for the *world* as a whole. Even sympathetic media reporting sometimes subverts this marking-out as a group – either by marking out individuals as celebrity eco-warriors such as 'Swampy' or 'Animal', or by erasing the boundary between them and wider society by saying they are just ordinary middle-class children (Paterson, 2000; Wykes, 2000). And as we shall see below even when the media does reproduce the marking-out of protesters as a group, readers can often view this not as legitimising the protest but delegitimising it, encouraging a reading of the protester's actions as the mere performance of a subcultural habitus. However, let us for now focus on this marking-out – how it is achieved through presentational codes and shared argots, how it might function to generalise the actions of the protesters into the political semiotic realm, but also how it might also sometimes subvert this political generalisation.

Kevin Hetherington argues that protest actions and more everyday behaviour within the protest subculture are performances of identity 'recognisable to others who share a particular identification' (1998). Such a move is one way to encourage a focus on what can be called *presentational* rather than representational codes in social movement action and communication.[6] *Representational* codes are referential, cognitive, or ideational; they can stand for something outside the act of communication and those involved in it, can convey information about absent things, past, future or possible events. They are generally inscribed in a durable medium, so that they can have an independent existence beyond the moment of performance. *Presentational* codes are usually made physically, bodily, in speech or gesture, by one person to a co-present other, although they can be encoded in representational media, and especially electronic media (McLuhan, 1962; Ong, 1982). They are highly indexical, not normally or directly standing for something outside the communicator or act of communication. They convey information (deliberately or otherwise) about the communicator – their identity, values, emotions etc. – and are also used in 'interaction' management (Goffman, 1972).

This distinction relates to one made in speech act theory (Austin, 1975; Butler, 1997; Evans, 1969; Searle, 1969; 1979; 1985) in terms of the difference between different classes of speech acts. Speech acts are 'things we do with words', which include not just making statements but also things like apologising, promising, requesting. Each class of speech acts has different 'felicity conditions', conditions that have to be met for them to succeed as acts of communication; unlike *statements*, for example, *apologies* cannot be judged as true or false, only as authentic or bogus, too early or too late. Similarly, self-revealing communications, which communicate who we are or how we feel, are not necessarily representing anything outside that. Any given act of communication might be anywhere on a spectrum of admixture between the purely representational and the purely presentational. Issues of style are clearly towards the presentational end – but what about the two emblematic gestures with which I opened this chapter? As presentational codes, are they confined in their significatory power to merely revealing inner, subjective feeling and commitment? Or can they also signify beyond the authentic act itself, without being encoded as a representational text? Eyerman and Jamison provide a direct link between presentational codes and political action in their notion of 'exemplary action' (Eyerman and Jamison, 1998: 23), the way that movements and their actions can symbolise what the movement stands for. Exemplary action is 'self-revelatory; through it an actor reveals her own intimate image of herself and how she would like others to see her'. But at the same time exemplary action also 'aims at communicating a vision of what the world could be like to others' (1998: 172).

Codes of all sorts can also be more or less bound to particular communities. All communication between two or more parties requires their co-membership of a speaking and interpreting community, but some forms of communication seem to be more rooted in community and context than others. This was the sort of idea that led Basil Bernstein (1973) to develop the notion of elaborated and restricted codes in his study of class and education, suggesting that middle class children tended to use elaborated code, and working class children restricted code. Although the distinction has been criticised for seeming to essentialise and denigrate working class linguistic capacities, nevertheless it is a useful way of attending to the different kinds of speech that can evolve in different contexts, where the work it has to do is of a very different kind. In comparison with elaborated codes, restricted codes are simpler, in vocabulary and syntax; are more oral and make more use of non-verbal cues; are more presentational and less representational; express concrete and present things rather than abstract and absent things; rely on shared background, cultural experience, assumptions; and reinforce similarities and group membership between speaker and listener.

Elsewhere I have argued that the use of shared argots helps to define group membership in environmental movements in a similar way to presentational codes (Szerszynski, 2002). I use the distinction used in relation to religious cultures between 'orthodoxy' and 'othropraxy' – between religions that place an emphasis on doctrinal conformity and those that place greater stress on external behaviour and appearance. Orthodoxic approaches are favoured by traditions that seek to transcend particular ethnic or other subgroups. Orthopraxy is found largely among subcultures, including communities such as the Amish within mainstream religions, which define themselves over and against the surrounding dominant culture (Bell, 1997: 193). In terms of this distinction, the established environmental NGOs can be seen as orthodoxic, in that they place greater stress on proposition and argument, and on having agreed 'positions' within the organisation on any given issue. Neo-tribal environmental movements, by contrast, are low on orthodoxy (as they permit great freedom of belief and have less interest in 'rational' political argument) and high in orthopraxy (in their emphasis on style and taste, codes of dress, comportment, shared argots, and so on). Within protest subcultures, adopting restricted codes can help bind together the movement and mark them out from wider society.

Marking-Out and Political Generalisation

However, I also want to suggest that marking-out not only helps with the reproduction of the movement itself, but also plays a role in the way the movement communicates to wider society. A crucial dimension of marking-out is, of course, its relationship to the unmarked. Roland Barthes discusses the way that signs in a given paradigm are often distinguished by being respectively *marked* and *unmarked* (Barthes, 1967: 76–7). The unmarked is generally the usual, the normal, the unremarked (for example, in racial terms 'white' is often cited as an unmarked colour in this way). Marked signifiers are those that are tagged in some way to mark them out as *not* normal, as *un*usual. In a further step, some unmarked terms can in fact be negatively marked, by lacking the features which constitute the 'markedness' of the marked signifier. In the political semiotic under consideration here, conventional modes of citizenship are the unmarked – what linguists and semioticians also call the *zero degree* of the field (Barthes, 1967: 77–8). Performative politics often works by trying to recode oppositions or paradigms so that this zero degree shifts – the natural and taken-for-granted becomes denaturalised and problematised. As Kershaw puts it, such protest dramaturgies function predominantly less through factual truth claims or normative prescription, but by placing the imaginary and the real in new relationships for the spectator, disrupting and thus exposing the performance of 'politics as usual' (1997: 263, 257).

In some cases, the culture of dramatic protest is itself one which is in a very specific sense reflexive, in that it folds back on and ironises itself, bringing its own cultural-ness more to the foreground (Seery, 1990). Such ironic styles of protest can be seen as creating a political semiotic field *without* a zero degree, one where there is no stable ground on which to stand, rather an ever-shifting surface of partial perspectives, in a similar way that, in the internal style of oppositional subcultures, the constant hyphenisation of identity can disrupt the simple homology of style (Hetherington, 1998). But more often in contemporary protest the zero degree is relocated away from 'actorly' notions of citizenship roles and resituated in more 'artistic' conceptions of citizenship as self-expression. For the protesters themselves, the marked and the unmarked swap places.

This distinction between the marked and the unmarked is necessary to 'tag' the actions of environmental protest groups as being of 'extra-ordinary' significance and legitimacy. There are parallels here that can be drawn from the study of ritual.[7] The ritualisation of behaviour has the general effect of marking it out as privileged, as embodying central cosmological codes for both actors and observers to an extent greater than other behaviour (Bell, 1992: 90). For observers, it is thus a form of 'ostensive' or 'overt' communication, communication that refers to itself and requests heightened modes of attention to be paid to it. But as well as ritualisation serving to signify unusual levels of *importance*, it also serves to signify unusual modes of *legitimacy*. Ritualisation is often employed where power and legitimacy are grounded not in a worldly authority, but in a higher moral law. In this sense these movements stand in the tradition of non-conformist radical religious groups such as the Anabaptists of the fifteenth century, who saw themselves as heralding a utopian society of moral and spiritual perfection (Purkis, 2000: 95–6). The important symbolic component of many protest actions, such as the heroic last stand, locked-on at the top of a lone tree, can be seen as providing a symbolic legitimation to acts that are not granted legitimacy from formal sources of legal authority. The very illegality of many protest actions is thus turned from a sign of illegitimacy into a different mode of legitimation, one deriving its moral force from the personal risk the individual is prepared to undertake to underwrite their commitment to protect nature. The stylistic marking-out of the movement can be seen as a materialised complement to this performative marking-out, both of which serve the semiotic function of helping to politically generalise their actions, to make them mean more than just the momentary expression of commitment and passion.

Returning to Sennett's argument about the fall of 'public man', then, we could suggest that his narrative of *decline* might need revising to one of *transformation*. Rather than the earlier actorly metaphor representing the only possible shared set of rules for interpreting the persons and actions of strangers in the public sphere, one which has been all but lost, direct action politics suggests a rather different shared political semiotic, one in which the material marking-out of the protest community plays a key role in linking private passion with public meaning.

However, those outside the movement do not necessarily read the marking-out of protesters in this way. To explore this we must turn another corner in the labyrinth of interpretation, attending to the interpretations of protest actions and identities held by their wider audiences. I will draw on two studies here, both of which suggest that the perceived legitimacy of protest actions can be undermined when their audiences identify the protesters as constituting a particular social group.

Rachel Einwohner (1999) examined two campaigns carried out by the Progressive Animal Welfare Society (PAWS) in the Seattle area in the early 1990s. One, directed at circus patrons, concerned the ill-treatment of performing animals; the other targeted hunters, trying to persuade them of the cruelty of hunting, but was less successful. Einwohner's analysis of the relative effectiveness of the two campaigns suggests that one feature of the hunting campaign's relative inability to persuade its targets of the legitimacy of its claims was the way the hunters perceived the protesters in class and gender terms – as middle-class, emotional women with no understanding of hunting. She generalises from this case to suggest that 'the identity that shapes social movement dynamics is not simply protesters' sense of who they are; it is also who their targets understand them to be' (1999: 73).

In a separate study Rose Capdevila explored the different attitudes taken by the public to eco-protesters by analysing the different readings that people made of an article in a young women's magazine written by a Newbury protester (Capdevila, 1998). She used Q methodology[8] to derive seven different narratives that readers seemed to be drawing on in their constructions of activism: *law abiding* (the protesters are naive and irresponsible), *liberal humanist* (the protesters are deeply committed and responsible, but maybe not helping), *activist* (the protesters are good role models and contribute to society), *radical* (working outside the system is necessary to produce change), *sceptical* (the issue is important but people should not break the law), *cynical* (the protesters are exciting but not really political) and *superficial motives* (the protesters are just enjoying themselves).[9]

A striking finding that emerges from Capdevila's study is that, although in almost all of the narratives the issue is seen as important, nevertheless the protests are rarely seen as legitimate. For most of the narratives, the protesters are 'othered' as a distinct social group within society in a way that undermines their claim to be fighting on behalf of the planet as a whole rather than just acting out their own positional *habitus*. The protests are interpreted as a simple clash of cultures and lifestyles, as trouble-making, or at best as misplaced but character-making youthful idealism. It is only the *liberal humanist* and *radical* narratives that play down identity dimensions such as age and gender, and see the protests as being carried out by every(wo)man, on behalf of society as a whole. It is in these narratives that the actions are most successfully generalised, in the political sense used above. However, it is also in these narratives that the marked-out-ness of the protesters is least visible. For the narratives that are most critical of the protesters, it seems to be the very marked-out-ness of the protesters, their group identity, which undermines the capacity of their actions to be viewed as authentic political action. In these cases, then, the political semiotic collapses, and actions are judged not as public acts with a claim to universal political and ethical legitimacy but simply as the expression of private sentiment in public. Rather than playing a role in the political generalisation of protest gestures, allowing such gestures to signify politically, beyond the moment and place of their performance, the typological marking out of protesters can also serve to lock protest actions more firmly out of the public sphere.

Conclusion

In this chapter I have argued that the political semiosis of contemporary environmental protest suggests an additional step in the narrative set out by Richard Sennett in *The Fall of Public Man*. Sennett describes a shift in the nineteenth century from 'actorly' to 'artistic' understandings of public expression – from shared impersonal codes of communication in which the private identity of the person remains a cipher, to notions of immanent meaning, where expressions are conceived of as immediate revelations of inner feeling in the moment. At least some forms of environmental protest, I suggested, seem to operate through interpretive codes that, however precariously, seem to allow 'artistic' forms of expression to enter the public sphere, to signify in a political way. I have suggested that in order for these protest actions to politically signify they need to transcend the time, place and person of their performance, and that the typological marking-out of the protest community has a role in making possible this political generalisation, through a kind of visual–aesthetic political logic. The cultural distinctiveness of the movement thus has a Janus-faced role; inwardly, it plays a role in the construction and maintenance of a cultural laboratory for the creation and reproduction of alternative cultural codes; outwardly, it potentially holds the meaning of protest actions in a middle position, neither collapsing into unique, unrepeatable expressions of emotion, nor being absorbed into the 'social', to be judged and weighed in the same way as other social gestures. In this way the protesters' actions claim a dual legitimacy – authentically performed, but universally grounded in ethical values that have a claim over all. However, an analysis of protest actions that attends to the complex interrelations between intentions and effects, between first-person and third-person accounts, suggests that this particular political semiotic brings its own problems. The notion of authentic performance makes the protesters highly vulnerable to criticisms of hypocrisy, inconsistency or inauthenticity; similarly, the subcultural marking-out of the protest community makes it open to being particularised in ways that render protest actions dismissable as merely the performance of subcultural habitus.

Notes

1 I am very grateful to Dorothy Holland, Wallace Heim, John Urry, Dave Horton, Tom Cahill and Baz Kershaw for helpful comments on an earlier draft of this paper.

2 Fay (1996: 136–54), for example, explores this relationship in terms of the tension between 'intentionalism', which grounds the meaning of an action in the intentions of the actor, and a more Gadamerian-hermeneutic approach, which focuses on the significance of acts for a particular interpretive community. Bourdieu and Wacquant (1992) turn such tensions into a research question in its own right, one that blurs the boundary between theory and method, by advocating that attention be paid to the complex dialectical interactions between the various pre-constructions of research objects (such as the kind of protest gesture being explored here) in different academic, institutional and vernacular fields of practice.

3 For Jackie Stacey's analysis of the 'global within' in consumer culture, and the way that exotic cultures are used to stand for certain global values and experiences, see Franklin, Stacey and Lury (2000).

4 I am not here suggesting that intentions, emotions and gestures *can* be judged as authentic or inauthentic in some final way. Such judgements are routinely made by participants in a given practice that is governed at least partly by a logic of authenticity, but are severely problematic when made by an analyst. I am here using 'authenticity' to delineate a specific logic that organises certain regimes of signification, ordering signs according to a distinction between authentic and inauthentic, itself relying on a particular metaphysic of the human person (Boltanski, 1999: 81).

5 Arendt points out that this marking-out through dress was not permitted in the case of slaves in imperial Rome, precisely to avoid their constitution as a collective political actor.

6 For a useful summary of the distinction between presentational and representational codes, see Fiske (1990: 67).

7 For more on ritual, see Szerszynski (2002).

8 This involved participants sorting statements about road protesters onto a 'quasi-normal' grid, arranged from those with which they most agreed on the left, to those with which they most disagreed on the right. Factor analysis was then used to identify patterns in how people sorted the statements, resulting in the seven factors discussed here.

9 Although the narratives are independent, each individual respondent might themselves draw on more than one of the narratives.

References

Arendt, H. (1998) *The Human Condition*. Second edition, Chicago: University of Chicago Press.

Austin, J.L. (1975) *How To Do Things With Words*. Second edition, Oxford: Oxford University Press.

Barthes, R. (1967) *Elements of Semiology*. tr. Annette Lavers and Colin Smith, London: Cape.

Bell, C. (1992) *Ritual Theory, Ritual Practice*. New York: Oxford University Press.

Bell, C. (1997) *Ritual: Perspectives and Dimensions*. New York: Oxford University Press.

Benjamin, W. (1973) 'The Work of Art in the Age of Mechanical Reproduction' pp. 211–44 in *Illuminations*. London: Fontana.

Bernstein, B. (ed.) (1973) *Class, Codes and Control*. Vol. 1: Theoretical Studies Towards a Sociology of Language, London: Paladin.

Boltanski, L. (1999) *Distant Suffering: Morality, Media and Politics*. tr. G. Burchell, Cambridge: Cambridge University Press.

Bourdieu, P. and Loic J.D. Wacquant (1992) *An Invitation to Reflexive Sociology*. Cambridge: Polity Press.

Butler, J. (1997) *Excitable Speech: A Politics of the Performative*. New York: Routledge.

Capdevila, R. (1998) 'Narrating Protest: A Q Study on Environmental Activism' paper presented to the conference Alternative Futures and Popular Protest IV, Manchester Metropolitan University, 15–17 April 1998.

Doherty, B. (1996) 'Paving the Way: The Rise of Direct Action Against Road-Building and the Changing Character of British Environmentalism' paper presented to the conference Alternative Futures and Popular Protest II, Manchester Metropolitan University, 26–28 March.

Doherty, B. (1997) 'Tactical Innovation and the Protest Repertoire in the Radical Ecology Movement in Britain' paper presented to the European Sociological Association Conference, Essex University, 27–30 August.

Doherty, B. (2000) 'Manufactured Vulnerability: Protest Camp Tactics' pp. 62–78. in B. Seel, M. Paterson, and B. Doherty (eds) *Direct Action in British Environmentalism*. London: Routledge.

Einwohner, R.L. (1999) 'Gender, Class, and Social Movement Outcomes' *Gender & Society* 13 (1): 56–76.

Evans, D.D. (1969) *The Logic of Self-Involvement: A Philosophical Study of Everyday Language with Special Reference to the Christian Use of Language about God as Creator*. New York: Herder and Herder.

Eyerman, R. and Jamison, A. (1991) *Social Movements: A Cognitive Approach*. Cambridge: Polity Press.

Eyerman, R. and Jamison, A. (1998) *Music and Social Movements: Mobilizing Traditions in the Twentieth Century*. Cambridge: Cambridge University Press.

Fay, B. (1996) *Contemporary Philosophy of Social Science: A Multicultural Approach*. Oxford: Blackwell.

Fiske, J. (1990) *Introduction to Communication Studies*. Second edition, London: Routledge.

Franklin, S., Stacey, J. and Lury, C. (2000) *Global Nature, Global Culture: Gender, Race, and Life Itself*. London: Sage.

Goffman, E. (1972) *Relations in Public: Microstudies of the Public Order*. New York: Harper and Row.

Hebdige, D. (1979) *Subculture: The Meaning of Style*. London: Routledge.

Hetherington, K. (1998) *Expressions of Identity: Space, Performance and the Politics of Identity*. London: Sage.

Hetherington, K. (2000) *New Age Travellers: Vanloads of Uproarious Humanity*. London: Cassell.

Kershaw, B. (1997) 'Fighting in the Streets: Dramaturgies of Popular Protest, 1968–1989' *New Theatre Quarterly* 13(51): 255–76.

Kress, G. and van Leeuwen, T. (1996) *Reading Images: The Grammar of Visual Design*. Revised edition, London: Routledge.

Lévi-Strauss, C. (1962) *The Savage Mind*. London: Weidenfeld.

Maffesoli, M. (1996) *The Time of the Tribes: The Decline of Individualism in Mass Society*. London: Sage.

McKay, G. (1996) *Senseless Acts of Beauty: Cultures of Resistance Since the Sixties*. London: Verso.

McLuhan, M. (1962) *The Gutenberg Galaxy: The Making of Typographic Man*. London: Routledge and Kegan Paul.

Melucci, A. (1989) *Nomads of the Present: Social Movements and Individual Needs in Contemporary Society*. London: Hutchinson Radius.

Melucci, A. (1996) *Challenging Codes: Collective Action in the Information Age*. Cambridge: Cambridge University Press.

Ong, W.J. (1982) *Orality and Literacy: The Technologizing of the World*. London: Methuen.

Paterson, M. (2000) 'Swampy Fever: Media Constructions and Direct Action Politics' pp. 151–66 in B. Seel, M. Paterson, and B. Doherty (eds) *Direct Action in British Environmentalism*. London: Routledge:

Peirce, C.S. (1991) *Peirce on Signs: Writings on Semiotics by Charles Sanders Peirce*. Chapel Hill, NC: North Carolina University Press.

Purkis, J. (2000) 'Modern Millenarians? Anticonsumerism, Anarchism and the New Urban Environmentalism' pp. 93–111 in B. Seel, M. Paterson, and B. Doherty (eds) *Direct Action in British Environmentalism*. London: Routledge:

Saussure, F. de (1966) *Course in General Linguistics*. tr. Wade Baskin, New York: McGraw Hill.

Searle, J.R. (1969) *Speech Acts: An Essay in the Philosophy of Language*. Cambridge: Cambridge University Press.

Searle, J.R. (1979) *Expression and Meaning : Studies in the Theory of Speech Acts*. Cambridge: Cambridge University Press.

Searle, J.R. and Vanderveken, D. (1985) *Foundations of Illocutionary Logic*. Cambridge: Cambridge University Press.

Seel, B. (1996) 'Frontline Eco-Wars! The Pollok Free State Road Protest Community: Counter Hegemonic Intentions, Pluralistic Effects' paper presented to the conference Alternative Futures and Popular Protest II, Manchester Metropolitan University, 26–28 March.

Seery, J.E. (1990) *Political Returns: Irony in Politics and Theory from Plato to the Antinuclear Movement*. Boulder, Colorado: Westview Press.

Sennett, R. (1986) *The Fall of Public Man*. London: Faber and Faber.

Szerszynski, B. (2002) 'Ecological Rites: Ritual Action in Environmental Protest Events' *Theory, Culture and Society* 19 (3): 305–23.

Szerszynski, B. and Urry, J. (2001) 'Visual Citizenship' pp. 111–15, in L. Short (ed.) *Thinkglobal: Cityscape><Landshape Symposium 2000*. Carlisle: Think Global Institute.

Taylor, C. (1991) *The Ethics of Authenticity*. Cambridge, Massachusetts: Harvard University Press.

Trilling, L. (1972) *Sincerity and Authenticity*. Cambridge Mass.: Harvard University Press.

Willis, P. (1990) *Common Culture: Symbolic Work at Play in the Everyday Cultures of the Young*. Milton Keynes: Open University Press.

Wykes, M. (2000) 'The Burrowers: News about Bodies, Tunnels and Green Guerrillas' pp. 73–89 in S. Allan, B. Adam, and C. Carter (eds) *Environmental Risks and the Media*. London: Routledge.

Index